John MacKenzie, William Killen

Mackenzie's Memorials of the Siege of Derry

Including his Narrative and its Vindication

John MacKenzie, William Killen

Mackenzie's Memorials of the Siege of Derry
Including his Narrative and its Vindication

ISBN/EAN: 9783337307165

Printed in Europe, USA, Canada, Australia, Japan

Cover: Foto ©ninafisch / pixelio.de

More available books at **www.hansebooks.com**

MACKENZIE'S
MEMORIALS OF THE SIEGE OF DERRY

INCLUDING HIS

NARRATIVE AND ITS VINDICATION.

WITH AN INTRODUCTION AND NOTES,

BY

W. D. KILLEN, D.D.

ASSEMBLY'S COLLEGE, BELFAST.

BELFAST: C. AITCHISON, 9, HIGH STREET.
LONDON: HAMILTON, ADAMS, & CO.
MDCCCLXI.

TO

The Rev. John Knox Leslie,

ONE OF THE SUCCESSORS OF THE REV. JOHN MACKENZIE IN THE PRESBYTERIAN
MINISTRY AT COOKSTOWN :

THIS REPRINT

OF THE

NARRATIVE OF THE SIEGE OF LONDONDERRY, AND ITS VINDICATION,

IS RESPECTFULLY DEDICATED,

BY

The Editor.

CONTENTS.

	PAGE.
INTRODUCTION	vii

NARRATIVE OF THE SIEGE.

PREFACE ... 3

CHAP. I.

The Transactions of the City of Derry, from the Shutting of the Gates to the Descent of the Irish Army ... 7

CHAP. II.

The Affairs of the other parts of Ulster and Sligo ... 17

CHAP. III.

What passed at Derry, from the Retreat of the British forces from Coleraine thither, till the time that King James' Army appeared before the town ... 29

CHAP. IV.

The Change of Government in Derry ... 35

CHAP. V

The Siege ... 39

CHAP. VI.

The New Establishment by Major-General Kirke ... 57

APPENDIX of Documents :—

1. Letter from the inhabitants of Derry to Lord Mountjoy 59
2. Letter from the inhabitants of Derry to the Society at London .. 59
3. Letter to David Cairns, Esq., from Enniskillen 60
4. Declaration of the inhabitants of Derry 60
5. Articles of Agreement between Lord Mountjoy and the City of Derry 61
6. The Antrim Association's Declaration 62
7. The King's Letter to Ireland by Captain Leighton 63
8. The Declaration of the Protestants of Sligo .. .. .. — 63
9. Colonel Lundy's Instructions 64

10. Captain James Hamilton's Instructions	64
11. The King's Letter to Lundy	65
12. Instructions to David Cairns, Esq.	65
13. Certificate to David Cairns, Esq.	65
14. Articles at a Council of War at Derry, 10th April, 1689	66
15. Orders and Instructions to John Cunningham, Esq.	66
16. Additional Instructions to John Cunningham, Esq.	67
17. Tiffin's and Lyndon's Certificate to Colonel Cunningham	67
18. Instructions to Robert Lundy, Esq.	68
19. Proposals to be made by the people of Derry to General Hamilton	68
20. Commission of the Deputies	70
21. Certificate to Lonther	71
22. Twisleton's Certificate	71
23. Account of the Officers killed and taken by the besieged	71
24. Account of the Bombs thrown into the city	72
25. Account of the Subsistence out of the stores to the soldiers	72
26. Names of Conforming and Non-conforming Ministers in the city during the siege	73

SUPPLEMENT—Osborne's Vindication ... 73

DR. WALKER'S INVISIBLE CHAMPION FOILED 83

INTRODUCTION.

The Siege of Londonderry in 1689 has been justly described by Lord Macaulay as "the most memorable in the annals of the British Isles." The city was closely invested from the 18th of April to the 1st of August; and though reduced by famine to little more than half their original numbers, and obliged to live on food to the use of which nothing but dire necessity could have reconciled them, its brave defenders continued fearlessly to withstand the foe, and to persist in their cry of 'No Surrender.' Their resolution was not sustained by the genius and enthusiasm of a great military chief; for neither Baker or Mitchelburn possessed more than average ability: it was the loftier inspiration of a love of truth and liberty. Animated by this principle every common soldier became a hero.

The announcement of the raising of the siege diffused joy throughout the Protestants of the three Kingdoms. The successful defence of the Maiden City had humbled a tyrant, and prevented him from extending to Scotland and England the horrors of civil war. No wonder that the victors were greeted with the applause of the Empire.

Upwards of six weeks before the termination of the siege, a fleet of thirty sail, carrying troops, arms, and provisions for the relief of the town, appeared at the mouth of the Lough. This armament was under the command of Kirke—a man of the worst character, who had already acquired a most unenviable notoriety by his cruelties in the West of England at the close of Monmouth's rebellion. It has been thought strange that William entrusted the care of such an expedition to so atrocious a scoundrel. But the new Sovereign did not well know whom to trust: he was surrounded by traitors; and he, perhaps, considered that the Major General might be as safely employed at Derry as elsewhere. Kirke's conduct soon showed that he had no heart for the service. Had he boldly proceeded up the Lough when he first came in sight of the beleaguered city, he could at once have relieved the garrison; for the boom across the river was not yet completed, and there was no obstacle of importance to obstruct the passage. A man of skill should not have been deterred by so puny an affair as the boom itself; as, at the Siege of Antwerp, upwards of a century before, means had been found to burst through a framework fifty fold more formidable. But Kirke had no taste for prompt action. James had lately arrived in Ireland with money and warlike stores from France: almost the whole country now acknowledged his authority; his partisans were in arms in Scotland; and many in England were beginning to look wistfully towards the expatriated sovereign. At such a crisis Kirke might deem it prudent to watch the course of events, and not to increase the irritation of his old master by displaying any superfluous bravery in the cause of William.* With the soldiers and citizens of Derry the Major-General had little sympathy. The men who were exhibiting such prodigies of valour in defence of the last refuge of Irish Protestantism, and who were meanwhile dining on salted hides or horse flesh, were, with some exceptions, the co-religionists of the Presbyterians

---

* Sir John Fenwick, who was executed in 1696 as a conspirator against the life of King William, states in his Confession that, "at his going into Ireland Major-General Kirke had promised to go in" for King James. *Dalrymple's Memoirs, III. Appendix,* 279. Though this Confession artfully implicates the friends of William, it is, as Lord Macaulay has stated, "made up of stories too true for the most part." *History of England, VII.* 351. London 1860.

of Scotland and the Puritans of England; and such were the men whom, of all others, Kirke abhorred. The rude soldier, who delighted to drink the health of Judge Jeffreys, could not be expected to peril his life for the friends of John Howe and Richard Baxter. It was, therefore, not at all singular that he remained so long inactive. When the besieged were perishing with hunger, even a Church Dignitary had been heard to say—"no matter how many of them die—they are but a pack of Scotch Presbyterians."*

Lord Macaulay ascribes the deliverance of Derry to a despatch signed by Schomberg, in which Kirke was peremptorily commanded to attack the boom. But if other agencies had not been at work it is probable that the Major-General would have contrived to evade the performance of the dangerous commission. He had long before been expressly required to relieve the place; and yet, when the difficulties were much less to be feared, he had found apologies for procrastination. There was now, however, a pressure from another quarter, which he did not deem it convenient to disregard. The minister who had persuaded the apprentice boys to shut the gates—the intrepid James Gordon, of Glendermot—had found his way on board the little fleet, and had been exhorting some of the officers and men to attempt the passage to Derry. Kirke heard of his proceedings; stormed, cursed, and threatened to hang him; but the God-fearing preacher was not to be intimidated by any blaspheming bully. Mr. Gordon, who was well acquainted with the locality, pointed out to the Commander how the impediment of the boom could be surmounted, and informed him that Captain Browning and others were prepared to encounter the hazard of the enterprise. Kirke now felt that his own head was in danger should he not make an immediate effort to aid the besieged. Were the city, in the meantime, captured, he could not hope, confronted with witnesses such as Gordon and Browning, to convince either Schomberg or the King that he had faithfully done his duty.† He was thus compelled to give the orders which issued in the relief of Derry.

Mr. Gordon, who had passed over to Scotland about the beginning of the year, returned there immediately after the siege, and became minister of the now far-famed parish of Cardross. He survived his removal from Ireland only a few years; but the tradition that he had instigated Kirke to attempt the breaking of the boom was long preserved among his Scottish parishioners. Wodrow, who was ten years of age at the time of the siege, and who was, subsequently, well acquainted with the people of Cardross, heard the story from more than one intelligent and respectable witness.‡ Lord Macaulay rejects it as "the gossip of a country parish in Dumbartonshire;" but the author of "The History of the Sufferings of the Church of Scotland," though not so brilliant a writer, was quite as good a judge of evidence as the great essayist; and many of the statements which adorn the most graphic descriptions of the "History of England," rest on the authority of "gossip" not nearly so well authenticated. That Mr. Gordon claimed the credit of the relief of Derry there can be no reasonable doubt; and that his version of the affair is clear, consistent, and correct as to details, cannot be disputed. His account of the manner in which Kirke at first resented his interference, contains internal evidence of its truth, for the Major-General is exhibited to the life when he is represented as pouring forth imprecations, and threatening to hang a Presbyterian minister.

---

* *Apology for the Failures charged on the Rev. Mr. Geo. Walker's Printed Account of the late Siege of Derry*, p. 18.

† As it was, he narrowly escaped a court-martial. "There was a Council of War designed between Major-General Kirke and Sir Henry Inglesby, about the business of Derry, the latter saying that Derry might easily have been relieved much sooner, with a great deal more to that purpose, but it came to nothing, and was no more talked of."—*Story's Impartial History of the Wars of Ireland*, p. 21. London, 1693.

When this brutal commander entered the rejoicing city a few days after the breaking of the boom, he fully sustained his infamous reputation. The men who had so nobly fought the battle of civil and religious freedom were entitled to an ample recompense. They were woefully disappointed. The weak and sick soldiers, who wished to resume their industrial occupations, were denied assistance out of the public stores; and many of them, on their way homewards, perished by starvation. The regiments were remodelled; and not a few of the officers, instead of obtaining promotion, were immediately reduced. Strangers who had taken no part in the siege supplanted captains who had endured its privations and perils. The treatment experienced by Colonel Adam Murray was superlatively base. Murray was the bravest of the bravo: he had charged Lundy to his face with treachery, and had compelled him to resign a trust which he betrayed: he had taken charge of the city during the short interregnum created by the traitor's expulsion; and, had he pleased, he might have continued Governor, as he had won the hearts of both citizens and soldiers. During the siege, wherever there was hard fighting, Murray's athletic form was seen, and his manly voice was heard cheering on the Protestant combatants: his very name carried terror through the ranks of the enemy: he was now slowly recovering from wounds received a few days before the deliverance of the city, and he had every right to expect the rewards of distinguished fidelity and valour. But it soon transpired that his regiment was to be joined to another under the command of a new colonel, and that he was to be deprived even of the favourite horse which had borne him through many a bloody struggle! His men, no longer permitted to follow a leader whom they loved as a father, and admired as the very soul of chivalry, withdrew in disgust from the service. It was in vain to attempt to remonstrate with such a despot as the Major-General. When one officer ventured to complain, Kirke, true to his character, ordered a gallows forthwith to be erected, and threatened to hang the murmurer.

But this unprincipled chief was not unmindful of his own interests. Aware that his conduct in the Lough was not above suspicion, he endeavoured to stifle inquiry by a piece of rather dexterous management. An address to the King and Queen was drawn up in the name of the officers and gentlemen of the city, and in this document there was a special acknowledgment of "the *indefatigable care* of Major-General Kirke." Some, probably, subscribed the paper without reading it; whilst others, who were aware of its contents, and who objected to the compliment paid to the commander, deemed it imprudent to incur the suspicion of disloyalty by withholding their signatures.

The next care of Kirke was the selection of a suitable representative to present the address to William and Mary. His choice rested on Mr. George Walker, a beneficed clergyman of the county of Tyrone, who had acted a conspicuous part throughout the siege. Many were dissatisfied with the selection of an agent who had himself fallen under some suspicion, but they did not care to oppose the nomination of the Major-General; and the reverend gentleman, after some well understood expressions of modesty, consented to undertake the mission.

Mr. Walker was born in 1618, so that at the time of the siege he was upwards of seventy years of age. He had not imbibed the doctrine of passive obedience so deeply as most of his episcopal brethren, and yet he possessed a considerable share of the spirit of a high-churchman. He was endowed with much natural eloquence; but his mind was indifferently cultivated; and the few tracts published in his name, if really written by him, display a very moderate amount of literary talent. He seems to have mistaken his profession, as he had a far greater taste for military occupations than for the functions of a minister of the Gospel; and during the siege, as well as afterwards, he delighted in the title of *Colonel* Walker. About the beginning of the Revolution he was employed by Lord Charlemont to raise soldiers for the defence of the Protestant interest—a commission which he undertook with great alacrity: he was afterwards placed at the head of the new regiment; and on more than one occasion, when under fire, he exhibited intrepidity and self-possession. When Lundy was set aside, Major Baker was elected in his stead; and the new Governor, with the concurrence of the garrison, nominated Mr. Walker as his assistant or deputy, and entrusted him with the care of the stores. The superintendence of the commissariat department was not so much at variance with the clerical character as direct interference with the stern realities of war; and it was, perhaps, thought that the aged divine would be less exposed to scandal were his attention confined to the distribution of the rations, and the husbanding of the provisions. He was a ready and popular speaker; and, when chosen vice-governor, the influence he was likely to exert over the mob of a besieged city was, doubtless, not overlooked.

But the pompous old man was not duly mindful of his secondary position. Soldiers and citizens soon saw that they could always put him in good humour by saluting him *Governor*; and as Baker was in declining health, Walker sometimes actually usurped the chief authority. He appeared to think that, as a clergyman and the most aged of the Colonels, he was entitled to take honorary precedence of all his military colleagues; and when public documents were signed by those in command of the garrison, he had more than once the assurance to foist in his name above that of the Governor. Baker, who was fast sinking into the grave, was willing to overlook his vanity; but others began to be much dissatisfied with his management; and at length four or five of the Colonels, with upwards of one hundred officers of lower rank, proceeded formally to prefer charges against him for misconduct,* with a view to obtain his removal from the post he occupied. Anxious at such a crisis to maintain peace among the defenders of the city, Baker prevailed on the complainants to withdraw their accusations, on the condition that Walker should no longer be permitted to act alone, and that the supervision of the stores, as well as of the garrison, should be vested in a Council of Fourteen, of which the Governor himself was to be president. About a month before the close of the siege, Colonel Baker died. When no longer able to perform the duties of his office, he had appointed Colonel Mitchelburn to take his place;† and this gentleman continued subsequently to act as Governor, though Mr. Walker still retained his former position. As the privations of the garrison increased, the absurdity of contending about questions of precedence became more and more apparent. The conduct of the military divine again created some uneasiness; but as matters stood, it was vain to think of investigation.

When Kirke entered the city, Walker became his confidant and counsellor. In public the voluble theologian lost no opportunity of extolling the services of the Major-General, and the Major-General returned these compliments by bearing testimony to the ability and bravery of *Governor* Walker. After a few days spent in mutual congratulations, Walker set out for

---

* See page 45.—To this day no attempt has been made to disprove this statement. In the tract, entitled, "Mackenzie's Narrative a False Libel," not a tittle of evidence is produced to show that Mackenzie has given even an exaggerated report of the transaction.

† Ash. in his Diary, thus describes this affair: "A council of war was held at Colonel Mitchelburn's to choose a Governor *in place of Governor Baker*, until he should recover of his sickness. When the council met, Colonel Lance and Lieutenant-Colonel Fortescue were sent to the Bishop's where Mr. Baker lay, to know whom he would depute. He named Colonel Mitchelburn, saying he was the fittest person to fill that station. The major part of the council consented, and Mitchelburn was confirmed Governor." Walker, as usual, magnifies himself when reporting the transaction: he says, "At this time Governor Baker is very dangerously ill, and Colonel Mitchelburn is chosen and appointed *to assist Governor Walker*."—*True Account*, p. 32. A house in Butcher's Street was long pointed out as the place where Walker resided during the siege. It has been recently rebuilt. Had he been Chief Governor he would have taken up his residence in the Bishop's palace.

London, travelling by way of Glasgow and Edinburgh, and bearing the address to the King and Queen from the officers of the garrison and the citizens of Derry. His fame had preceded him, for at least one letter* written by himself during the siege had already been widely circulated; and Kirke had taken good care to inform the English Government of the merits of a gentleman to whom the Empire owed such a debt of obligation. When he reached the British capital, every one was anxious to obtain a sight of the clergyman who, in the hour of danger, had exchanged the surplice for the sword, and maintained his post with such unflinching resolution in the Thermopylæ of Protestantism. He was most graciously received by William and Mary, presented with a gift of £5,000, and given to understand that he was to be promoted to the rich see of Derry, then supposed to be vacant by the abdication of Bishop Hopkins.†

It was not extraordinary that Mr. Walker was elated by the praises heaped on him so profusely. In an evil hour his vanity overcame his prudence. Very shortly after his arrival in the English metropolis he was induced to put his name to a publication which eventually involved him in great obloquy, and exposed him to much sharp criticism. It is entitled, "A True Account of the Siege of Londonderry, by the Rev. Mr. George Walker, Rector of Donaghmore,‡ and late Governor of Derry, in Ireland."§ Several writers have intimated that the diligent old warrior kept a diary during the siege, and that the work presented to the public is merely an expansion of notes taken down by him from time to time, as the operations proceeded.‖ But the reputed author himself makes no such averment, and it is obviously destitute of foundation. It is even somewhat doubtful whether Walker was the sole compiler of "The True Account," for though it bears his name, it has been thought that, during his short stay in England immediately before its publication, he was kept in a state of such excitement that he had little time for composition. He, no doubt, furnished the materials, and perhaps dictated a portion of the narrative, but he was probably assisted in its preparation. Some of his contemporaries were impressed with the conviction that others had a share in the performance. One of his assistants was believed to be Vesey, Archbishop of Tuam, a native of Coleraine, known to the student of Irish ecclesiastical history as the author of a life of the intolerant Bramhall, Archbishop of Armagh. Vesey was, at this time, an exile in England, having been driven out of his Archdiocese by the party of Tyrconnell; and as he was of an officious disposition, as well as a violent partisan, it is not at all improbable that he aided Walker in drawing up "The True Account."¶

---

* See this letter appended to the "True Account of the Present State of Ireland, by a Person that with great difficulty left Dublin, June 8th, 1689." London, 1689. The letter is republished in *Derriana*. "The True and Impartial Account," written by Walker's friend, Bennet, had also already appeared.

† After all Hopkins did not resign. He took the oaths to William and Mary, and died a very few days before the battle of the Boyne, in the following year.

‡ Walker here conceals the fact that, in addition to the parish of Donaghmore, one of the richest rectories in Ulster, he held the living of Lissan, and perhaps another.—See *Ulster Journal of Archæology*, II. 132. The Donaghmore of which he was rector is not that near Strabane, but the parish of the same name at Dungannon.

§ Licensed, September 13, 1689. It passed through several editions in the course of a few weeks.

‖ The "True Account" is often called Walker's "Diary" by parties anxious to add to its historical authority, and the reputed author himself once gives it that title, but he never ventures upon any more particular statement. The gross chronological blunders it contains supply clear proof that it was drawn up afterwards. Thus, it misrepresents the date of the breaking of the boom, assigning it to the 30th, instead of Sabbath, the 28th of July. Again, it makes Darcy, as a *prisoner*, sign a letter to Hamilton about the beginning of July, when it is well known that he was liberated in the end of April. It states, farther, that Kirke's ships were discovered on the 15th of June, but it is well known that they were seen on the 13th. The keeper of a diary would not be thus perpetually giving incorrect dates.

¶ He himself admitted that the manuscript had been submitted to him. "I often heard him say," writes a friend, "he could safely be deposed *he never read half of it before it was printed.*"—

Never was the spirit of sectarianism in a state of much greater excitement than about the time when this pamphlet appeared. Whilst the Irish army lay encamped around the walls of Derry, the English Parliament had passed the Act of Toleration; but other measures, recommended by William for the relief of Dissenters, had met with strenuous opposition; and the breach between the Established Church and the Non-conformists was wider than ever. In Scotland, Presbyterianism, after nearly thirty years of proscription, had recovered the ascendency; and the ministers who, shortly before, had been hunted among the mountains and the moors, expected soon to meet under royal auspices, and hold another General Assembly. As their co-religionists constituted the major portion of the Protestants of the North of Ireland, some of them were, perhaps, so sanguine as to hope that their ecclesiastical polity would be established by law in Ulster; for the King regarded the Presbyterians as his best friends, and the service they had rendered to the Empire by the defence of Derry had signally illustrated their claim to political encouragement. When Walker reached London with the Address from the Maiden City to the new Sovereigns, the public mind was mightily agitated by politico-religious controversies. An Act of Parliament had been passed requiring all functionaries, whether of the Church or State, to take the oath of allegiance to William and Mary, and it was understood that the Archbishop of Canterbury, and other prelates, were prepared to refuse. The Episcopal clergy in Scotland were unfavourable to the revolution settlement,* and the Episcopal clergy in Ireland had acted most equivocally, for when the Presbyterians were manning the walls of Derry in the service of the Prince of Orange, four of the Protestant Bishops were sitting in Dublin in the Parliament of King James. But Walker, happily for his party, had acted otherwise; and had thus, to some extent, redeemed its reputation. When he reached London he was, therefore, received by his prelatic brethren with the utmost enthusiasm. The friends of "the Church" did not well know how to do him sufficient honour. The University of Cambridge hastened to tender him the degree of Doctor of Divinity.† The University of Oxford soon afterwards bestowed on him the same academic distinction. Derry, it was said, owed its preservation to a churchman. The city was saved by the vigilance, courage, and capacity of the great Doctor Walker.

"The True Account" is designed to promote this impression. The very title page is deceptive. Though Walker was only Colonel Baker's assistant, and never, even according to the testimony of his most ardent partisans, had any thing more than a joint command, he does not scruple to style himself "Governor of Derry." In the Dedication to William and Mary he quietly appropriates to himself all the credit of the struggle, as he informs his royal patrons that God "by making use of a poor minister, the unworthiest of the whole communion of which he is a member, would intimate to the world *by what hand he would defend and maintain*" their Majesties' interest and the Protestant religion. The story of the siege is written in this style of self-glorification; and, in his statement of matters of fact, Walker is

---

"*Mackenzie's Narrative a False Libel*," p. 18. He affirmed, also, that he had not "altered one word of what he read;" but he may, notwithstanding, in various ways have assisted Walker.

* In a letter from Mr. Hugh Magill to Sir Arthur Rawdon, dated London, March 25, 1690, it is stated that "one of the frigates cruising near Dublin took a Scotch boat going into the bay, wherein were thirty-five passengers, with several letters of inte,ligence, and £8,000 in silver, sent to King James *by the Episcopal clergy of Scotland.*" Rawdon papers, p. 314. London, 1819.

† A writer in the *Ulster Journal of Archæology* has disputed this statement.—(See Vol. II. p. 272, note). It is attested by Walker's particular friend a few months afterwards. Thus we read— "They [the Universities of England] unanimously confer on him the honourable degree of Doctor in Divinity. Cambridge begins, and presents him with a degree, though absent: it was done when the King was there last summer at the commencement. Oxford makes him a solemn invitation to give them a visit, and on the 26th of February, 1689, he is created Doctor in Divinity.—*Mackenzie's Narrative a false Libel; in defence of Dr. Geo. Walker written by his friend in his absence,*" p. 12. London 1690.

not particularly scrupulous. The author himself stands out in the foreground of the picture. *He* issues the orders, *he* negotiates with the enemy, *he* plans the military operations, *he* heads the sallies, *he* rushes to the rescue, *he* preaches, *he* promises victory. The citizens of Derry had before been ignorant of the grand achievements in which he here speaks of having figured. Every one who had survived the siege could tell that Colonel Adam Murray was distinguished above all others by deeds of surpassing heroism, but the Derry Achilles happened to be a Presbyterian* who was known to entertain a very humble opinion of the Rev. George Walker; and, in connexion with the exploits of the garrison, he is accordingly mentioned only *once* in the "True Account." Even there he is noticed apparently for the purpose of introducing a compliment to the Narrator, who represents himself as mounting a horse, and hastening to the deliverance of the Colonel when in imminent danger. This tale must, at least, be an absurd exaggeration; for many in Derry denied his interference altogether, and the sceptics asserted that no one could tell where Walker was to be seen on the occasion, or how he was arrayed, or what was the colour of the horse which carried the reverend champion.† "The True Account" is chargeable with several strange omissions. It makes no mention of some of the greatest feats of prowess performed during the siege, and it takes no notice of the establishment of the Council of Fourteen. It does not state that the Rev. James Gordon, the Presbyterian minister of Glendermot, instigated the Apprentice Boys to shut the gates; nor that the Right Rev. Bishop Hopkins protested against such a proceeding, telling the citizens that, at all hazards, they were bound to render obedience to King James, "their *only* lawful sovereign." In his Account Walker gives a list of the Episcopal clergy who were in Derry during the siege, but he states that he could not learn the names of the Presbyterian ministers! One of these gentlemen, whom he thus ignores, had been invited by him to become chaplain to his own regiment, as most of the soldiers belonging to it were Presbyterians; others of them had acted in a similar capacity; all of them had been occasionally requested to meet with the military council; and they had preached every Lord's day in the Cathedral, where he himself officiated. His inability to give their names was, therefore, rather extraordinary. It was still more singular that, though he knew so little of men with whom he was holding such frequent intercourse, he could repeat the names of other Irish Presbyterian ministers who were *not* in Derry during the siege,‡ and that he could travel out of his way to make a most unwarrantable attack on the Rev. Alexander Osborne, one of the Presbyterian ministers of Dublin.

In "The True Account," we are told that the garrison "unanimously resolved to choose Mr. Walker and Major Baker to be their Governors during the siege," and the author re-

* This fact has been recently denied on the authority "of one of the family of that officer;" but individuals are sometimes unacquainted with the true history of their ancestors. The earnest Presbyterianism of Adam Murray was well known to both friends and foes.—See pp. 37 and 94, and notes. See also *Mackenzie's Narrative a False Libel*, p. 2.

† It is remarkable that in the "True and Impartial Account of the most material Passages in Ireland since December, 1688, with a particular relation of the Forces of Londonderry," licensed July 22, 1689, there is no mention of Walker's interference, though the circumstances of the sally are minutely related. The flight of the besiegers is ascribed to another cause. "The guns from the town forced the enemy's horse to retreat," p. 25. Other contemporary accounts are equally silent as to Walker's services. He may have taken some part in the affair, but not such as to attract any notice. Had he taken a prominent part, his behaviour would not have been overlooked by his friend Bennet in "The True and Impartial Account."

‡ Leland, Macaulay, and some other writers, speak of David Houston's interference during the siege; but they have obviously mistaken the meaning of a passage in "The True Account," page 21. Walker's language implies that Houston was *not* in Derry—a conclusion established by the fact that his name does not appear in the list of Presbyterian ministers who were there, as furnished in Walker's "Vindication," p. 33. Houston was in Scotland at the time of the shutting of the gates, and he was not in Derry during the siege.

peatedly styles himself "*the* Governor."* Lord Macaulay conceives that the Rev. Colonel has been unjustly assailed for thus assuming the possession of supreme authority. "There was afterwards," says the noble historian, "some idle dispute about the question whether Walker was properly Governor or not. To me it seems *quite clear* that he was so."† The question is certainly of little consequence in itself; but otherwise it is not altogether unimportant; for, if it can be determined, the solution will enable us to estimate the value of Walker's "True Account," and supply us with a test by which we may judge of his character. Those who carefully examine the evidence will, we believe, see cause to adopt a conclusion different from that announced by Lord Macaulay. The novelty of a minister of religion in high military command attracted universal notice; and as Walker magnified his position in the correspondence which he contrived to carry on during the siege with parties outside the town, it is not extraordinary that some, who were strangers to the actual state of matters, as well as others, gave him the title he coveted. The royal letter, dated Hampton Court, 16th August, 1689, congratulating the people of Derry on their successful defence, is directed in its published form, to "George Walker and John Mitchelburn, Esqs., Governors of Londonderry;" but the argument based on this address is illusory, as *no names* were inserted in the document when it left England, and the blank was filled up by Kirke at his discretion.‡ It is, too, noteworthy, that the citizens in their reply ignore the governorship of the reverend warrior, and style him "*Colonel* George Walker." The fact that his name stands first in the list of officers appended to two or three documents drawn up during the siege is by far the most plausible argument in his favour; and yet even this is not decisive; for in none of these cases does he venture to subscribe himself *Governor;* and it appears that, at the time, when he placed his name above that of Baker or Mitchelburn, he was deemed guilty of a breach of propriety.§ Everything we know concerning him concurs to prove that he was presuming and officious, and that it was exceedingly difficult to keep him in his own position. In "The True Account" he lays claim to the same authority as Baker; and after the death of that officer he uniformly describes himself as "*The Governor*"-in-chief, but not a single witness can be adduced to sustain him in this latter assumption. The weight of testimony goes decidedly to show that, throughout the siege, he was only second

---

* The following may be given as a specimen of the style in which Walker exhibits himself:— "On Sunday, the Major-General (Kirke) came into the town, and was received by *the Governor* and the whole garrison with the greatest joy and acclamations. *The Governor* presents him with the keys, but he would not receive them. The next day *the Governor*, with several of his officers, dined with the Major-General at Inch."—*True Account, p.* 42. Ash, who was an Episcopalian, gives a very different account of these transactions, and represents Walker as occupying only the *second* place. "Major-General Kirke came to Derry, accompanied by Colonel Stuart, and several English officers: they alighted at Bishop's Gate, and went through Bishop Street, the Diamond, and Butcher's Street, to *Governor Mitchelburn's*. The Governors, *Mitchelburn* and Walker, were with him, one on each hand. . . . . A guard was formed on both sides of the street, the officers standing at the head of their poor, half-starved soldiers, all the way from Bishop's Gate *to Governor Mitchelburn's house, where Major-General Kirke dined*." No wonder that Mitchelburn was indignant at the presumption of Walker. A reader of the *True Account* could draw no other conclusion than that Walker was *the Governor*, and Mitchelburn only his assistant.

† *History of England, IV.* 202. *Note. London,* 1860.

‡ Postcript of a letter from the Earl of Shrewsbury to Major-General Kirke, dated at Hampton Court, 16th August:— "The King's letter, being intended for the officers-in-chief commanding at Derry in the time of the siege, and *it not being known here who those are,* I desire you to fill up the superscription with such names as are proper to be addressed to." See *Memorial,* by William Hamill, Gentleman, p. 15. London, 1714. The fact that Walker when in London was styled Governor by the Irish Society and others is equally inconclusive, as parties in the metropolis were led astray by Kirke and himself. Even the English Parliament was for a time deceived.

§ Officers at this time did not always sign their names to public documents in the order of their rank. Thus, at the Council held in Londonderry, on the 10th of April, 1689, the name of Lundy, who was Governor, is far down in the list.—See p. 29 of this volume.

in command. Mackenzie, who was respected by contemporaries as a pious and intelligent minister, deposes that he held merely a subordinate position. His evidence is corroborated by Captain Roche, who, at great hazard, made his way from the ships into the city during the siege, and who affirms that he acted, when there, " by the command of Colonel Baker, THE THEN GOVERNOR."* When Kirke made his entry into Derry there seems to have been no doubt as to the individual who was chief Governor, for the Major-General proceeded to the house of Mitchelburn, *and dined there.* The officer who commanded the soldiers in the Phœnix, when Derry was relieved, attests that, during his stay in the place, Colonel Mitchelburn "acted as *sole* Governor."† Mr. William Hamill, the brother of Colonel Hamill, avers that Baker alone was elected Governor.‡ A number of officers, equally competent and trustworthy, who authenticated Mackenzie's Narrative, thus virtually declared that Walker was only Assistant Governor.§ Colonel Murray told Walker to his face, in the presence of the Committee of the British Privy Council, that he was not Governor of the garrison ; and when the reverend gentleman, then in the zenith of his popularity and power, attempted to sustain himself by appealing to Colonel Hamill and Lieutenant-Colonel Blair, who were also in the room, and who had good reason to be afraid of disobliging him, these officers maintained a most significant silence.|| But, according to Lord Macaulay, Walker alone is to be credited, and all other witnesses utter falsehood !

The history of the controversy which now ensued, as given by this writer, is most unfair and erroneous. He intimates that the only objection urged against "The True Account" by the Presbyterian ministers was that Walker had "omitted to mention their names."¶ They were not so silly as to imagine they could sustain much injury by so trivial, though so invidious an oversight. Neither were the Presbyterian ministers the only parties who complained of the production. It was felt by the brave men who had fought at Derry to be an uncandid and a party performance. Though professing great impartiality. it was calculated to mislead the public mind ; it did gross injustice to Baker, Murray, Mitchelburn, and other chief actors in the siege; and at their expense, it glorified Walker and "The Church." As might have been expected, it led to a war of pamphlets. A tract soon appeared, entitled, "An Apology for the Failures Charged on the Rev. Mr. George Walker's Printed Account of the late Siege of Derry, in a Letter to the Undertaker of a More Accurative Narrative of that Siege." In this piece, which is anonymous, the writer comments ironically on the statements contained in the "True Account." A rejoinder was speedily forthcoming, which is also anonymous, and which is styled, "Reflections on a Paper pretending to be an Apology for the Failures Charged on Mr. Walker's Account of the Siege of Londonderry."

Walker now felt it necessary to resume the pen, and endeavoured to meet the objections urged against his first performance, in a pamphlet to which he attached his name, and which is designated, "A Vindication of the True Account of the Siege of Derry."** The author

* See the case of Captain James Roche, in the appendix to "Harris' History of the Life and Reign of King William," p. 30. Dublin, 1749.
† See his testimony, p. 71.
‡ See " Memorial, by William Hamill, gentleman," p. 9. London, 1714.
§ See pp. 84, 85, of this volume. The fact that Walker was the Governor's assistant is also established by the evidence of the old historical drama, called " The Siege of Derry," where he is described as " Evangelist," and " Commissary of the Stores." This drama, in a modified form, may be found in " Graham's Ireland Preserved." It is, by some, attributed to Mitchelburn.
|| See page 86. Colonel Hamill, who was in extremely embarrassed circumstances, was induced to sign a paper stating that Walker " executed the place and officer of Governor *joint* with Colonel Henry Baker, until the said Baker's sickness, whereof he died, and after with Colonel John Mitchelburn ;" but it is evident that "his poverty, and not his will, consented" to the signature, though, as Walker was really Assistant-Governor, he perhaps felt himself justified in putting his name to the document. As to the certificate of Gervais Squire, see pp. 87 & 95.
¶ *History of England,* V. 132. ** London, 1689.

most ostentatiously professes moderation, but throughout displays a large amount of cool insolence, mingled with no little evasion and special pleading. "Mr. Walker," says the publisher in the Preface, "has at last been persuaded to write this Vindication, in which he is forced to reprove and rebuke with some authority, and resent,* but hopes none will take it to themselves, but those he intended it for of his own country." The Reverend gentleman (who writes in the third person), does not hesitate in this tract to avow the sectarian spirit of his previous production. "He does confess that in the writing of that book (The True Account) he thought it *necessary* for him, with as little offence as possible, to discover that he was a true son of the Church of England."† A private communication, couched in a friendly spirit, had already been addressed to him, complaining of his attack on the Rev. Alexander Osborne, whom he has represented as "a spy upon the whole North employed by Lord Tyrconnel ;" and proof had been tendered to convince him, that the excellent minister thus stigmatized was one of the best friends of Protestantism in Ireland ;‡ but, instead of making an honourable apology, he refuses to withdraw his indictment. "He has heard of the gentleman's (Mr. Osborne's) good intentions in his proceedings : Mr. Walker is sorry they were no better understood, that he might clear him from the imputation of those mischiefs his management and advices brought on that part of the kingdom."§ In "the True Account" he had taken care not to mention that, during the siege, the Presbyterians had enjoyed the use of the Cathedral every Lord's-day from twelve o'clock at noon ; but the fact had now transpired, and he most disingenuously endeavours to turn it to the advantage of his party. "If they (the Presbyterians) were in Derry the greater number and more considerable, would they have chosen Church of England men their Governors, and been contented with so moderate a share of the church and in the afternoons ?"∥ Adam Murray, as we have seen, might have been the Governor ; but he declined the honour, as he felt he could better serve the common cause by retaining the command of the cavalry. Besides, Presbyterians had long been denied military promotion ; and if, in this emergency, they had no officers of the same experience in war as Colonel Baker or Colonel Mitchelburn, they exhibited their good sense when they conferred the command on those who possessed the highest professional qualifications. It was absurd to infer their inferiority in numbers because they met in the Cathedral in the afternoon. The Episcopal worship was over every Lord's-day at twelve o'clock, and the Non-conformists would have been most unreasonable had they not been satisfied with the use of the building for the remainder of the day. Walker himself knew right well that the Presbyterians were by far the majority of both citizens and soldiers, and it is to be regretted that he permitted his sectarian feelings to betray him into equivocation as to a fact so notorious. But the notice taken of the Presbyterian ministers in this Vindication is, perhaps, the most discreditable part of the performance. Under the pretext of supplying his original omission in not giving a list of those who were in the place during the siege, he tries to turn them into ridicule by metamorphosing their names, or otherwise recording them inaccurately. Thus, Mr. Gilchrist of Kilrea, who is placed at the head of the catalogue, has the awful designation of Mr. W. Kil-Christ ;¶ and Mr. Mackenzie of Cookstown, who stands next, is styled Mr. Jo. Machiny. Mr. Mackenzie was as well known in Derry as Mr. Walker ; and, on a most important occasion, when it was deemed prudent to enter into negotiations with the enemy, he was one of six commissioners chosen to form the deputation.** Such a puerile attempt to annoy the

---

* *i.e.*, resentment. † p. 13. ‡ Vindication of the Rev. A. Osborne by Boyse, p. 2.
§ p. 16. ∥ p. 15.
¶ The name is here given exactly as printed by Walker. The mischevious intent cannot be mistaken.
** See pp. 52 & 70.

Presbyterian ministers by tampering with their names was unworthy of a man who had reached the age of upwards of threescore years and ten, and who expected soon to be consecrated bishop of Derry.

Lord Macaulay's version of this controversy is remarkable for its flippant inaccuracy. "Walker's accusers," says he, "in their resentment disregarded truth and decency, used scurrilous language, brought calumnious accusations which were triumphantly refuted, and thus threw away the advantage which they possessed. Walker defended himself with *moderation and candour.*"* The two words here employed by the great historian exactly express the qualities in which the "Vindication" is most deficient. The Rev. Joseph Boyse, of Dublin, a Presbyterian minister of eminent ability, well known by his various contributions to theological literature, now interfered, and published "A Vindication of the Rev. Mr. Alexander Osborne, in reference to the affairs of the North of Ireland."† This tract, in spirit and style, is much superior to any of the preceding pamphlets. Mr. Walker's most absurd attempt to underrate the numbers of the Presbyterians is met by the following plain statement:—"In the Cathedral, in the forenoon, when the Conformists preached, there was but comparatively a thin auditory; in the afternoon it was very full, and there were four or five meetings of Dissenters in the town besides; and how any man will reconcile this with the number of Conformists being more considerable, or indeed near equal to that of their brethren, I cannot well imagine."‡ In other parts of this tract Boyse adduces facts which might well have abashed and confounded an individual even less sensitive than the intended Bishop of Derry. Walker, as has been stated, had excused himself for the omission of a list of the Presbyterian ministers who were in the place during the siege, on the ground that he could not learn their names; but Boyse proves that the Reverend Colonel, when passing through Edinburgh, on his way to London, had repeated to two clerical visitors the names of them all, with one exception.§ His vindication of the Rev. Alexander Osborne is most triumphant. Mr. Walker had not only assailed Mr. Osborne's character, but had also, with a view still farther to stain his reputation, inserted in "The True Account" a letter addressed by him to several persons of distinction in the north of Ireland. The letter was written under very peculiar circumstances, so that it was liable to misconstruction,‖ but a few words would have disclosed its true design; and yet not a syllable of explanation was appended. Such treatment of one who had rendered good service to the Protestant cause excited the disgust of all possessed of right-feeling; and a number of gentlemen fully acquainted with the details of the transaction, including Lord Massareene, Sir Arthur Rawdon, and Colonel

---

* *History of England*, V. 132. The following is a specimen of what Lord Macaulay describes as "moderation and candour." Speaking of the only adverse pamphlet which had yet appeared Walker says that it "discovers so much ignorance, malice, and falsehood, that it is not worth the notice; only that he should be glad the author could be known, that he might be duly corrected for so scandalous a paper, reflecting most unjustly, not only on the Church, the Reverend Bishops and Clergy, and Mr. Walker himself, but upon the present Government, with very little credit to the party he seems to defend; and all performed with such a strain of dulness, such impudence, and so many lies, and so vulgarly writ, that he is below anything like an answer, or any further notice, unless of a magistrate." P. 34. It may occur to some readers that, had the magistrate been swift to punish vulgar writing, Walker himself was in danger.

† London, 1690. Licensed, November 22, 1689. Mr. Boyse was, at this time, only about twenty-nine years of age.

‡ See p. 79 of this volume. It would appear that there were two or three Presbyterian meetings in the forenoon, as well as in the afternoon, in different parts of the town. Mackenzie speaks of "two or three other meetings," in addition to that in the Cathedral in the afternoon. Boyse speaks of both forenoon and afternoon.

§ See p. 80 of this volume.

‖ See a more particular account of this matter, at pp. 26 & 76.

Upton, now came forward to bear testimony in Mr. Osborne's favour. "In regard, some of late," said they, alluding to the language employed by Walker, "have represented Mr. Osborne in a public manner as an ill man and spy upon the whole North, employed by the Lord Tyrconnell, and as serving two masters, the British and the Irish, and the like, to his great disadvantage, we cannot but own that we, who had, as we suppose, good reason to understand him therein, had, and still have, better thoughts of him, and are so far from looking on him as guilty of any such matters, that we are well assured of his having intended, and done therein, the best service he could to the Protestant interest there, and that he was very faithful to the same to his utmost."*

The mis-statements advanced by Walker suggested to Mackenzie the propriety of supplying the public with a more accurate history of the siege; and, accordingly, soon after the appearance of "The True Account," he commenced the preparation of his "Narrative." As a memorial of one of the most important events connected with the Revolution, it is a document of great value. From it almost all subsequent writers, on the same subject, have derived a large portion of their materials. It is more complete and circumstantial than any other contemporary record of the transactions it describes. Before its publication the whole of what properly relates to the siege was read over, paragraph by paragraph, to a number of the colonels and captains engaged in the defence of the city, and as they are known to have concurred in its statements, it thus possesses an authority which it could not otherwise challenge.† By the Protestants of Ulster it must ever be perused with the deepest interest, and many of them will here find the names of their ancestors most honourably registered.

This Narrative strips Walker of not a few of the plumes in which he had decked himself. It furnishes the clearest evidence that he would more than once have capitulated, had he not been baffled by the vigilance and resolution of the garrison. The statements of the "True Account" and of the "Narrative" are often directly contradictory. Walker, for instance, boasts that, when his house was searched for provisions, none could be found: Mackenzie tells us that the examination was not quite so unproductive, as "beer, mum,‡ and butter" were discovered in it, and conveyed to the public stores. Walker represents himself as heading the sallies of the garrison: Mackenzie alleges that he confined himself to his duties within the city, and engaged outside the walls in no sanguinary conflicts. "As to the enemy," says he, "he was a man of peace all the time, and was guilty of shedding no other blood to stain his coat with, but that of the grape."§ Walker states that, when the garrison were almost in despair, he preached in the cathedral, and declared, "that God would at last deliver them," and that "about an hour after sermon" the ships in the Lough were

---

* See this document, at pp. 77 & 78. As Boyse's Vindication of Osborne has long been a very scarce pamphlet, it has been deemed proper to republish a large portion of it in the present volume. —See *Supplement to the Narrative*, p. 73.

† See the attestations in the "Invisible Champion Foiled," p. 85. It was compiled from various diaries kept during the siege.

‡ *i.e.*, "Ale brewed with Wheat"—*Johnson's Dictionary*. It may be that, at a subsequent search, nothing was found, and that Walker, without mentioning the previous discovery, takes credit for this fact. But it is plain, from a pamphlet published in defence of Mitchelburn in 1692, that Walker to the last was suspected of tampering with the stores. See "Account of Transactions in the North of Ireland, 1691," By J. H.

§ See p. 89 of this volume. This statement is confirmed by what we find in a vindication of Mitchelburn, published in 1692, and quoted in the preceding note, where it is said that Walker "appeared more conspicuous in the eating part than the fighting part." There is reason to believe that his inebriety, one of the "personal vices" mentioned in the Narrative (p. 45), created much uneasiness and dissatisfaction during the siege. It is plainly suggested by the words quoted in the text. We find it subsequently noticed by a brother clergyman, not unfriendly to him. The Rev. Dr. Davis, in his diary, informs us that, on Saturday evening, May 31st, 1690, he and his friends "met Dr. Walker coming from Belfast, *after taking a plentiful refreshment*."—*Ulster Journal of Archæology*, IV. 83, 87.

seen approaching the boom. Mackenzie alleges that "about this time Walker preached a discouraging sermon." The account of Walker cannot bear the test of impartial scrutiny, for the Episcopal service in the cathedral was over at noon, and the ships did not approach the barrier till seven o'clock in the evening. The sermon which Walker is said to have preached on the occasion, and which is designated the "Christian Champion," was obviously prepared for the public eye after the victory was won. It is somewhat suspicious that, according to the printed entry on the back of the title-page of the first edition, it was licensed for the press the very day on which its author attests that the boom was passed! At that agonising crisis, Walker thought little about printing or licensing sermons.*

The history of the siege of Derry published by the minister of Cookstown quickly drew forth a reply replete with scurrility, and entitled "Mr. John Mackenzie's Narrative a False Libel." Walker had acquired considerable political influence, and as he continued to act in concert with his friend Kirke, persons from the North of Ireland looking for situations under Government, and especially for military promotion, were anxious to secure the favour of the bishop elect, and the Major-General. Under the influence of this feeling, some needy Derry officers were induced to signify their dissatisfaction with Mackenzie's Narrative; and their certificates of disapproval, though rather equivocally expressed, were paraded in the new pamphlet.† But this manœuvre was unsuccessful. Mackenzie again presented himself before the public, and in his rejoinder, designated "Dr. Walker's Invisible Champion Foiled,"‡ exposed the arts employed to get up the signatures, as well as the worthlessness of the testimonials themselves. He produces a document subscribed by Sir Arthur Rawdon, Sir Arthur Langford, Colonel Upton, and other gentlemen of the highest character, attesting that his Narrative had been read in their presence, at a meeting of Colonels and Captains then in

* "The Christian Champion," though represented as licensed July 30th, 1689, was evidently published after Walker's appearance in London. The title-page is ornamented with a rude likeness of the author.

† Some of these certificates are so meagre and unsatisfactory, that it is only wonderful they were ever published by the friends of Walker in his vindication. The following appear at the head of them:

"*We, the underscribers*, officers of Londonderry, in the following list mentioned, do hereby declare that Mr. John Mackenzie or any for him, never read all that part of his pamphlet, intituled, "A Narrative of the Siege of Londonderry," to them, that related to Londonderry, before the same was printed, as, in the preface to the said pamphlet, is set forth; nor did the said subscribers assent to what they heard read, but on the contrary, objected against *several things* they heard read, and having seen the said pamphlet since it was printed, *do not assent to, or approve of it.* As witness *our hands,* this 9th day of April, 1690.   "RICHARD CROFTON."

This certificate, drawn up in the plural number, indicates by the solitary name appended to it, that the greater number of the individuals to whom it was presented, refused to sign it; and yet its statements are so vague and general, that an officer, who was convinced of the truth of almost the whole Narrative, might have subscribed it.

The next certificate is still more cautiously expressed:—

"I, the under-written, did not assent to two particulars in Mr. John Mackenzie's book, viz., the articles against Dr. Walker, and the discouraging sermon, *not knowing anything of them.*
"ALEX. SANDERSON."

Mackenzie has *named* no less than seven colonels or captains (see page 45), concerned in bringing forward charges of a very grave character against Walker, and yet we find that not one of these gentlemen has appeared to deny the fact. Instead of honestly meeting the charge that Walker had repeatedly attempted to capitulate, or showing that he had acted with fidelity, his vindicator can only bring forward certificates stating that the reverend gentleman had "executed the place and office of Governor," joint with Colonel Baker and Colonel Mitchelburn, and that certain parties, after having read Mackenzie's Narrative, did "*not approve of it.*" The grounds of their disapproval are not stated, but may be easily conjectured. It offended Kirke and Walker, and its appearance at this juncture alarmed and perplexed those seeking for public employment. They did not approve of it, for they apprehended that, in as far as they were concerned, its publication was unseasonable.

‡ This title was suggested by the circumstance that his assailant was anonymous.

London, who had served at the siege of Derry, and that they had *all* acquiesced in its statements. From such an authority there could be no appeal.

The "Invisible Champion Foiled" terminated the controversy. A few days after its publication, Walker fell at the battle of the Boyne. The King, who, on his first appearance in London, had treated him with singular respect,* seems subsequently to have formed a more correct estimate of his character. When he heard of his death he evinced no concern. "William," says Lord Macaulay, "thought him a busybody who had been properly punished for running into danger without any call of duty, and expressed that feeling with characteristic bluntness on the field of battle. 'Sir,' said an attendant, 'the bishop of Derry has been killed by a shot at the ford.' 'What took him there ?' growled the King."†

Thus died George Walker, a man whose character has been strongly misunderstood, and whose services have been vastly over-estimated. During the siege he never enjoyed the confidence of either the bravest soldiers or the best citizens; and, though he survived only eleven months, he lived long enough to prove that he possessed none of the attributes of true greatness. Walker had a glorious opportunity of doing something to consolidate and advance the Protestant interest in Ireland. He had seen Conformists and Non-conformists shut up within the same walls; united in opposing the same enemy; and worshipping in the same Cathedral. It might have occurred to him that the Presbyterians, who were prepared to die on the walls of Derry rather than submit to Popery, were men whose religious convictions were entitled to respect; and that they might henceforth be placed, at least on a footing of ecclesiastical equality, with their Episcopal brethren. He was aware that Dr. Ezekiel Hopkins, whose income exceeded that of all the six and twenty ministers shut up in the town, had, in the first instance, exhorted the citizens to bow their heads to Popish domination; and had then, like Lundy, fled from the scene of danger. He might thus have been led gravely to doubt whether Episcopal government were worth the cost of its maintenance; for, had the people submitted to the bishop, they would have betrayed the cause of their country. But within a few weeks after the struggle, he outraged all propriety by his vainglorious boasting and his sectarian folly. Instead of seeking to bind Protestants together by the memory of their common sufferings, and the ties of their common faith, he absurdly sounded the trumpet of division. Instead of modestly passing over his own performances, and doing justice to the exploits of his valiant associates, he presents himself as the great

---

* He had the promise of the Bishopric of Derry a few days after he reached the metropolis. The excellent Lady Russell, in a letter dated 19th September, 1689, thus speaks of Walker, when his real character was yet unknown in England—"The King, besides his first bounty to Mr. Walker (£5,000), whose modesty is equal to his merit, hath made him Bishop of Londonderry, one of the best bishoprics in Ireland. It is incredible how much everybody is pleased with what his Majesty hath done in this matter, and it is no small joy to me to see that God directs him to do wisely."

† *History of England*, V. 271. Burnet, in his "History of his own Time," when speaking of the Siege of Derry, mentions Lundy and Kirke, but takes no notice of Walker. "The Oxford editor of Burnet's History," says Macaulay, "expresses his surprise at the silence which the Bishop observes about Walker. In the Burnet MS. Harl. 6584 there is an animated panegyric on Walker. *Why that panegyric does not appear in the History, I am at a loss to explain.*"—*History of England*, V. 133. note. The explanation is simple. Burnet, as well as the King, had seen cause to change his mind. In a letter from Queen Mary to William, congratulating him on the victory at the Boyne, and dated July 7th 1690, there is a passage apparently referring to the death of Walker, and to the haste with which, in the autumn of the preceding year, he had been nominated to the bishopric of Derry. "I must put you in mind of one thing," says the Queen, "believing it *now* the season, which is, that you would take care of the Church in Ireland. *Every body agrees that it is the worst in Christendom:* there are now bishoprics vacant, and other things. I beg you will *take time* to consider who you will fill them with." *Dalrymple's Memoirs, III. Appendix II. p.* 154. The late Bishop Mant was not an admirer of Walker. He was "more valued *at the time,*" says that prelate, "for his military exploits, than for his peaceful and *clerical* character." *History of the Church of Ireland*, II. p. 10. Mackenzie (see p. 00) refers to a change in public opinion respecting Walker, and the facts now stated show that he does not speak at random.

champion and appropriates to himself almost all the glory. No wonder that "The True Account" was as unsatisfactory to the soldiers as to the citizens. As the controversy proceeded, the English Tories, in their ignorance, might believe, as Lord Macaulay expresses it, that Dr. Walker, " an Anglican divine of eminent merit, was rabbled by a mob of Scotch Covenanters ;"* but in Edinburgh, as the noble historian has intimated, public opinion was "against him ;" and in Derry, where he was still better known, he was deemed by many a fitting companion for Kirke and Hopkins.

In a few years many of the defenders of Derry were no more. Some of them sunk under disease, brought on by the hardships of the siege ; and others, who were beggared by the war, and left without hope of aid from Government, died of broken hearts. Very few of those who had so faithfully served their country were suitably remunerated.† Provision was made for the family of Governor Baker, and his son obtained a grant of one of the forfeited estates in the county of Louth. The widow of Captain Browning, whose ship, the Mountjoy, broke the boom, received a gold chain and a pension. But the greater number of the officers were neglected. Upwards of twenty years afterwards Colonel Mitchelburn was thrown into the Fleet prison, in London, for a debt contracted by him when employed in seeking some acknowledgment out of the public purse. In 1721 a pamphlet appeared, with the ironical title—" A View of the Danger and Folly of being Public-spirited, and Sincerely Loving one's Country"—in which the disgraceful treatment experienced by the men who, against such fearful odds, had maintained the cause of King William in Ireland, is fully detailed. This little work, written by Mr. William Hamill, the agent of the Londonderry and Enniskillen regiments, states that a debt, amounting to nearly £140,000, had never been discharged. Even the sums expended by the officers and men in purchasing horses, arms, and accoutrements—taken from them by Government when they were disbanded—remained unpaid ; and no compensation was made for the plundering of their houses, and the destruction of their property during the revolutionary war. Mr. Hamill himself, the heir to an estate of £1,000 per annum, died in poverty.

Mackenzie's Narrative, in an unmutilated form,‡ has long been a very rare volume, and his other work, " Dr. Walker's Invisible Champion Foiled," can seldom be procured on any terms. They are now reprinted, that they may be made more generally accessible, that the facts attested by them may be preserved from oblivion, and that the present generation may have the means of tracing more correctly the proceedings of the various parties connected with one of the most critical struggles in our national history.

We have few materials remaining for a biography of the Rev. John Mackenzie. He was ordained Presbyterian minister of Cookstown in 1673. During the siege of Derry he acted as chaplain to Walker's regiment, and he thus became well acquainted with the character of the Reverend Colonel. The works now reprinted attest that he possessed good sense, as well as no small share of acuteness ; and several of his manuscript sermons, still extant, supply evidence that he was a faithful and able preacher. He died in 1696, aged forty-nine years. Several descendants in the neighbourhood of Cookstown, and elsewhere, still bear the name, and revere the memory, of the historian of the siege of Derry.

The public are indebted for this edition of his works to the Rev. John Knox Leslie, one of Mackenzie's successors in the Presbyterian ministry at Cookstown. Mr. Leslie, in the first instance, suggested the reprint, and then generously patronised the undertaking.

---

* *History of England,* V. 133.
† Calamy, in his account of his Life and Times, says :—" The inhabitants of Londonderry, on the account of their being Dissenters, were not rewarded as they deserved."—l. p. 186.
‡ In the *Derriana,* published in 1794, a considerable part of it is omitted. The present is the only unmutilated edition that has appeared since the Revolution.

A NARRATIVE
OF
THE SIEGE OF LONDONDERRY,
OR
The Late Memorable Transactions of that City.

Faithfully represented, to rectify the Mistakes and supply the Omissions of Mr. Walker's account.

BY JOHN MACKENZIE,
Chaplain to a Regiment there during the Siege.

The most material passages relating to other parts of Ulster and Sligo are also inserted from the Memoirs of such as were chiefly concerned in them.

WITH ALLOWANCE.

LONDON: Printed for the Author, and are to be Sold by Richard Baldwin, in the Old Bailey. 1690.

PREFACE.

The small city of Londonderry having been the last year the scene of so great and remarkable actions, it is hoped that an impartial account of them will not be unacceptable to the public. Gratitude to Almighty God obliges us to record so many signal instances of His power and goodness in the preservation of that people. And it is no more than justice to those who either lost or eminently hazarded their lives in that cause to transmit the memory of those services, by which they have so generously expressed their zeal for the Protestant religion, and their affection to the present Government. It is true, indeed, an Account of the Siege has been published several months ago;[*] and had there not been, besides several material mistakes in it, many passages entirely omitted that were of great importance to set those affairs in their true and native light; or had those faults of that Account been since fairly corrected instead of being vindicated, it would have superseded my labour in preparing this Narrative for the public view, in the writing whereof I am so far from being conscious to myself of being biassed by any affection to a party, that I have been sparing in representing some matters of fact with all the advantage they were capable of, lest they should have that aspect.

I have in this Narrative of Derry inserted the most material passages in the other parts of Ulster (except Enniskillen, of which a distinct account has been given by another hand[†]), and of Sligo, from the memoirs of some persons of quality, and others that were actors in them—a piece of justice due to the nobility and gentry in those parts, who, with so great expense of their fortunes, and some of them with no less hazard of their lives, endeavoured the preservation of their country. For, by this Account, the reader may see they did all that could be expected from them; and the chief causes to which their ill success must be ascribed, were their too great confidence in Colonel Lundy's promises and conduct, and their too early expectations of relief from England. And the behaviour of those of them that stayed in Derry, and made up almost the whole of that garrison, is sufficient to put that reproach of cowardice out of countenance, which some (out of design to exclude them from being employed in the reduction of Ireland) have been so industrious to load them with. I have added in the end his Majesty's letters and instructions, because they so fully manifest his royal care and concern for the preservation, not only of Derry, but of the whole kingdom.

In the Account of the Siege itself I have not only compared other diaries with what I was an eye-witness of, but for fuller satisfaction offered this part of the Narrative to be reviewed by such of the officers of Derry as are now in town,[‡] several of whom, as Colonel Crofton, Colonel Murray, Lieutenant Colonel Blair, Captain Alexander Sanderson, &c., having heard it read in the presence of Sir Arthur Rawdon, Sir Arthur Langford, Colonel Upton, and several other gentlemen, and being desired upon every material paragraph to object against anything either misrepresented or omitted in the relation, freely professed their assent to it: and Dr. Walker was acquainted with the design of publishing it some time before he left the town.

I foresee, indeed, that some who are concerned may be offended with several passages that seem to reflect on some particular persons, especially Colonel Lundy, Dr. Walker, and Major-General Kirk, to which I need only say that, as I have mentioned nothing relating to them but matters of fact that are capable of all the demonstration that can be reasonably expected, so this narrative would have been palpably imperfect and

---

[*] *The True Account*, by Walker.
[†] *The Actions of the Enniskillen Men*, by the Rev. Andrew Hamilton.
[‡] *i.e.*, in London, where Mackenzie published his Narrative.

defective without them. What is said of Colonel Lundy is no more than what was necessary to vindicate the forces at Clady from the imputation of cowardice with which he endeavoured to palliate his own conduct, to give the true reason why the chief officers left the place, and to justify the multitude in casting off his authority, when they saw him resolved on giving up the town to King James. I may allege the same as to Dr. Walker. It was necessary to take notice of the articles against him, because they occasioned that material change in the government by the establishment of the Council of Fourteen. And the other passages were no more than requisite to disabuse the world that had been so grossly imposed on in the ridiculous attempts used to make not only a chief governor in the garrison, but a mighty hero of that gentleman, not only in the Account published in his own name, but in the papers of others who wrote their panegyrics upon him. I shall only produce one instance of this kind out of the Observations printed on Mr. Walker's Account; for among other links in the author's chain of miracles (as he calls it) this is the sixth: "The unanimous suffrage of the people in electing and constituting Mr. George Walker their commander-in-chief, than whom they could not have pitched on a person more completely adapted to so capricious an employment, being a man of exquisite parts, having a neat dexterity in accommodating the humour of the rabble, a discreet temper in moderating the diversity of persuasions, a prudent managery of the common provisions, a vigilant care in the order of guards, watches, and exercise, and an undaunted courage in leading them on to the most dangerous enterprises." A very eloquent paragraph, that gives us the true idea of a complete Governor; only the author had done better to bestow it on Dr. Walker in some part of the world where he is not yet so well known; for if all the other links in his chain of miracles were like this, I am afraid that even in London, as well as at Derry, it would be mistaken for a small legend. For he does not seem so much in this character to have considered what was true, as what would represent his imaginary Governor and General as great and extraordinary. But since Governor Baker has been thus injuriously pilfered of several of his deserved plumes, and Dr. Walker adorned with them, it was but common justice to restore them to the right owner. For what Major-General Kirk did after the siege, it could not be omitted without disappointing the just expectations of the reader, to know what treatment the greatest part of that deserving people met with from him, especially when so very different from his Majesty's declared sense of their services; and the rather because his carriage since to the gentry, and other inhabitants of the North of Ireland, has been but too agreeable to it. And I may justly add, that I have been so far from aggravating these matters beyond just bounds, that I have omitted several things relating to these three gentlemen that were not inconsiderable, because not so necessary or pertinent to this Narrative.

Lest any should think there is, on the other hand, too much said of some particular persons, who were active in the siege, I shall so far prevent that objection, as to assure the reader that as there is nothing mentioned concerning them but what they really did, so several things have not been taken notice of, though to their advantage, because less considerable than what is here related.

One defect, indeed, I must acknowledge in this account—viz., That several, especially of the inferior officers and common soldiers, did excellent service, and showed great courage in the sallies, whose names and particular actions it was impossible for me to recover. But what I could learn that was most remarkable, I have represented with all the impartiality I could, having been rather sparing than lavish in the few characters given of such as were most useful.

Having said thus much to obviate any cavils against the ensuing relation, I shall conclude this Preface with a few reflections on the contents of it.

1. The first attempts of Derry for its own preservation were very justifiable.

There were but too strong grounds to suspect a general design of the Irish Papists against the British Protestants, and particularly of the Ultoghs,* who had given the earliest demonstrations of their cruel dispositions in the rebellion of '41,† and engraven it in the most bloody characters. Of what sort of men the Earl of Antrim's Regiment (designed to garrison there) was made up, the Narrative gives a short but true account. And as these presumptions of their extraordinary danger were the only argument that induced a few youths at first to shut the gates, and the graver citizens soon after to concur with them for their own defence, so the argument carries that weight and strength with it that will sufficiently clear them from any imputations of disloyalty or sedition, in the judgment of all that are not bigots for unlimited non-resistance. To assert that, in these circumstances, they might not justly deny entrance to the Irish soldiers, till they had remonstrated their danger to the Government, is in effect to say, they should have taken no measures to prevent their own imminent ruin, but such as were sure to come too late. And perhaps if those gentlemen that have so freely censured them, had been in their case, their fears would for once have brought them into their wits; for whatever passion they seem to have for a notion they have so long valued themselves upon, as their Shibboleth, I do not see that they are more fond of slavery and destruction than other men, when themselves are in any danger of it. For what they did afterwards, in proclaiming King William and Queen Mary, and consequently in opposing King James's army, the example of England, with the dependence that Ireland has on it, sets those actions above the need of any apology for them.

2. It is not very easy to find a parallel instance in history where so great issues depended on the defence or surrender of so small a place.

Had Derry been surrendered, the whole kingdom of Ireland had been entirely lost, and particularly that brave people of Enniskillen (whose resolute opposition did not a little contribute to the preservation of Derry) had been unavoidably exposed as a sacrifice to the fury of the Irish. King James might have poured so considerable a force into Scotland as would not only have embroiled that kingdom (for that was done by a few), but in all human probability either overrun it, or at least turned it into a field of blood; and how difficult a task it would have been in those circumstances to have secured the peace of England, where there were so many dangerous symptoms of disaffection among too many, and a strange ferment among all, is too easy to imagine. But the defence of that place, as it obviated all these dismal evils, so it has in a great measure blasted all the other designs of the Popish faction against Britain, and facilitated the reduction of Ireland, the very flower of King James' army having perished, and the courage of such as survived, sunk before those walls.

3. And yet scarce ever did a people defend so weak a place with so invincible resolution under greater discouragements.

The English forces sent for their assistance, upon Colonel Lundy's representing the condition of the town as desperate, returned, and all their principal officers, perceiving how affairs were managed, came with them. After which Colonel Lundy and his Council were only solicitous to make the best terms they could for themselves. When their authority was broken by the threats of those whom they called the rabble, there was scarce a man left of any considerable reputation for experience or conduct in military affairs. They had too great reason given them to fear some treacherous friends within, as well as a powerful enemy without, their gates. They could scarce reasonably expect any assistance from England, when those sent before had left the place as hopeless. The ships that came afterwards under the command of Major-General Kirk never made any attempt to come up, when they had no obstacle but what the Castle of Culmore could give them, and had all the advantages of wind and tide to favour them. (Nor did they make any essay till the time we were relieved, notwithstanding the frequent signs we made to them of our distressed condition.) And some weeks after their appearance in the Lough, most of them were gone out of our sight, so

* *i.e.*, Ulster Romanists.   † *i.e.*, of 1641.

that we had little hope of relief by them. And yet, though sickness and famine then daily swept off great numbers (for it is thought that no less than ten thousand died during the siege, besides those that died soon after), we would not hear of surrendering while there was any possibility for the garrison to subsist.

4. The conduct of Divine Providence, in the preservation of that city deserves our admiration and thankful acknowledgments.

Besides what has been already suggested, or is more fully observed in the relation itself, I may add, That those few youths should first shut the gates against the Earl of Antrim's Regiment, when not one person of note in the town durst openly concur with them—that the multitude should obstruct the surrender of it when signed by Colonel Lundy and his Council, after the principal officers had left it, and resolutely adventure on the defence of it, under so many and great disadvantages—looks like the effect of some extraordinary impulse on their minds. To what can we ascribe it, that in so many sallies we should lose so very few men (not above eighty in all), and kill so considerable numbers of the enemy, many more of whom are also reckoned to have died of their wounds than fell in the field, and it is supposed betwixt eight thousand and nine thousand in all perished during the siege; that so many bombs thrown into the town should do no more mischief (nay, some of them, by tearing open the ground, discovered some concealed provisions, which put us on searching for more, with good success); that so many thousand Protestants, whom the enemy had driven to the walls, should be so soon dismissed again, and the shot we made at them, while at a distance and unknown, only single out their enemies. To what can we attribute this, but the immediate care and protection of Heaven. And that when we were reduced to such desperate necessities, those two ships should so boldly attempt, and so successfully (even though the wind failed them) effect our relief after the enemy had made the utmost preparation to oppose them, looks as if the Almighty chose our extremity, and the very difficulties of our deliverance, to enhance the glory of his power in it. The French cruelty in driving so many of our friends before the town, confirmed, instead of weakening, our resolution to maintain it. Those many Protestants that at the beginning of the siege left the city, and took protection, and even the great numbers that died the last six weeks of the siege, made those provisions last the longer, which, had they failed sooner, necessity would have forced us to submit to an enraged enemy, whose treaties we had so little ground to rely on, and from whom we could expect so little mercy after so obstinate an opposition.

5. How disingenuous, as well as foolish, have the attempts of some been, to engross the honour of those actions to a party. Especially, when this was done with so gross partiality as to monopolise it to that party, which, though about equal to the other in the number of field officers, yet was far exceeded by the other in the number of inferior officers, and could not, according to the exactest computation we could make, claim above one in fifteen of the common soldiers. I should not have taken the least notice of this, if the palpable misrepresentation in the Dedicatory Epistle* of the former Account, renewed in the vindication of it, had not obliged me to do it.

6. The treatment that people met with from Major-General Kirk seems very hard and unaccountable. But on this, and the former remark, it is needless to enlarge; for where things so plainly speak themselves, it is but officious impertinence to make any seditious comments upon them.

Several circumstances have concurred to delay the publication of this Narrative. I saw not Dr. Walker's Account till December, and could not come hither† before the end of January, and have since spent some time in waiting for papers, and consulting such as were capable of giving me any further information.

If I have omitted the mentioning of any persons' names who might have merited well in the garrison, I declare it is not done of design, but for want of just information.

* Walker prefaced *The True Account* with a Dedicatory Epistle to William and Mary.
† *i.e.*, to London.

CHAP. I.

THE TRANSACTIONS OF THE CITY OF DERRY, FROM THE SHUTTING OF THE GATES TO THE DESCENT OF THE IRISH ARMY.

THE noise of the Prince of Orange's intended descent into England in autumn, 1688, and the preparations made in Holland for that purpose, extremely alarmed the late King James. He, to strengthen himself the more effectually against this expected invasion, commanded over from Ireland several regiments of the standing forces there, who were by that time so modelled, that they consisted almost entirely of Irish Papists; and on these he seemed to rely as his surest friends—a fatal mistake in his politics, though all of a piece with those other measures which his own inclinations, as well as the great zeal of his priest-ridden cabal, suggested to him. For his army here could not bear it —to see themselves outrivalled by a crew of scullogues* in their prince's favour—and he could not have brought any guests into the English nation more unwelcome to it than Irish cut-throats. To supply the room of these regiments in Ireland, the Earl of Tyrconnel, then Lord Deputy, issued out commissions for levying four new regiments in the four provinces of that kingdom. Of that to be raised in Ulster, the Earl of Antrim (an eminent Papist in the North) was made Colonel; which regiment (as it was commonly reported) he was ordered to have complete and ready about the 20th of November then ensuing. The Lord Mountjoy's Regiment of Foot (a well disciplined battalion) was then garrisoned in and about Londonderry, and their colonel, several of the officers, and some of the soldiers being Protestants, the inhabitants of that city looked on their being there as a great security to them, and dreaded the thoughts of their removal. But the Lord Tyrconnel, either out of design to secure himself the better at Dublin, or, as was said, with an intent to send that regiment over to England, ordered them to march up from Derry towards Dublin by the 23d of November. It was expected the Lord of Antrim's Regiment would by that time be in readiness to succeed them, and garrison in their stead; but it fell out very happily that they were not completely raised until above

a fortnight after the Lord Mountjoy's left that city. Some ascribe this delay partly to a report then current among the Irish, that the new levied soldiers were to be all transported for England, to which few of them had any great stomach (their countrymen having never made any lucky expeditions thither, and seldom returned back with a whole skin), and therefore they came in but slowly; partly to the curiosity of the government, in appointing a standard for the stature of their new levied soldiers, who were to be all near six foot high, it is probable out of design of having their army the more uniform, and formidable for their bulk, whatever they were for their courage.

But whatever occasioned that delay, it cannot but be owned as a remarkable providence, that a vacancy so seldom known before, should so strangely happen there in this juncture. The Lord Mountjoy's regiment being gone, the care of the city was committed to John Buchanan, Deputy Mayor to the Irish corporation,* a person of no good reputation in the town, who modelled the town-guards as he thought fit. But the news of this new regiment of the Earl of Antrim's being intended to quarter there was very unwelcome to the inhabitants. They had a certain account that they were all of them entirely Papists, and many, both of

---

* The *Scullogues* were the lowest class of Irish farmers.—See *Ulster Jour. of Archæology, VI.*, 113.

* In October, 1688, the Protestant Mayor, Mr. Campsie, was removed, and Mr. Cormac O'Neill, of Broughshane, near Ballymena, succeeded. The Corporation was now remodelled, and the greater number of the new members were Roman Catholics. Hence Mackenzie speaks of it as "the *Irish* Corporation." Mr. O'Neill remained in Derry only a few days after he was sworn in as Mayor; and, on leaving, appointed Mr. Buchanan, one of his partizans, as his deputy. The Presbyterians who belonged to the Corporation in 1688, before it was remodelled, were John Campsie, Mayor; John Craig, William Smith, and Alexander Leckey, Aldermen; John Burnside, James Fisher, James Cunningham, William Kyle, Henry Long, James Simpson, David Cairns. John Ewing, and Robert Shannon, Burgesses; Horace Kennedy and Edward Brooks, Sheriffs.—*Presb. Loyalty, p.* 426. The Sheriffs were not changed by Tyrconnell's government.

the officers and soldiers, the offspring or near relations of those who in the Rebellion of 1641 had so deeply imbrued their hands in British and Protestant blood. And they had too just reason to believe that these rakehells (who were the very scum of the country) had the hereditary inclinations, as well as the blood of their ancestors running in their veins; and their particular aversion to this regiment was heightened by the apprehensions which they generally had of some mischievous project hatching among the Irish Papists against the whole body of British Protestants. And these fears did not want very probable grounds to support them; some of which it will not be improper to suggest. Many of their priests at their ordinary masses had declared publicly to their people, that they had some great design in hand, which would highly concern them and all their nation, whereof they should have particular notice, as soon as it was convenient; that it was their indispensible duty, at the peril of their salvation, to do whatever their priests should direct and enjoin them, requiring them in the meantime to buy and furnish themselves with the best weapons they could. And the stories of this kind, told by some of the Irish themselves, gained the more credit, when it was observed that generally, through the whole kingdom, not only the men, but the women and boys, too, began to furnish themselves with skeines and half-pikes, it being the great business of the Irish smiths in the country to make this sort of arms for them. These were afterwards called Rapparees, a sort of Irish vultures that follow their armies to prey on the spoil. I shall not mention the many bold and threatening discourses that dropped from many of them, especially when good liquor had a little warmed their blood, or upon occasional quarrels: but I must not omit, that as several consultations of the Irish clergy were discovered, particularly in the county of Donegal, not far from Derry, where the great debates were said to arise betwixt the priests and friars, about the execution of some great design; so a particular sermon preached by a certain friar in Derry itself to the Popish part of the garrison in the open market-house, October, 1688, did not a little alarm the Protestants there, some of whom were, out of curiosity, his hearers. The main subject of his discourse was about Saul's destroying the Amalekites, where he showed how dangerous it was to spare one of those whom God had devoted to destruction, God having deserted Saul, taken the kingdom from him, and ruined both him and his family, for that very reason, as he certainly would all that were guilty of the like disobedience; and that they were obliged always (as then from Samuel) to take their directions from their clergy, as from God, and punctually observe the same, at the peril of their souls.

The application was thought very easy and obvious.

Some of the clergy, also, were observed to buy up fire-arms, and procured several chain-bridles to be made, some whereof were accidentally found, and seized by George Phillips, Esq. And though the news of the Prince of Orange's landing in England, Nov. 5th, gave the Protestants a reviving prospect of the happy change of the Government of that Kingdom, yet it rather increased their fears of their present danger, because they concluded, if the Irish should make any attempt while England was in a combustion, they could expect little relief from thence. But that which made the deepest impression on them was a letter dropped at Comber, December 3d, in the County of Down, where the Earl of Mount-Alexander then resided.* The superscription thus—"To my lord: this deliver with haste and care." The letter was as follows:—

"December 3d, 1688.

"GOOD MY LORD,

"I have written to you to let you know that all our Irishmen through Ireland is sworn; that on the ninth day of this month they are all to fall on to kill and murder man, wife, and child; and I desire your lordship to take care of yourself, and all others that are judged by our men to be heads, for whosoever of them can kill any of you, they are to have a captain's place; so my desire to your honour is, to look to yourself, and give other noblemen warning, and go not out either night or day without a good guard with you, and let no Irishman come near you, whatsoever he be; so this is all from him who was your father's friend, and is your friend, and will be, though I dare not be known, as yet, for fear of my life."

There was no subscription, and the ill writing, as well as the style, seemed to argue it was penned by one of the meaner sort of the natives. There were letters written to others to the same purpose, as Mr. Brown, of Lisburn, and Mr. Maitland, of Hillsborough, besides divers informations. Whether the first letter was really intended by some well-meaning Irishman as a warning, or was a contrivance, I shall not dispute; but the next

* The ruins of Lord Mount-Alexander's residence are still to be seen in the vicinity of Comber. The title became extinct in 1757.

day after this letter was dropped, Sir W. Franklin,* Arthur Upton, Esq.,† W. Conningham, Esq., and Mr. Thomas Knox,‡ sent an express to Dublin with copies of it, not only to alarm the Protestants in that city, but to give them the opportunity of communicating the notice of it to all other parts of the Kingdom. Letters were also dispersed to the Dissenting ministers of the adjacent counties to alarm the country; and accordingly the copies of it thus spread through the several parts of the Kingdom (added to the strong presumptions that the fore-mentioned passages gave of such a design) frighted a great number of Protestants out of it, especially about Dublin, and other parts that were more entirely under the power of the Irish. The memory of the miseries of '41§ was fresh, and they were loath to trust themselves now in the same hands that seemed to have now more power, and better pretence to act those barbarities over again. The copy of this letter was sent by William Cunningham, Esq., from Belfast, enclosed in a letter of his own, to George Canning, Esq.,‖ desiring him to send this to Derry with all expedition. Mr. Canning sent to Alderman Tomkins. A gentleman, meeting with this messenger, was informed of it, and sent his information to George Phillips, Esq., of Newtonlimavady, on the 6th of December, on which day a great part of the new Irish regiment came to quarter in that village. Mr. Phillips, late that night, sent a messenger to the city with what account he had heard of the fore-mentioned letter, and to acquaint them withal, what untoward guests they were like to have the day following: there being, instead of six or eight companies, as they were called, of Irish and Highlanders, about double the number, besides a huge number of women and boys; and, what is remarkable, the messenger came into the town the next morning, being the 7th of December, about the same time that Alderman Tomkins communicated to the city the copy of the letter to the Lord Mount-Alexander. This morning early Mr. Phillips sent another messenger, expressing his sense of their danger from so ill a crew, and advising them to take care of their own safety. The messenger also told them that he had left some of the foremost companies within two miles of the town, the rest being on their way. These circumstances concurring, struck a mighty terror and consternation into the Protestant inhabitants. Several cabals were held in the streets; all were persuaded there was such a design as the fore-mentioned letter suggests, and they looked on these new levied men as the most likely tools for the execution of it. Alderman Tomkins, who brought the copy of the fore-mentioned letter, consulted Mr. Gordon, a Nonconformist minister,* what was expedient to be done, who not only advised to the shutting of the gates, but wrote that day to several neighbouring parishes, to put themselves into a posture for assisting the city, if there should be occasion for it. There was some muttering among the mobile† about shutting the gates, which Alderman Tomkins at first privately encouraged; but when he, with Alderman Norman, and some others, had consulted the Bishop,‡ and found him altogether averse to it, they were unwilling to be concerned; and indeed however divers of those who made some figure in the town wished the thing were done, yet none of them thought fit to be themselves active in it. But in the little cabals which several of the city youth had, when they put it to the question, Whether they should shut the gates, most of them were inclined to it, so much the rather because Mr. Gordon had encouraged and incited several of them thereto. By this time about three companies of the fore-mentioned regiment were come to the water-side, with two officers, a lieutenant and ensign. The officers, leaving the men, ferried over, and came to the Deputy-Mayor and sheriffs, with their Potent.§ One of the sheriffs (Mr. Kennedy) suspected the design of these youths, and intending to quarter the soldiers that

* Sir W. Franklin was the second husband of the Countess of Donegal.
† Arthur Upton, Esq., of Castle Upton, near Templepatrick, was a zealous Presbyterian. Lord Templeton is the present representative of the family.
‡ Mr. Thomas Knox was one of the Burgesses of Belfast, and one of the leading merchants there. Shortly after the Revolution he purchased from the Earl of Donegal an estate, then worth about £1,000 per annum, at Dungannon. He was brother-in-law to Captain Edward Brice, grandson of the Rev. Edward Brice, of Broadisland.—See *Presbyterian Loyalty*, p. 402. The present Bishop of Down and Connor and Dromore belongs to this family of Knox.
§ *i.e.*, 1641, the year of the great Irish massacre.
‖ This Mr. George Canning was the ancestor of the great Statesman of the same name, and of the present Lord Garvagh.

* Mr. Gordon succeeded Mr. John Woole as Presbyterian Minister of Glendermot. Mr. Woole, who was ordained in 1654, had also the charge of Fanghanvale and Cumber.
† *i.e.*, the multitude.
‡ Alderman Tomkins was an Episcopalian.— See *Presbyterian Loyalty*, p. 428. Alderman Norman was of the same denomination. Hence they were so much under the influence of the Bishop.
§ *i.e.*, Warrant, or official order.

B

night on the other side of the water, had given them a secret hint to be prepared next morning, if they intended to prevent their coming in. But whilst they were about consulting their strength, the Irish soldiers having, as is supposed, some intimation of their design, made all the haste they could over, and came to the landing-place, about three hundred yards from Ferry Gate. The youth observing this, about eight or nine of them (viz :—Mr. Henry Campsie, Mr. William Crookshanks, Mr.Robert Sherrard, Mr. Dan. Sherrard, Mr. Alexander Irwin, Mr. James Steward, Mr. Robert Morrison, Mr. Alexaander Cunningham, Mr. Samuel Hunt, with whom soon joined Mr. James Spike, Mr. John Cunningham, Mr. William Cairns, Mr. Samuel Harvey,* and several others) drew their swords, ran to the main guard, seized the keys without any great opposition, and came with them to the Ferry Gate, drew up the bridge, and locked the gate, the Irish soldiers being advanced within 60 yards of it. From thence they went to secure the other three gates, and, having placed guards at each of them, met in the market. So happily did these resolute youths nick the very minute of their design, and upon so seemingly rash and desperate action, did the preservation of that important place out of the hands of the Irish depend—the greatest events in the chain of providence being often so contrived by exquisite wisdom as to hang upon the slenderest links in it. This sudden turn extremely surprised the graver citizens of the town, who, though loath enough the Irish soldiers should enter in, yet dreaded the consequences of shutting them out. But the Deputy-Mayor, the Sheriff, the two Irish officers, with other Papists, and some Protestants accompanying them, came to the market-place, and both by promises and by threats endeavoured to prevail on the mobile to desist from so rash an enterprise, but all in vain. They had, in the meantime, sent some to secure the magazine, which, the mobile perceiving, sent a party to seize it, one of whom (viz., Mr. Campsie) being shot by the sentinel, one Linegar, a reputed Papist, Linegar was seized and sent to jail, and the noise of Campsie's being wounded increased both the number and the resolution of the mob. In the meantime, the Bishop of Derry, with others, came to the market-place, and made a speech to the multitude to dissuade them from so inconsiderate an undertaking,* wherein he represented to them both the danger of it to themselves, and the unwarrantableness of it, as it was a disobedience to their Sovereign. But the dangers they saw at present made greater impression on them

* It would appear that almost all, if not all, the Apprentice Boys who shut the gates were Presbyterians. Hence they disregarded the advice of the Bishop, and acted on the recommendation of the Rev. James Gordon. The Congregation of Derry was now vacant, in consequence of the removal of the former minister, the Rev. Robert Rule, to Scotland, early in the year 1688, so that Mr. Gordon, who lived in the immediate vicinity of the city, was at present virtually the spiritual guide of the Presbyterian inhabitants. Henry Campsie, whose name is here first mentioned, was, no doubt, placed in this honourable position because of his near relationship to Mr. Campsie, the Presbyterian Mayor, supplanted shortly before by Mr. Cormac O'Neill, of Broughshane. William Crookshanks appears to have been of the family of the Rev. John Crookshanks, the Presbyterian minister of Raphoe, who was a native of Derry, and who was killed at the battle of Pentland.—See *History of Presbyterian Church in Ireland*, II., 285, 287. John Cunningham was one of the Presbyterian Burgesses driven out of the Derry Corporation by the Test Act in 1704. He was in all likelihood of the same lineage as the Cunninghams of Castle-Cooley, Burt, who, as there is reason to believe, are descended from one of the early Presbyterian ministers of the same name, settled in that part of Ulster. Joseph Morrison, another of the Burgesses ejected from the Corporation for his Presbyterianism in 1704, seems to have been related to Robert Morrison, the Apprentice Boy. In a pamphlet, published in 1689, the shutting of the gates is ascribed to " one Irwin, a young Presbyterian Scot, *with some others of his fellows.*"—See *Apology for the Failures charged on the Rev. George Walker's Account*, p. 13, 14. The Rev. William Irvine, of the Sinclair Seaman's Church, Belfast, is descended from Alexander Irwin. The watch and the sword of the Apprentice Boy are still preserved in the family. It is well known that the orthography of proper names was at that time very unsettled. Hence the name of this young man is written Irwin, Erwin, Irwyn, Irwine, and Irvine.

* The Bishop was Dr. Ezekiel Hopkins. The *Londeriad* describes this Right Rev. gentleman as thus addressing the citizens :—

"Dear friends, a war upon yourselves you'll bring :
Talbot's deputed by a lawful king ;
They that resist his power do God withstand.
You'll draw a potent army to this land."

This rude poem was written very shortly after the siege by a person minutely acquainted with the state of matters in Londonderry. It was printed in Dublin, in 1699, under the following title :—

" Londerrias : or a Narrative of the Siege of Londonderry, which was formed by the late King James, the 18th of April, and raised the 1st of August, *Anno. Dom.*, 1689. Written in verse by Joseph Aickin. 12mo." It is reprinted in an imperfect form in *Derriana*.

than any feared for the future; and their dull heads could not comprehend how it could be so great a crime to shut the gates against those whom they believed sent thither to cut their throats; and they were too much concerned to make good what they had now done, to hear any longer harangues about it. The Deputy-Mayor also attempted once more to dissuade them, but to no purpose. The Irish soldiers, in the meantime, stood at the gate, fretting at their present disappointment, that they should be forced to wait like scoundrels, where they hoped to domineer as lords, till one, Mr. James Morrison, a citizen, having in vain warned them to be gone, called out aloud, "Bring about a great gun here," the very name whereof sent them packing in great haste and fright to their fellows on the other side the water. Hitherto the multitude acted without the least public countenance from any of considerable note or figure in the town, till that afternoon came in David Cairns, Esq.,* who, having received a full account of what was done, and their inducements thereunto, declared openly his approbation of it, commending their courage, and assuring them of his utmost assistance; and thereupon went round the walls, and to the gates, encouraging their guards and sentinels, and returned to the main guard again to show his concurrence with them. He endeavoured also to possess others of note in the town, with a just sense of the necessity of taking this course to secure themselves at that dangerous juncture, and several began to appear more openly in the matter, as entertaining the same apprehensions, so as that night he, Mr. Norman, Mr. Jemmet, Mr. Thomas Moncreiff, Mr. James Lennox, and several others, being come into the guard-house, upon some discourse there as to their inability to defend themselves, without considerable assistance, wrote to several gentlemen in the country, to acquaint them with what was done, to represent their common hazard, and the necessity of their concurrence for their common defence and safety; to which letters they received various returns, some approving the action, and promising their assistance: others discouraging what they thought so bold an enterprise. Besides these, one letter came afterwards, directed to Mr. Cairns, from a Nonconformist minister in Enniskillen, which, because it shows how early the inhabitants of that town agreed with those of Derry, both in their resolutions, and the reasons of them, I shall here insert:—

"Enniskillen, December 15, 1688.

"Sir,

"After an alarm of an intended massacre, there are two foot companies sent to be quartered in this small place, and though we be deserted by our magistrates, yet we intend to repulse them. You are therefore entreated in this common cause to look on our condition, and if we come to be made a leading card, sit not still and see us sink. The bearer can more fully inform you of our condition. The Lord direct and preserve you and us, who intend hurt to none, but sinless self-preservation.

"This from, yours, &c.,
"Robert Kelso."*

About the same time the principal inhabitants of Enniskillen wrote a letter to the same purpose to their friends at Derry (which see at the end). Others in the town wrote to the Government to excuse themselves, and

* David Cairns of Knockmany, in Co. Tyrone, the first gentleman in Ulster who went to Derry on the arrival of Antrim's regiment at the Waterside, was distinguished alike by piety and talent. He was for several years representative of the Maiden City in the Irish Parliament. He was a steady Presbyterian, and he states in his will that, had he "bartered his conscience for allurements" held out to him, he might have left behind him a much more ample provision for his posterity. In this document he bequeaths a memorial of his regard to the Rev. Samuel Ross, Presbyterian minister of Derry, and a like memorial to the Rev. Nehemiah Donaldson, the Presbyterian minister of Derg. Counsellor Cairns died in 1722, aged 77. He was married to Margaret Edwards, a member of a highly respectable family, from which the Rev. E. T. Martin, of Dundonald, is descended. David Cairns was nearly related to Sir Alexander Cairns, a companion in arms of the famous Duke of Marlborough. This Sir Alexander Cairns left an only daughter, from whom Lord Rossmore is descended. The sister of Sir Alexander was married to John Henderson, Esq., of Castletown, near Strabane, and one of the daughters of Mr. Henderson by this lady was married to Mr. Laird, the Presbyterian minister of Donoughmore, near Strabane, from whom the Rev. W. M'Clure, of Londonderry, is descended. Another of the daughters of Mr. Henderson, of Castletown, was married to a Mr. Singer, the ancestor of the Right Rev. Dr. Singer, Bishop of Meath.

* Mr. Kelso was ordained at Raloo, in the County of Antrim, in 1673. He demitted this charge in the following year, and removed to Wicklow, where he was settled in 1675. He passed from thence to Enniskillen, where he died shortly after the Siege of Derry.

lay the blame on the mobile. I should add here that the l'otent being more narrowly inspected, was found defective; for it was in the body of it to provide quarters for the captains hereafter named, and their men, whereas there was no captain named at all.

And thus ended this remarkable seventh of December.

Good guards are kept within and without the walls that night. And the next day, the 8th of December, since they wanted both arms and ammunition, they broke open the magazine, and took out thence about 150 muskets, with some quantity of match, and one barrel of powder, and bullets proportionable. There was in the magazine at that time but about eight or nine barrels of powder in all, and about two more in the town (two or three of those in the magazine were not fit for use). There were but few arms fixed, and those designed for the Irish regiment, the rest, being about a thousand more, were much out of order. The Bishop that day left the town, and went to Raphoe;* but the sight of several from the neighbouring parts of the country, whom the fear of an intended massacre drove thither for security, the rumour of a design among the Papists in town to fire the city, and the rude carriage of some of the Irish soldiers in their quarters over the water, drew many more of the town to join with the mob for their common preservation. And yet I must add, that when towards the better settling of their guards, they took an exact account of all within the walls able to bear arms, they did not in all amount to three hundred, so depopulated was the town at that time: the suburbs were not numbered, but it was believed they could not make near so many more. This day the city was cleared of the greatest part of the Papists in it, and a convent of Dominican friars packed off. The Earl of Antrim lodged that night at Newtownlimavady, with Mr. Phillips, whom he carried with him next day in his coach towards Derry (being the 9th, the fatal day for the expected massacre). The post letters that morning brought the news of the Prince of Denmark and the Duke of Ormond's, &c., going over to the Prince of Orange, which give us no small encouragement; and Alderman Tomkins, by the assistance of Mr. Gordon's influence on his people, sent in a considerable number into town, under the command of young Mr. Tomkins, as their captain. For joy of their good news from England, the gunner was ordered to discharge two of their best guns,

which he accordingly did. This put the Irish soldiers on the other side of the water into no small consternation. About the same time, one George Cook, a butcher, drew up fifty or sixty boys on the shore, at the Ferry Quay, whom the Irish took for Laganeers* (famous for the victories they obtained over the rebels in 1641); soon after Mr. Tompkins and Mr. Gordon appear on a hill near them, with about thirty or forty horse, having no design of disturbing them. But all these circumstances so unluckily concurring to heighten their fears of some sudden destruction coming on them, put them on so hasty a flight, that many of their officers left their boots, and soldiers their coats behind them. Their colonel, the Earl of Antrim, accompanied by Mr. Phillips, met them about a mile off the town, and having heard from his men a very frightful story, thought fit to send Mr. Phillips into town before him, to bring him word whether they would admit himself, and who commanded the town. Mr. Phillips, as coming from the enemy, was with some difficulty admitted under a guard; but finding he was no way disaffected to the design, but rather inclined to join with them in their own defence, the guard was taken off; yet upon his desire to Mr. Cairns, who then commanded in town, that some colour of force might be put upon him in what he did, he was publicly threatened with confinement if he did not concur with them. He was permitted to acquaint the Earl with his being detained there, whom in his letter he discouraged from coming thither; upon receipt thereof the Earl went back to Coleraine, where he endeavoured to rally his scattered regiment. And the city considering their own circumstances, to encourage the gentlemen in the country whose aid they expected, and to engage Mr. Phillips the more to their interest, with Mr. Cairns's concurrence, bestowed on him the title of their governor, which he accepted.

In the meantime it was thought expedient to write up to the Lord Mountjoy, then at Dublin (in whose friendship they had great confidence), some account of what had passed, that he might interpose with the Lord Tyrconnel on their behalf, and do his utmost to allay his resentments; and accordingly they sent his lordship a letter (which, because it confirms the foregoing relation, I have annexed at the end), expecting that he would communicate it to the Lord Deputy.

* The Lagan was the name given to a district of country near Derry, and its inhabitants, among whom were many Protestants, were called Laganeers.

* He subsequently passed over to England.

On the 10th, Captain Forward,* and Mr. William Stewart,† brought about two or three hundred horse into the city, and Mr. John Cowan,‡ of St. John's Town, a company of foot, which they offered to our service. But finding the need not only of more men, but chiefly of arms and ammunition, the city unanimously chose David Cairns, Esq., to send over as their agent to England, giving him a large letter of credence, and full instructions under the hands and seals of the chief then in town. He had with him also a letter to the Society in London, which I have in the end inserted ; a private key was also contrived to hold correspondence with them.

This day the townsmen were formed into six companies of foot, under the command of

I. Captain Samuel Norman.
Lieutenant William Crookshanks.
Ensign Alexander Irwin.
II. Captain Alexander Leckey.
Lieutenant James Lennox.
Ensign John Harvey.
III. Captain Matthew Cocken.
Lieutenant Henry Long.
Ensign Francis Hunt.
IV. Captain Warham Jemmet.
Lieutenant Robert Morrison.
Ensign Daniel Sherrard.
V. Captain John Tomkins.
Lieutenant James Spaight.
Ensign Alexander Cunningham.
VI. Captain Thomas Moncrieff.§
Lieutenant James Morrison.
Ensign William Mackey.

* Captain Forward had considerable property at Newtowncunningham and Burt. The Earl of Wicklow is the present representative of the family.

† Mr. William Stewart, of Ballylawn, was the father of Alexander Stewart, father of the first Marquis of Londonderry. Mr. William Stewart's sister was married to Alderman Cowan.

‡ Mr. John Cowan, who was an influential Presbyterian, and one of the ten aldermen subsequently driven out of the Derry Corporation by the Test Act, was the father of Mary Cowan, the mother of the first Marquis of Londonderry. Mr. Cowan's father's name was also John, and both served in Derry during the siege. It is probable that the elder Cowan is the gentleman mentioned in the text.

§ The celebrated Dr. William King, who was Bishop of Derry from 1691 to 1703, and who was subsequently Archbishop of Dublin, greatly widened the breach between the Episcopalians and Presbyterians; and, at his instigation, this Captain Thomas Moncrieff in 1697 complained to the Lord Chancellor that the Presbyterians of the Derry Corporation appointed none but members of their own Church to municipal offices.—See

December the 11th, Mr. Cairns went for London. The same day Governor Philips went to Newtown, and in a few days returned with about three or four hundred horse. William Hamilton, of Moyagh, brought near two hundred more, which they tendered to our service. Soon after, letters from Dublin inform us that the Lord Tyrconnel had ordered the Lord Mountjoy and Lieut.-Colonel Lundy, with six companies of their regiment, to come down and reduce this city to its former obedience. But our friends there cautioned us against the receiving of them, and the city was generally averse to it, and yet, that their actions might not be misinterpreted, they endeavoured to represent the reasons of them in a declaration, which they published about this time.—(See in the end.)

When the Lord Mountjoy came to Omagh, he sent Captain MacCausland with a message to this city, desiring two or three of their number to meet him at Raphoe, upon which Captain Norman and Mr. John Mogridge were sent to hear his proposals, who at their return gave assurance of his lordship's being fully empowered to capitulate, and that he would, on the surrender of the garrison, with our arms, procure a free and general pardon for what was past. These terms our two envoys did earnestly solicit us to accept, though in vain. But because these two had no power to conclude anything, his lordship desired there might be commissioners with full power to treat with him at Mount-Gavelin. Accordingly, the Governor, George Philips, Esq., Captain Alexander Tomkins, Horace Kennedy, Esq., Lieutenant William Crookshanks, and Lieutenant James Lennox, were empowered by the city to treat and conclude, who, after a full hearing of his lordship's proposals, would comply on no other terms than the getting a Protestant garrison, and liberty to keep their watches and arms as formerly, as also a free and general pardon under the Great Seal, which his lordship declared he could not grant, and so they parted without any conclusion, his lordship then saying, he would next morning come to the gates and demand entrance. They returning with the

History of Presbyterian Church in Ireland, II., 445. The charge was shown to be unfounded. Captain Moncrieff, who was an alderman, was dissatisfied because he had not been chosen Mayor. Among the other Episcopalians about this period members of the Derry Corporation were, in addition to those named in preceding notes—Gervais Squire, James Hobson, John Mogridge, James Stroug, Henry Ash, William Newton, and Samuel Leeson.—See *Presbyterian Loyalty*, p. 426, 427.

report of these passages, we began to examine again the stores of ammunition, and found only six barrels of powder, a few arms unfixed, and most of the guns unmounted for want of carriages. Soon after, his lordship appears at the Bishop's Gate, where, for some time, he was made to stand (upon a warm debate within whether he should be admitted). At length, out of respect to his lordship, he was suffered to enter, who being very importunate for an accommodation, there were eleven persons of the city and country appointed to treat with him—viz., George Phillips, Governor, Horace Kennedy, Esq., Captain Alexander Lecky, Captain Warham Jemmet, Captain John Forward, Captain George Canning, Lieutenant Henry Long, Lieutenant James Lennox, William Cunningham, Esq., and James Steward. His lordship, after some debate, that he might prevent any more forces coming down upon us, was at last prevailed on to agree to such articles as the city proposed, which articles are annexed in the end.

Upon the perfection of these articles, his lordship, for our better satisfaction, ordered Lieutenant-Colonel Lundy* to repair to Strabane, there to stop his six companies, till the full moiety, being Papists, were turned off, and some officers of the city were sent to see it done, and Protestants enlisted in their stead. Yet there were but two companies (all Protestants) under command of Lieut.-Colonel Lundy and Captain Stewart received at first into the city. The other four, consisting of one half Papists, were ordered to quarter at Strabane, Newtownstewart, and Raphoe, till thoroughly reformed, which so fully satisfied us that the Protestant interest would be much strengthened by the interposition of the Lord Mountjoy, that our Governor freely resigned his charge to him, and we all resolved to follow his orders and directions. Accordingly his lordship heartily concurred with the citizens, advised them to repair the carriages of the guns, fix the old arms that lay in the stores, and everything else that might be found necessary for the preservation of the city. Whereupon there was a meeting in the Guild-hall, of all the inhabitants, in order to the levying of moneys for that purpose. And a voluntary subscription being there made (about £100), a select number was chosen to dispose thereof, as also to regulate the concerns of the city, viz., Samuel Norman, alderman, Alexander Lecky, alderman, Matthew Cocken, alderman, Horace Kennedy, sheriff, Mr. Francis Nevill, Mr. Frederick Coningham, and Mr. James Lennox, to whom Mr. John Mogridge was secretary. The Lord Massareene also, some time after, freely contributed a considerable sum of money towards the defence of the place. They studied all possible means for the preservation and safety of the city and country; and since they still apprehended a descent of the Irish, they kept up a good correspondence with the neighbouring counties in what concerned their common interest. And that our friends in the country might be encouraged with a speedy supply of powder and arms, money was freely advanced (by Horace Kennedy, Esq., Edward Brooks, Esq., Lieutenant Henry Long, Ensign William Crookshanks, Ensign William Mackey, Ensign John Harvey, Francis Hunt, Alexander Gordon, Hugh Davey, and William Maxwell, Merchants*), and sent with James Hamilton, Merchant, to Scotland, to buy powder and arms. He could procure no more than forty-two barrels of powder, which (except ten left in the county of Down) happily came, and was secured in the magazine. Being also informed that a small bark which was sent from Dublin, with thirty barrels of powder for the Earl of Antrim, lay windbound at Killough, in the county of Down, there were persons appointed to seize and bring the same about for our use, who did so; and leaving a share in some trusty hands for the country's service, brought the remainder, being about twenty barrels, to this city. But all being too small a quantity, pressing letters were despatched to our agent at London, to solicit their Majesties for succour.

The Lord Mountjoy is sent for to Dublin by the Lord Tyrconnell: his friends here all dissuade him from going up. But the advice of some in Dublin prevailed more upon him. Upon his coming there, it was proposed to him by the Lord Tyrconnell that he should go with Lord Chief Baron Rice on a message to King James in France, to desire leave of treating with England for that kingdom; upon which he procured the following articles on our behalf to be perfected, a copy of

* Lundy was a Scotch Episcopalian.

* Most of the persons here mentioned were ejected from the Derry Corporation in 1704, as Presbyterians who refused to qualify under the Test Act. Among the Aldermen thus disqualified, were Horace Kennedy, Edward Brooks, Henry Long, William Mackey, and Hugh Davey. At the same time, John Harvey, the Chamberlain, who was a Presbyterian, was also ejected.—See *History of the Presbyterian Church in Ireland*, Chapter XXII, Note 37. Mrs. Hay, of Derry, relict of the Rev. George Hay, late senior minister of the First Presbyterian Church, is the lineal descendant of Alderman Hugh Davey.

which he sent down to the North, with the ensuing letter, which I shall here add, because it discovers how miserably he, as well as many other well meaning gentlemen were imposed upon by Tyrconnell, who, though he was sufficiently afraid of the issue of things, yet was doing all he could by the increase of his new levies to defend King James's interest there, even while he pretended to others that he was ready to surrender the sword to any commissioned to receive it. And this intrigue of sending to King James is said to be the contrivance of Rice and Neagle, to amuse and divert others of the Popish party in the Council, whose fears inclined them to an earlier submission.

"January 10th 1688-9.

"Until his Majesty's pleasure be further known, it is humbly proposed to your Excellency:—

"1st. That no more levies be made in this kingdom, no more arms given out, nor no commissions signed.

"2nd. That all the new raised forces be kept in their present quarters (if no enemy lands here, and that the kingdom is quiet), and that no more troops be commanded into Ulster than are at present there.

"3rd. That no nobleman, gentleman, officer, or common man in the kingdom, shall be imprisoned, seized, or in any wise molested for any tumultuous meetings, arming of men, forming of troops, or attempting anything that may be called riotous or rebellious, before this present day.

"4th. That no private gentleman's house shall be made a garrison, or soldiers quartered in it."

"Dublin, January 10th, '88-9.

"You have had an account how long I stopped on the way after I left you, and the reasons which made me since come forward; and whatever my jealousies were at my first arrival, I am now fully satisfied with my coming, and, with God's blessing, hope it will come to good to us all. As soon as I saw my Lord Deputy, he told me he intended to send me to the King, jointly with the Lord Chief Baron, to lay before him the state of the Kingdom, and to tell him, if he pleased, he would ruin it for him, and make it a heap of rubbish; but it was impossible to preserve and make it of use to him; and therefore to desire his leave to treat for it. The objections I made to this were two, my being not so well qualified for this as another Roman Catholic, one to whom in all likelihood the King would sooner give credit; and the improbability of being able to persuade the King, who is now in the French hands, to a thing that is so plainly against their interest. To the first of these I was answered what is not fit for me to repeat; and the other was so well answered that all the most knowing Englishmen here are satisfied with it, and have desired me to undertake this matter, which I have done this afternoon: my Lord Deputy having first promised me upon his word and honour to perform the four particulars in the enclosed paper. Now, because a thing of this nature cannot be done without being censured by some, who perhaps would be sorry to have their wishes by quiet means, and by others who think that all that statesmen do are tricks, and that there is no sincerity among them, I would have such consider that it is more probable, I, and the most intelligent men in this place, without whose advice I do nothing, should judge righter of this than they who are at a greater distance, and it is not likely we should be fooled, so I hope they will not believe we design to betray them, ourselves, and our nation. I am morally assured this must do our work without blood, or the misery of the Kingdom. I am sure it is the way proposed in England, who depend so on it, that no forces are appointed to come hither; and I am sure what I do is not only what will be approved of in England, but what has its beginning from thence. I do therefore conjure you to give your friends and mine this account, and for the love of God keep them from any disorder or mischief, if any had such a design, which I hope they had not. I shall write to this effect to some other parts, and I desire you would let such in your county as you think fit see this. Let the people fall to their labour, and think themselves in less danger than they believed."

His lordship went soon after, with Chief Baron Rice, to France, where, instead of obtaining an order for the Irish to lay down their arms, he was made a prisoner in the Bastile.

The Lord Tyrconnel, designing to muster up all his strength against us, orders Lieut.-Colonel Lundy to send up the four companies which were not brought into the city, as well as the other two; but, rather than lose so many good arms, we were induced to receive them; and, having well purged them of Papists, we unanimously concur, and keep our joint guards by detachments out of these six companies, and our own six town companies; which the Lord Tyrconnel being advertised of, issues a proclamation to all parts of the North, discharging the British therein from assembling together, by way of troops and companies, &c. But the Protestants were too sensible of the necessity of defending themselves to pay any great deference to such a proclamation; and particularly at Derry, they went on with their preparations for their own safety, having been early encouraged thereto by the nobility and gentry of the Counties of Down and Antrim (who by a message sent them by William Cunningham, Esq., declared their approbation of what they had done, and assured them of their utmost assistance); but they were not altogether pleased with Lundy's management of affairs. He had, against the mind of the committee for the city, chosen Mr. Norman, Lieut.-colonel, and one Hill, major to his regiment. He soon after discharged the city companies from keeping their guards, and refused them ammunition. And when upon complaint made he restored them, he would but allow one city officer to the guards, and endeavoured to bring them under the command of his own officers. These things disgusted the city, but they thought it not a fit time to contend about them.

Having given this brief account of what passed at Derry, from the first shutting the gates till the descent of the Irish army, it will not be improper to give some relation of the most material passages that happened in other parts of Ulster, before they approached those walls.

CHAP. II.

THE AFFAIRS OF THE OTHER PARTS OF ULSTER AND SLIGO.

THE news of the Prince of Orange's landing was very acceptable to the generality of the Protestants of Ireland, whose success they hoped would soon alter the scene of affairs in that kingdom. The Presbyterian Ministers in the province of Ulster, with several gentlemen of note there, were the first that agreed to send an address to the Prince. To this end they empowered Mr. Osborne and Mr. Hamilton,* being then at Dublin, to fix on the person; who sent Dr. Cumming,† Dec. 8th. The purport of the address (wherein they desired nothing in particular for themselves) was, to congratulate his arrival and success hitherto in so glorious an undertaking; to represent the deplorable condition of the Protestants in that kingdom, and particularly in that province; and beg some speedy relief—assuring him of their readiness to serve his interest to the utmost of their power. All the ministers afterwards in behalf of themselves and their congregations, sent another congratulatory address, dated January 22nd, by two of their number, Mr. Patrick Adair and Mr. John Abernethy.‡ The nobility and gentry of that province were universally sensible of the dangers that then threatened them; for besides those mentioned before, they observed that the Lord Tyrconnell was daily issuing out vast numbers of Commissions for levying of men; that the colonels were empowered to make up as many companies as they could; that the captains were to maintain their own companies for three months at their own charge, who were most of them so unable to support themselves, that the Lord Tyrconnell ordered they should have their commissions without paying any fees; and many of them were forced to leave them in pawn, for what they had already run on the score. They soon saw how such a necessitous crew were designed to subsist. While they were only Rapparees,* they were well versed in the arts of theft and rapine; and being now lifted into the army, they thought they might practise them with some kind of authority; so that in a month or two there was scarce a Protestant in most counties (where the British were not upon their own defence) that had either any stock left on their land, or any horses in their stables. And all complaints of these villanies met with so little countenance or redress, that the Lord Deputy seemed to have raised so many swarms of banditti and robbers, rather than soldiers under discipline, and commissioned them to plunder and ruinate the country, rather than secure and defend it.

All this alarmed the Protestants of the North, who saw their numbers were their only security against the same violences being as generally practised among them. They therefore consulted their own safety, and ordered strong guards to be kept. The first project they fell upon was the disarming of Sir Thomas Newcomen's regiment quartered at Belfast and Lisburn, in order to their making themselves masters of Carrickfergus. Sir Arthur Rawdon discoursed and prevailed on several of the Protestant officers in the regiment to concur with them in this design. He had ordered also a considerable party to be ready at the same time for surprising the Irish garrison at the Newry. The 4th of

---

* The Rev. Alexander Osborne, who had previously been minister of Brigh, was now settled in Dublin, as pastor of the congregation of Newmarket. The Rev. Archibald Hamilton was minister of Armagh.

† Dr. Duncan Cumming, or Comyng, was a Dublin Physician.

‡ The Rev. Patrick Adair was minister of Belfast, and the Rev. John Abernethy of Moneymore. When Mr. Abernethy was in London, his wife and family were obliged to fly for refuge to Derry. Her son John (afterwards a Presbyterian minister, settled first at Antrim, and then in Dublin, and celebrated as the author of various sermons and other published works) had been previously conveyed by a friend at Ballymena to the house of her father, Mr. Walkinshaw of Renfrew, in Scotland, and was thus preserved. Mrs. Abernethy sustained all the horrors of the siege, and all the distress who accompanied her to the city died there.—*History of the Presbyterian Church in Ireland*, III, 157. After the Revolution, Mr. Abernethy removed from Moneymore to Coleraine, where he died, in 1703.

* "These are such of the Irish as are not of the army, but the country people armed in a kind of an hostile manner, with half-pikes, and skeines, and some with scythes or muskets."—*Story's History of the Wars of Ireland*. p. 16.

January was the day for putting it in execution; the Protestant guards were advertised of it; Sir Arthur Rawdon and Sir John Magill* marched from Moira at the hour they had appointed with five hundred horse and foot; Lieutenants Tubman and Berry took the guard at Lisburn; Tubman put all the Papists' arms under the Protestant guard. Captain Obrey of Lisburn, had a small party of horse ready, and actually seized twenty-five of the soldiers' muskets. But when all things were thus ready, and the execution of this design was, as they thought, so easy and secure, Sir Arthur Rawdon, and Sir John Magill, were met within three miles of Lisburn, by Mr. Hamilton, of Tullymore,† who came to acquaint them that the gentlemen at Belfast could not do what was desired from them; they said they had not notice early enough (Mr. Hamilton not coming thither before nine o'clock that night, when the soldiers were in their quarters). They objected the ill consequences which might ensue from the doing of it to the town of Belfast, if they should afterwards fail of securing Carrickfergus; and therefore urged the delaying it till they had more fully concerted their measures, and put the country into a better posture of defence. Upon this, Sir Arthur Rawdon and Sir John Magill were forced to disperse their men, though not without great reluctancy and regret at the disappointment. Mr. Hamilton of Tullymore, upon his return, thought fit to try Sir Thos. Newcomen, who professed himself a Protestant, to engage him to join with him in their common defence—which discourse so alarmed his suspicion, that he put himself on his guard, barricaded the streets of Lisburn, sent to the garrison of Carrickfergus to take care of themselves, who upon his warning sent for the Earl of Antrim's Regiment, and part of Cormack O'Neill's, to strengthen the garrison. But several of the Protestant officers in Sir Thomas Newcomen's Regiment, with one hundred and twenty soldiers, deserted, and the officers sent their commissions to the colonel. Sir Thomas Newcomen soon after took his opportunity, when most of the gentlemen in that part of the country were at Mount-Alexander, to march off with his regiment towards Dublin, and he narrowly escaped being disarmed by the rabble themselves. The Protestant nobility and gentry could not but foresee these proceedings would incense the Government, and draw down an army on them as soon as the Lord Tyrconnel could be ready with his new levies. And, therefore, to be better prepared for what they expected, they agreed to enter into associations in the several counties for self-defence against these illegal outrages. (See in the end.) The counties of Down and Antrim nominated the Lord Mount-Alexander, and the latter added Mr. Skeffington,* for their Commander-in-Chief; as those of Armagh and Monaghan, did the Lord Blaney; those of Derry, Donegal, and Tyrone, Colonel Lundy and Major Gustavus Hamilton.† They chose Councils or Committees for every county, and appointed a general Council of Union, at Hillsborough, for all the associated counties of Ulster. These councils or committees chose the field officers, and applied themselves to those ministers that had the greatest influence on the people for raising their men. Some of the gentlemen that raised regiments, having no public fund, armed and maintained them at their own charge. The Consult ordered the following regiments to be raised in Down and Antrim.

A regiment of horse, consisting of twelve troops, out of both these counties, the Earl of Mount-Alexander, Colonel.

A regiment of Dragoons out of the County of Down, Sir Arthur Rawdon, Colonel.

A regiment of dragoons out of the County of Antrim, Mr. Clotworthy Skeffington, Colonel; but this regiment was not raised, but a regiment of foot instead of it.

Four regiments of foot out of each of the said counties. In the County of Antrim, Sir William Franklin, Mr. Upton, Mr. Leslie,‡ and Mr. Adair§ raised each of them a regiment. There was another in and about Lisburn, designed for Captain Leighton, and three hundred foot were raised by Mr. Edmonstone.‖ In the County of Down, Sir John Magill, Sir Robert Colville,¶ James Hamilton, of Tully-

---

* Sir Arthur Rawdon resided at Moira. The Moira estate is now the property of Sir Robert Bateson, Bart. Sir John Magill resided at Gill Hall, near Dromore. It is said that, a few years after the battle of the Boyne, he gave leases for lives renewable for ever, at the rents which they had previously paid, to all his tenantry who would accept them. The Earl of Clanwilliam is his descendant, and the heir of his property.

† This gentleman was the ancestor of the Earl of Roden, of Tullymore Park, Co. Down.

* Mr. Clotworthy Skeffington was the son of Lord Massareene.

† Major Gustavus Hamilton was subsequently created Viscount Boyne.

‡ This Mr. Leslie resided near Ballymoney. The family seat is still there.

§ This was Mr. Adair, the proprietor of the Ballymena estate.

‖ Mr. Edmondstone resided at Red-Hall, near Ballycarry, in the County of Antrim.

¶ Sir Robert Colville was the son of the Rev. Dr. Colville, of Galgorm, near Ballymena. He was

more, and James Hamilton, of Bangor,* Esqrs., raised each a regiment; and Captain Francis Annesley raised some horse and foot.

The rest of the counties of Ulster were equally forward in their levies.

It was resolved also in the General Consult to send a gentleman into England with an address to the then Prince of Orange, and Captain Baldwin Leighton was chosen, who accordingly sailed from Belfast, January 19th.

The frontier garrisons of Down, being but inconsiderable and unwalled villages, were at first maintained by Sir Arthur Rawdon (his Lieutenant-Colonel, Mr. Hawkins, concurring with him), but afterwards the country contributed to the expense.

The Consult had ordered the surprisal of Carrickfergus. Some Protestants in the town were acquainted with it, and the design laid Feb. 21st. In the night, one thousand foot march from Belfast towards it, under the command of Lieutenant-Colonel Bremicham, and Major Baker; but the weather being bad, and the way tedious, it was clear day before they reached the town. When they were within a mile of it, Bremicham stopped them, on pretence of two passages in a letter he had from the Lord Mount-Alexander, Sir William Franklin, and Mr. Hamilton, of Tullymore. The one was, that he should do nothing in Carrickfergus, without Mr. Henry Davis's advice, who was then in the town; the other, that they would be with him at the hour of action. The garrison, through this delay, had so much notice of their approach, as enabled them to put themselves in some posture of defence. The Earl of Mount-Alexander, Sir Arthur Rawdon, and other gentlemen, came with four or five hundred horse, not doubting the success of the foot, but found the foremost party of them and those on the walls firing at one another. Mark Talbot, Lieutenant-Colonel to the Earl of Antrim, came out to know the reason of this attempt. He was told the stores of Carrickfergus had been always under a Protestant governor; that being now in other hands, they came to demand it for the Prince of Orange, especially to prevent the insolencies and robberies of the soldiers. They also offered terms to the garrison, which Talbot promised to acquaint the Earl of Antrim with. Upon his return it was agreed "That Colonel Cormac O'Neill, who had then his regiment in town, should disband it, and lay down his commission — he and they having protections to return to their several dwellings; that the garrison should be kept by a few of the Earl of Antrim's regiment, who should never have above a week's provisions at once; that the Protestants in town should have a guard as well as the Papists, of equal number, without any disturbance from the castle; that the value of what had been plundered should be restored; that all letters from the Papists to Dublin should be sent open to the Consult at Hillsborough, and particularly such a letter sent from the Earl of Antrim and Cormac O'Neill, by one of their number, to give the Lord Tyrconnell an account of that affair as the Protestants should approve of." A letter was accordingly sent, signed by both sides, but Friar O'Haggerty was (upon Mr. Randal Brice's* recommendation) suffered to be the bearer, who understood as much as any in the garrison could dictate to him, and gave the Lord Tyrconnell the following (too true) account of the condition of the North, viz:—That they were untrained, and had few experienced officers; that the most part were without arms; and, such as had them, their arms were unfixt and unfit for service; that they were very much scattered, and their number not near what had been written, and was confidently reported in Dublin; and that they wanted all ammunition and necessary provisions for appearing in the field. The Lord Tyrconnell (who had deferred for twenty days to send down his army, after it had been first agreed on in Council), upon this information, resolved to despatch the most considerable and best trained part of it, under the command of Lieutenant-General Hamilton.

From the 23rd of February till the 11th of March, several skirmishes happened between the Irish garrison at Newry, or the Rapparees, and the frontier garrisons of the North—the latter being frequently employed to rescue preys of cattle which those ravenous beasts seized and endeavoured to carry away.

Two letters from Dublin, one of the 22nd, the other of the 25th of February, arrived in the North, one giving an account of the preparations making against them at Dublin, the other relating the disarming the Protestants there. But their confident expectation of succours from England, and their conceit of Tyrconnell's fears, made them too slow in their measures. They did indeed

---

now the proprietor of the estates of Comber and Newtownards, subsequently purchased from the family by the ancestor of the present Marquis of Londonderry.

* Lord Bangor is descended maternally from this Mr. James Hamilton.

* Mr. Randal Brice was grandson of the Rev. Edward Brice, the first Presbyterian minister settled in Ireland. He was afterwards M.P. for Lisburn.—See M'Comb's Presbyterian Almanac for 1859, p. 68.

send to Colonel Lundy, at Derry, to bring down what he could spare of the forces of Derry, Tyrone, and Donegal to their assistance, and offered him the command of their whole army. Colonel Lundy promised to bring with him one thousand men well appointed out of each of the three counties, with a train of artillery, and to be with them on a certain day, which was about a fortnight before the descent of the Irish army. Upon which the Consult ordered Hillsborough to be stocked with all necessary provisions for an army; but Colonel Lundy failed their expectations in this, as he did in everything else afterwards, that concerned their common safety.

The 9th of March Captain Leighton returned with a letter [see in the end] from his Majesty to the Earl of Mount-Alexander, to be communicated to the rest of the nobility and gentry, approving their endeavours for their own defence, &c. He brought over also commissions for all the regiments in the counties of Antrim, Down, Armagh, and Monaghan (except two that were not raised when Captain Leighton left the North), and assured them of speedy relief; telling them that some of the cannon and ammunition were shipped, and fifteen thousand men ready at the water side, &c. Upon his coming, King William and Queen Mary were proclaimed in the towns that were in the North-East part of Ulster (with all the expressions of duty and affection, which became their high obligations to their Majesties, as well as their hopes from them); and, in some, before his arrival.

The same day, Mr. Osborne arrived at Hillsborough with a message which the Lord Tyrconnel had permitted him to deliver. But the real design of his coming was to prevent their being surprised with the descent of the Irish army, to give them the best information and advice in order to their defence, to which he earnestly urged them; a fuller account whereof the reader may see in his Vindication.*

11th of March, the Irish army came to Newry, Sir Arthur Rawdon being then at Loughbrickland, sent to the Consult for more forces to defend that place. But, being that night informed that the whole Irish army would be there next morning, and the Consult acquainting him that they had no forces ready to be sent, and advising him to retire to Dromore, he ordered the inhabitants that night to pack up their goods, sent his foot to guard them, and with his horse secured their retreat. The inhabitants went on to Belfast and the sea coasts.

12th of March, the garrison at Rathfryland, with the inhabitants, abandoned the place, and came to Dromore, and that night the Irish army came to Loughbrickland. This day Captain Hugh Magill brought his troop of eighty dragoons from the Ards to Dromore. Sir Arthur Rawdon sent to Hillsborough for a hundred good musketeers, but they came not, nor the other forces expected from other parts.

13th of March, the Irish army marched towards Dromore. This night Major Baker brought four companies of foot to Dromore, but very ill armed. The officers put what horse and foot they had into the best posture they could, and sent to Hillsborough for powder and arms.

14th of March, the express returned with some powder, but the bullets were unsuitable to their unsizable arms. The express also brought Sir Arthur Rawdon orders to retire next night with his men to Hillsborough— upon which they resolved to quit the town, expecting that the rest of the forces of Down and Antrim would be that night at Lisburn,

* Mackenzie here refers to the "Vindication of the Rev. Mr. Alexander Osborne," by the Rev. Joseph Boyse, mentioned in the Introduction to this volume. The circumstances which led Mr. Osborne now to visit the North are thus described by Dr. Reid—"The first notice which the northern Protestants received of Tyrconnel's determination was through the medium of the Rev. Alexander Osborne, already mentioned as one of the Presbyterian ministers of Dublin. Since the landing of the Prince of Orange in England, he had maintained a regular correspondence with his brethren in various parts of Ulster, and by letters in cypher had informed them of the proceedings of the deputy and the progress of affairs in the sister kingdoms. Finding, however, the communication with the North both by sea and land entirely cut off, from the beginning of March, and fearing the cause in Ulster would be ruined through want of timely notice of the impending invasion, he availed himself of an offer of the deputy to employ him in conveying a message to the leaders of the northern association, that he might have an opportunity of apprising his friends in the fullest manner of their imminent danger, and of putting them on their guard against the artifices of Tyrconnel to induce them to lay down their arms. For this purpose he left Dublin on the 7th of March, and, though pursued by a party of marauding Irish near Newry, he arrived at Loughbrickland in safety on the second day afterwards. From this place he wrote to Lord Mount-Alexander, Sir Arthur Rawdon, and others, informing them of Tyrconnel's proposals, but prudently withholding his opinion of the course which they ought to pursue, till he should 'fully discourse with them in person.'"—*History of Presbyterian Church in Ireland*, II., 845, 2d ed.

and advance from thence the next day to Hillsborough.

The same day the Presbyterian Ministers appeared before the Consult with the proposals mentioned in Mr. Osborne's Vindication,* and the country was summoned to appear on the 19th, at Blarismore.

One of the scouts acquaints the officers at Dromore, that about two troops of Irish horse were marching towards the town, upon which the horse and dragoons were drawn up in the street. The four companies of foot were also drawn up at the entry of the town. The horse and dragoons went on and faced a party of the enemy, till they discovered the whole body of the Irish army coming on them, and, having no strength capable to oppose them, their foot went off, and their horse endeavoured to make good their retreat. Some few of the horse and dragoons, and some of the country people that were carrying off their goods, were killed.

* These proposals are thus recorded at page 18 of the " Vindication"—" On the 14th of March last, 1689, nine Presbyterian ministers (Archibald Hamilton, of Bangor, Alexander Osborne, of Dublin, Henry Livingstone, of Drumbo, William Legat, of Dromore, Alexander Gordon, of Rathfriland, Alexander Glass, of Dunmurry, George Lang, of Loughbrickland, Alexander M'Cracken, of Lisburn, and Patrick Adair, of Belfast) came to such of the Consult as were then present at Hillsborough. They apologised for their offering their advice in such affairs, which nothing but a deep sense of the common danger and distress of that great body of Protestants whereof they were members, could have put upon them. The Consult received them very kindly, and desired them to proceed. They then acquainted them that there were in their several parishes many able men, fit for military service, who had arms and were not yet enlisted in the army, and yet were very willing to venture their lives for King William and Queen Mary, and the Protestant religion. They therefore proposed, if the Consult approved of it, that they would presently repair to their several parishes and admonish all men in their limits between sixteen and sixty, that could bear arms, to meet and rendezvous on such day and place as the Consult should think fit, with such arms as they could procure, and ten days provision with them. For they found by the information of their brother, Mr. Osborne, one of their number, that the Lord Tyrconnel's army would certainly attack them on the refusal of his proposals, which proposals they could by no means advise them to comply with, but rather advised them to make a vigorous and resolute defence. To this advice, those of the Consult then present readily assented, and presently employed clerks to write orders for summoning the country to meet at Blarismore on the Tuesday following, being the 19th."

The same day the Lord Mount-Alexander, Colonel Upton, and Mr. Hamilton of Tullymore, upon advice hereof, got together what horse they could at Hillsborough, which were not many, and were marching out of town to assist those of Dromore, when they met their foremost party on their retreat. They rallied as many as they could of that flying party, and sent to Lisburn for the forces that were there, to the number of near four thousand. Sir Arthur Rawdon rode thither to hasten them up; but the precipitant motion of the Irish army struck such a terror into the people, who were but ill armed, that few would stay at Hillsborough, so that they were forced to leave it to the Irish, who seized the provisions and the little ammunition laid up there, besides the papers of the Consult. Most of the forces also at Lisburn shrunk and stole away; their leaders in this confusion could not agree on any post thereabouts which they were able to defend against a well appointed army; their hopes of speedy assistance from the other counties as well as from England were frustrated; and so they resolved upon shifting for themselves. All the gentlemen of the lower parts of the county of Down (except Captain Hugh Magill* and his brother) endeavoured to transport themselves. Others resolved to stay and defend their country to the last extremity, as Sir Arthur Rawdon and most of his regiment; part of Sir John Magill's regiment, under the command of Lieutenant-Colonel Whitney; part of Sir William Franklin's, under the command of Major Tubman; Colonel Arthur Upton with part of his regiment; Colonel Adair's regiment, under the command of Colonel Edmonstone; Major Stroud with his own troop; Captain Clotworthy Upton with his troop, being one of the Earl of Mount-Alexander's regiments; and one troop of Belfast, commanded by Captain White. All these forces, being about four thousand in number, marched to Coleraine. The rest either removed into England, or took protections from the Irish; but all the colonels went either to Derry, or out of the kingdom, except Colonel Leslie,† who chose rather to take protection, and helped to victual the Irish Camp before Derry.

Of the garrison of Dungannon, I need give only this short relation: Dungannon, in the county of Tyrone, being in great danger from the Irish garrison in Charlemont, that had

* This Captain Hugh Magill was killed at Athlone in July, 1690.—*Rawdon Papers*, p. 327. It is stated subsequently in this Narrative that Captain James Magill was killed in the fight at Portglenone.

† This was Colonel Leslie of Ballymoney.

above thirty companies in it, the defence of it by a good garrison was thought very necessary. And accordingly the counties of Tyrone, Derry, and Donegal, sent in several troops and companies by turns, which were maintained partly by the country, partly by their officers. About the 11th of February, the Irish gathered together in great numbers, near Stewartstown and Gleno. Colonel Stewart commanded a detached party of our men (about twenty-four, some of Captain Stewart of Killymoon's troop, and some foot) to go and view them, who killed some of the Irish, and took thirteen or fourteen prisoners. Soon after a considerable party of the forces of Charlemont, joined with other Irish of the country near Benburb. A party of our men, both foot and horse, beat them off, and took a prey of cattle from them, as they did several afterwards. Colonel Lundy about the 14th of March, sent his orders to Colonel Stewart to quit the town, which accordingly he did, though against the opinion of most of the officers. Nor was there any care taken to carry off that great quantity of provisions which the country about had sent in, so that they fell into the enemy's hands. About the 16th or 17th of March, some of the garrison marched towards Coleraine, others towards Derry, as Mr. Walker and his company, &c. The 11th, a party of our men beat off a party of the Irish, who had taken up the pass at Toome.

Of the forces raised by the Lord Blaney I shall give the reader a brief account out of a memoir of his own.

"Being chosen by the counties of Armagh and Monaghan to command all the forces raised, and to be raised, for the Protestant service there, after the disarming the Irish dragoons at Armagh, I posted myself there, and at a general rendezvous of the inhabitants of the county, found their number to be about eighteen hundred men, indifferently well armed.

"There was at this time at the fort of Charlemont, which is within five miles of the town, near three thousand of the enemy who were very insolent, upon the account they received of an army's being sent from Dublin, to reduce the Northern rebels, as they called us, to obedience.

"This made them for a fortnight together attempt the plundering all the Protestant houses near the town, and being obliged to defend them, several skirmishes happened between our parties, the Protestants always prevailing, insomuch that considerable numbers of the enemy were every day killed, and we only suffered the loss of one man.

"Thus it continued till Wednesday, the 13th of March, at which time I heard that my own house at Monaghan was taken by the Irish, that all the forces of the county were retreated to Glasslough, and besieged there by the enemy. Sir Nicholas Atchison came the same day from the North, and informed me that Sir Arthur Rawdon had quitted Loughbrickland, and that the Irish army, under the conduct of Lieutenant-General Hamilton, had possessed themselves of that place. A Council of War was then called of all the officers in the town, where it was resolved that we should the next day march towards the relief of those who were besieged at Glasslough; and if we could bring off the Protestant party there, we should march through Dungannon to Toome, and so to Antrim, to join with our friends there. The same day a party of the enemy was beat off by the Protestants at Tandragee, and several of them killed."

Of the affair at Glasslough, I shall beg leave to insert the following relation from another hand:—

"Those of Glasslough having orders from my Lord Blaney to march towards Antrim, notice was given to the country to be there that night or the next morning. The Irish having intelligence of it, beset the roads to rob them; upon which Captain Anketel mounted twenty of his horse; and Captain Richardson, with seven files of foot, went out and fell on the robbers; they killed six, the rest flying to the woods and bogs. Captain Cole, with his troop of horse, and two foot companies, came hither, and it was concluded to march that day; but we were immediately alarmed with the account of a body of Irish foot coming towards us. It was agreed to go out and fight them. The enemy had possessed themselves of an old Danish fort, within less than half a mile of the town. We detached one hundred fire-locks, and all the horse of two troops fit for service. The enemy, who had fired at us while at a great distance, upon our nearer approach, sallied out, and fired a volley at our men. But Captain Anketel, with his horse, came so suddenly on them, and pursued them so close as they were retreating into the fort, that the enemy within, seeing several killed, and others trod under the horses' feet, threw down their arms, and betook themselves to their heels. They were about five to one in number, and yet there were (as Mr. Anthony, who stayed in the country, told us) one hundred and eighty of them killed, among whom was Colonel M'Kenna, four captains, six lieutenants, and six ensigns. We only lost that brave man, Captain Anketel, who, after the enemy was routed, was unfortunately shot by a fellow that lay in a bush. More of the enemy had been cut off, if they had not had a bog to retreat to. But after this encounter, we had only so much ammunition left us as served to charge our arms on our march.

"On Friday, the 15th, I heard that the forces of the counties of Down and Antrim were broken, and retired to Coleraine. Upon which advice I marched thither with three hundred horse, and as many foot, being all that were left me of the eighteen hundred I mentioned before, the others having taken protection from the enemy. On the road between Dungannon and Moneymore, I met, at Artrea, one thousand of the enemy, who attacked us, but we were so successful as to beat them, and kill 140 of them. All the country people thereabouts generally fled to Coleraine with the army, except a few. The gentlemen in the country in other parts were very active, particularly Sir Francis Hamilton and Captain Robert Sanderson, in the County of Cavan, who were two of the ten excepted from pardon in the Lord Tyrconnel's proclamation."

Of the forces raised by the Lord Kingston, I had the following relation from his lordship:—

"On the 4th of January, 1688, the gentlemen of the County of Sligo met and associated themselves, and chose the Right Hon. Robert Lord Baron of Kingston, and the Hon. Captain Chidley Coote, their chief commanders, and promised obedience to both or either of them; and then formed themselves into troops and companies; and furnished their men with horses, arms, ammunition, and provisions; and ordered frontier garrisons to be kept, as Grange, in the way to Ballyshannon, to hold correspondence with Derry and the places adjacent. Garrisons were also put into Newtown and Mannorhamilton, to keep correspondence with Enniskillen, my Lord Bellimont's house at Killoona, Dr. Leslie's and Mr. Cooper's at Mercury, were the frontier garrisons toward the Boyle and Ballymote, to prevent the incursions of the Irish from those parts. There was also a garrison at Cottlestown, in the farthest part of the county of Sligo, to observe the motions of the new-raised army in the county of Mayo, which was very numerous. Soon after the Bishop of Killala had quitted his house, there was one Tremble, a servant to Sir Arthur Gore, barbarously murdered by Captain Walter Burke and his soldiers.

"Colonel Macdonald, being garrisoned at Boyle, and not permitting any of the Protestants to pass with their goods and provisions towards the garrison of Sligo, but ordering all such goods and provisions to be seized, it was thought fit he should be writ to, desiring him to let the Protestants have free passage to Sligo, as all the Papists had from thence to Boyle, Athlone, and other places, to their Irish friends, without any molestation from the garrison of Sligo. But he not performing what was desired, it was resolved that the Lord Kingston and Captain Chidley Coote should with a party of horse and foot march to Boyle, and demand a free passage for the Protestants, which the Colonel readily granted, but never performed, though we looked on him as one of the fairest reputation among the Irish in those parts. It is to be observed that the Colonel, upon the approach of our party, drew all his horse, foot, and dragoons within the walls of Lord Kingston's house and gardens, though with his old troops and Rapparees he had at least five to one in and about the place.

"About five of our horse, commanded by Captain Arthur Cooper, went to view what the Irish designed at Ballimont, then garrisoned by a company of foot, under the command of Captain Terence Macdonagh. He drew them up to face our men; but they firing on them, and with the shot of one blunderbuss killing one, and wounding five more, the Irish threw down their arms, and ran to the castle, our men pursuing, and beating them to the draw-bridge.

"About five or six hundred shewed themselves before Ballintobcr, Dr. Leslie's house—upon which he drew out about thirty horse and forty foot, and then the Irish fled to the bogs.

"During the stay of the forces at Sligo, frequent correspondence was kept with Derry, sometimes with Colonel Lundy, and sometimes with the Committee; and at Enniskillen, with the governor of that place, Colonel Gustavus Hamilton. Many letters came to Sligo from Colonel Lundy and the Committee, to march the forces to Derry, it being alleged by them that, if the Northern forces were conquered, that must fall of course. By this time the stone fort at Sligo was finished, and the sod fort new made up, at the cost of the officers, and labour of the soldiers.

"Whilst the English were at Sligo there was an open market kept, where the Papists as well as the Protestants had the selling and disposing of what commodities they brought thither. Yet some time before Sligo was quitted, several of the British coming thither from Tirreanragh, with great store of meal, cattle, &c., a party of Irish that were got into an old castle belonging to Captain Henry Crofton, an inveterate Roman Catholic, robbed and plundered all the British of their corn,

&c., and made a store of it in the castle. Of which an account coming to the Lord Kingston, his lordship immediately sent in the night Captain William Ormby and Captain Francis Gore, with a detached party of men out of every troop and company under their command, and the next morning before day the Lord Kingston marched with another party to assist them, if there had been occasion. But his lordship met Cornet Charles Nicholson, who gave him an account that our party had got the castle by setting fire to the gate, and smoking the enemy out, who at first fired very briskly upon our men, yet we lost none. We found great store of provisions of meal, &c., and seventeen muskets belonging to the Irish army, with several half-pikes, Irish daggers, and Rapparee's swords. The Protestants had their corn and cattle returned them, or a market rate paid them for so much of their corn as they could spare.

"Several letters were written from time to time to Colonel Lundy for a supply of arms and ammunition for the garrison of Sligo, but none could be had, until at last a ship came to Derry from Scotland with ammunition, and then Colonel Lundy consented to let Sligo have three barrels of powder, and Ballyshannon one, provided five pounds per barrel were paid for it. But though a bill of twenty pounds was immediately sent for that end, none of it ever came to Sligo.

"About the 20th of March, an express came to Sligo from Colonel Lundy, to hasten our march with all speed to Derry, which letter, as all others that came from Colonel Lundy or the committee, were communicated to all our officers, but the last letter that came was mislaid by Captain Coote; and on the same day a Council of War (if then it might be so termed) was called, and a speedy march to Derry was voted by the officers who had no commission to make them so, but such as the gentlemen they had chosen for their chief had given them. The names of the subscribers of that Council were as follows: Major Owen Vaughan, Major Thomas Hart, Captain Hugh Morgan, Captain Percy Gethins, Captain Edward Woods, Capt. William Ormesby, Captain William Smith, Captain William Griffith, Lieutenant Richard Brooke, Lieutenant Adam Ormesby, and Cornet Oliver Brookes.

"On the 21st, being the next day following, the Council was called again, when it was hotly pressed and voted to march northward, and accordingly all things were prepared against the next day, and then a march began. The foot baggage, with some horse in the rere, marched out early in the morning, the rest attending the Lord Kingston till they had broken the trunnions, and nailed the heavier guns, and sent off the smallest by boat, and staved all the rest they could find. But those sent away were put into an island by storm, which next day were taken by the Irish, by help of some boats that were concealed by them.

"On the 24th, the forces, with bag and baggage, arrived safe at Ballyshannon. Lieut.-Colonel Connell Farrell was ordered to hinder and oppose us with one hundred and eighty firelocks from Boyle, with the Dartry-Irish, to the number of four or five hundred, who attempted the breaking down of Boudrou's Bridge, which they quitted upon the approach of about fifty of our horse, and took the bogs, and never opposed us in our pass, though there were many dangerous ones, wherein a few might hinder the passage of a great many, had they had courage to do it.

"Either on the way, or at Ballyshannon, a letter came to the Lord Kingston from the committee at Derry, with orders, as they said, from Colonel Lundy to stay at Ballyshannon, and keep the passes on the Erne Water, which was obeyed, he having his present Majesty's commission.

"The garrison of Ballyshannon, under the command of Captain Folliot, was now reinforced, and the ferry-boat of that place sunk. And the Lord Folliot's house, with other houses on Connaught side the water, were burned, to prevent the enemy's sheltering themselves therein, and from thence annoying us with their shot. And one arch more of Balleck Bridge was pulled down, part being so served by Sir James Caldwell before, and a garrison left there under the command of Major Vaughan and Lieut. Arthur Cooper, and another garrison left at Mulick, being the house of Lieutenant Walter Johnson, under the command of Captain William Smith, Captain Francis King, and Lieutenant Toby Mulloy, to observe and guard a ford at the mouth of Lough Erne. And at the same time another party was ordered to keep the castle and town of Donegal, being commanded by Captain Francis Gore and Captain Edward Woods. During the time of the Lord Kingston and his party's being at Ballyshannon and the places before-mentioned, there came several expresses, inviting the Lord Kingston with eighty of his choicest horse and three hundred foot to Derry, with promises that provision should be made for them. But the party, having been all along together, they were all of them against breaking until something should happen by which they might show their zeal to his present Majesty's service and the Protestant religion;

and accordingly stayed there until a letter came to the Lord Kingston, signed at a Council of War at Derry, April the 13th, ordering the forces under his command, as well as all others to be at Clady, Lifford, and Long Causey, or the places near them, on Monday, the 15th of April, by ten o'clock in the morning. This letter came not to the Lord Kingston till the 14th of April, at ten o'clock that night, and the nearest of his forces were thirty miles from the place of rendezvous. Upon this the Lord Kingston called a council of war, wherein it was concluded that though it was impossible for the Lord Kingston and his party to be at any of the places above-mentioned, in twice the time limited, yet the Lord Kingston himself, with ten or twelve horse, should the next morning go towards Derry, to see how matters were, and to give directions accordingly to his party. Very early the next morning his Lordship went; but when he came to Stranorlar, within five miles of Raphoe, his Lordship met with several of the British running from Cladyford, who gave his Lordship an account that the British were fled with Colonel Lundy into Derry, and the Irish were got to Raphoe, between his Lordship and that place; whereupon his Lordship hastened back to Donegal, and sent an express with orders for the horse to secure themselves in Enniskillen, and the foot at Donegal, Ballyshannon, and other places. And then the Lord Kingston, with some of his officers, went to Killybeggs, and took shipping, and were put into Scotland—from whence his lordship hastened to give his Majesty an account of affairs, hoping to have made a quick return to his party, with his Majesty's commissions and orders."

So unhappily were the designs of that Noble Lord (who inherits the courage as well as the honour of his father) for the preservation of that part of the country, which he prosecuted with extraordinary zeal and resolution, frustrated by the confused, but peremptory orders which he received from Colonel Lundy.

What happened of moment from the time of the forces of Antrim fleeing to Coleraine, to the time of their deserting, I shall extract out of a diary of Sir Arthur Rawdon's, only the relation of what passed at Portglenone was drawn by another hand.

"March 1689.

"Friday, 15.—The forces of the north-east parts of Ulster came to Coleraine, of which immediate notice was sent to Colonel Lundy, then at Derry.

"Saturday, 16.—The next day several of the north-east officers went to see Colonel Lundy, to advise what measures should be taken, and met with Colonel Lundy, about two or three miles from Newtownlimavady, and turned back with Colonel Lundy and Colonel Gustavus Hamilton to Coleraine. Colonel Lundy said that he could not spare ammunition to defend Coleraine, and therefore thought it advisable to quit the town as soon as it should be attacked; for he said he had not forty barrels of powder, but assured us he had provisions to hold out a year: and further added that he would take care to bring all the stacks of corn and hay into Derry, which were then in great numbers on the road, but never did it.

"The commonalty at Coleraine suspected Colonel Lundy, and when he was going towards the bridge, to view the town, they imagined he was going away, and drew up the bridge, and the guard presented their muskets and pikes at him.

"It was concluded that, because there was much to do at Derry, to fortify and provide it with stores, that Colonel Lundy should remain in Derry, and Colonel Gustavus Hamilton manage the field, he having been chosen governor of the county of Donegal before.

"Monday 18.—Lieutenant-Colonel Whitney was ordered to be upon the guard with his men, at the bridge of Coleraine, fearing lest the townsmen should again draw up their bridge, to hinder Lundy's going away, who that day went to Derry.

"Wednesday, 22.—It was ordered by the Committee of Derry, that a ravelin should be built to defend the Bishop's Gate, and money was ordered for it.

"Several sums of money were also raised for the garrison of Coleraine.

"And because it was suspected and given out by some that, in case the forces were beaten at Coleraine, the town of Derry would not let them into their gates, a paper was drawn up by the Committee, and signed by the chief of the inhabitants and officers, both of the town and country, being an agreement to stand together and succour each other, and this was proclaimed in the Market-house, to the great satisfaction of all.

"Thursday, 21.—Captain James Hamilton* arrived with four hundred and eighty barrels of powder, arms, and ammunition, (as was said for two thousand men), money, and a commission to Col. Lundy to be governor of Derry.

* Captain James Hamilton is thus described in the *Londeriad*:—
" He's son to the great Lady Hamilton,
Who hath estates on either side the town."
The present representative of the family is the Marquis of Abercorn. Of these 480 barrels of gunpowder, scarcely 80 remained at the close of the siege.

D

"The instructions which Captain Hamilton had were to summon the Mayor and all other officers, civil and military, on board him, and there, before them all, to give the oaths of fidelity to Colonel Lundy, before he should give him any arms, &c. But instead thereof, most of the gentlemen on board were desired to withdraw, on pretence of private business, so that if Lundy was sworn, it was very privately. And it was much wondered at, that when the Committee of Derry and the officers next day desired that Lundy might take the oaths before them all, for their greater satisfaction, he absolutely refused it, on pretence of having taken them on board the day before. Mr. Charles Hamilton, Mr. Wm. Stewart, and others refused them; but the Mayor, Sheriffs, Aldermen, and all the officers, were sworn, and the King and Queen were proclaimed with great solemnity and joy, the Bishop* being present.

"It was not fully known what arms or money came to Derry, nor how disposed of, there being but thirty muskets given to each regiment, and though (besides the money which came over) considerable sums were raised in town, yet it was believed that little of it was disposed for the public use.

"Sunday, 24.—Colonel Gustavus Hamilton called a Council of War at Coleraine, and represented to the officers that the want of ammunition would make them a prey to the enemy, and that therefore it was best to quit the town, and retire to Derry. In the meantime, the enemy appeared with some squadrons of horse before the town, which made all repair to the ramparts, and hindered quitting of the town, which else had been done. Some rambling shots were made at the enemy, who thereupon retired.

"Monday, 25.—About two o'clock in the morning a fire happened in an out-house near our magazine, which made us suspect treachery, and we all got to the ramparts; but, the fire being extinguished, and no enemy appearing, all was quieted.

"Wednesday 27.—About eight in the morning, the whole army, under the command of Lieutenant-General Hamilton, appeared before our ramparts, and advanced within about fifty yards of them, under shelter and covert of hedges and ditches, which particular interest had hindered us from throwing down. This was on Blind Gate side, and near the church, the mill sheltered them within forty yards of a bastion. They raised two batteries, one of three guns, which played upon the bridge and Blind Gate, their design being to break down the bridge, and hinder our escape, they not doubting of making themselves masters of the town, and to that end made several shots at the bridge and several at Blind Gate, one of which split the upper beam and broke the chain, which Captain Archibald MacCullough, with great hazard, fastened, the enemy firing very warmly at him. The other battery did little mischief, but killing one man, and battering down a few chimneys, and making a few breaches in the church roof. Their gunner was killed with a musket shot, by Captain Hugh Magill. About four o'clock in the afternoon there fell much snow, which covered the ground in an instant. About five the enemy retired in great confusion, but we (having been forced to block up the gates with timber, earth, and rubbish, which was not to be removed suddenly) could not pursue them, only some of our men leaped over the ramparts, and took several prisoners, particularly one Courney, who went to the enemy after they came to Derry, with some arms, commissions, and red coats, two tents, &c. We lost but three men, which is very little, considering the continual firing of the enemy. What they lost is uncertain, because they carried off their dead. It was reported by the country people, that they burned many of their dead in a house.

"Thursday, 28.—We foraged within two miles of the enemy's camp, and brought in cattle, &c.

"Friday, 29.—Sir Arthur Rawdon's regiment was ordered to go to Moneymore, about twenty-six miles from Coleraine, to oppose Gordon O'Neill, who, it was said, was marching towards Coleraine with two thousand men.

"Mr. Skeffington's regiment was ordered to Bellaghy, Dawson's Bridge, and the passes on the Bann above Portglenone. One battalion of that regiment, under the command of Lieutenant-Colonel Houston, was ordered to keep the pass at Toome; but because of the floods which overspread the woods of Creagh, they could seldom get to their posts, or relieve their guards. The other part of it, under the command of Major Mitchelburn, was sent to guard the pass at Newferry, four or five miles below Toome, to which there was easier access. Colonel Edmondstone was ordered to defend and secure the pass of Portglenone, by hindering the enemy's repairing the bridge, which is fourteen miles from Coleraine.

"Colonel Canning's regiment was also ordered to Magherafelt and Moneymore; Sir John Magill's was sent to Kilrea, and that part of the Bann; care had been taken before to sink most of the boats and cots on the

---

* This should be *the Mayor.*—See *The Invisible Champion Foiled.*

Banu river. Sir Tristram Beresford's* regiment, with Colonel Francis Hamilton's, and several detachments, to the number of three thousand men, were left to defend Coleraine. The Protestants at Fagivie, under command of Captain Blair,† beat back some of the Irish who had crossed the river there.

"April, Tuesday, 2.—We went to Moneymore, the Irish quitting it upon our approach, and we got great quantities of provision in the country, and saw no enemy. Colonel Edmonstone sent word to Sir Arthur Rawdon that his men were almost starved for want of provisions, and that none could be had, unless he would furnish him, and withal desired to see him; and accordingly he sent provisions, and went there late that night (Friday 5th), and found that he had entrenched himself so well, that the enemy could not annoy them, either with great or small shot, and he had destroyed great part of the bridge. There was a continued firing on both sides.

"Saturday, 6.—We killed near twenty of the enemy, and with hot iron bullets fired the town where they lay, and drove them all out of it.

"Sunday, 7.—About two o'clock this morning we had notice that the Lord Galmoy, Colonel Gordon O'Neill, and Colonel MacMahon were come to Dungannon, with three thousand foot and one thousand horse, in order to surprise and cut off the garrison at Moneymore, and Sir Arthur Rawdon was desired to hasten thither. The letter being communicated to the officers, it was resolved Sir Arthur Rawdon should go towards Moneymore; but he, with Major Baker, Captain Hugh Magill, and Captain Dunbar, had not rode above a mile before they had an account sent them that the Irish in five or six great boats, had in the night time passed by the guards that were kept on the river side, by Colonel Skeffington's regiment, and were then coming down within a mile of Colonel Edmondstone's trenches. Sir Arthur Rawdon immediately sent notice of it to Colonel Edmondstone, to Lieutenant-Colonel Whitney, and to Major Mitchelburn.‡ One company of Colonel Edmondstone's regiment that lodged in some country houses, got to the river, and fired at them till their powder was all spent. When the boats came within half a mile of the trenches, they landed the men, and took in more Irish on the other side the river, till they had landed a considerable party. Two or three companies of the grenadiers advanced first through the bog, towards Colonel Edmondstone's trenches, he having but a hundred and twenty men in them, went out with sixty of them to line a ditch on the side of the bog towards the enemy, leaving Lieut.-Colonel Wm. Shaw to guard the trenches, and vigorously opposed them till both their ammunition was spent, and the Irish overpowered them with their numbers, which were continually increasing. About this time Sir Arthur Rawdon and Captain Dunbar came to the trenches, and were surprised with a volley of shot from the Irish, who immediately sent one hundred grenadiers to line the hedges on the way to that only pass by which they could retreat, and to keep that pass against a party of Protestants that they saw marching towards it. This party was five companies of foot, under command of Lieutenant-Colonel Whitney, coming to Colonel Edmondstone's assistance, who commanded three young captains to lead on the men; but when he observed the enemy, he commanded his men to face about and retire, which all did except one, Capt. James Magill, who, ashamed of so base a retreat, went on. About this time, Sir Arthur Rawdon and Captain Dunbar came to the pass, and, having no other way to escape, ventured through all the shot poured in upon them from the hedges till they met Captain James Magill, but as they were charging again, they spied another party of Irish behind them, and they had not gone far before Captain James Magill was unfortunately shot off his horse. A captain of the grenadiers came up and run his sword several times through him, and another of them dashed out his brains with a musket. So barbarously did they kill that deserving young gentleman, whose early valour would have met with other treatment from any enemy but the Irish. By the time Sir Arthur Rawdon had got over the pass, Major Baker and Captain Hugh Magill were come up with what men they could get together, and had stopped Colonel Whitney's party. Colonel Edmondstone also, and Lieutenant-Colonel Shaw had by several ways got up to them, but the soldiers, having little ammunition or match left, the body of the Irish being increased, and especially the Lord Galmoy's march towards Moneymore being con-

---

* Sir Tristram Beresford, who was born in 1660, was now only about twenty years of age. He was ancestor of the present Primate of Armagh, and of the Marquis of Waterford, and brother-in-law to Sir John Magill, of Gill-Hall.

† Captain Blair was an elder of the congregation of Aghadoey. He was in Derry during the siege, along with his minister, the Rev. Thomas Boyd. Fagivie is also called Agivey.

‡ Afterwards Governor of Derry. He was the grandson of Sir Richard Mitchelburn, of Brodhurst Stanmer, in Sussex.

firmed, it was resolved that Colonel Edmondstone and Lieutenant-Colonel Whitney should march to Coleraine ; that Sir Arthur Rawdon, with his own regiment of dragoons, Colonel Skeffington's and Colonel Kenning's regiments of foot (the last of them was under command of Lieutenant-Colonel William Cunningham) should march towards Derry, which was accordingly done."

Besides Captain James Magill and several common soldiers who were lost, one Captain Henly was wounded and taken prisoner. And Sir Arthur Rawdon, by continual fatigue and want of rest cast himself into a dangerous illness, which afterwards forced him to leave the kingdom — a gentleman who in all those affairs of the North of Ireland, showed himself a true lover and friend of his country, by his extraordinary zeal and courage, his great expenses and indefatigable diligence in the defence of it. Colonel Edmonstone also contracted those distempers in the trenches at Portglenone, of which he afterwards died at Culmore, April the 14th, having behaved himself there, and on all other occasions, with great gallantry and resosolution.

The Irish having crossed the Bann, all those of the army above at Moneymore and Magherafelt (except a few captains that took protection), as well as those at Toome and Newferry fled over the mountains to Derry. Coleraine was deserted, lest the Irish should intercept betwixt the forces there, and those at Derry ; part of the bridge was cut down, part of it burnt ; and all the country came towards Derry as their last refuge.

CHAP. III.

WHAT PASSED AT DERRY, FROM THE RETREAT OF THE BRITISH FORCES FROM COLERAINE THITHER, TILL THE TIME THAT KING JAMES' ARMY APPEARED BEFORE THE TOWN.

April 9.—THE body of our army came to the ferry that leads over to the town, and it was no small trouble to see so many brave and resolute men, both horse and foot, without a general. The horse and dragoons were that day ordered by Colonel Lundy to march to Lifford and Strabane, and the next the dragoons were ordered to march to Letterkenny. The horse and dragoons brought in good store of meal and other provisions to Derry.*

April 10.—Mr. Cairns being sent from England with instructions and a letter from the King to Colonel Lundy, came this day to Derry. He met some officers and a great number of people going off. Colonel Lundy had offered passes to the officers, and spoke so discouragingly to many of them concerning the indefensibleness of the place, that they strongly suspected he had a design to give it up, and they could see little hope of preventing it, in such a confusion, if he proved treacherous; and therefore were unwilling to stay, only to be betrayed into the enemy's hands. Mr. Cairns delivered the King's letter to Governor Lundy, and acquainted him and others with the cause of his coming, and the forces following him at sea for their aid; and though this good news put new life and resolution into many of them; yet since others, and particularly some of the chief officers, were said to be on the wing to depart, he was earnest with Governor Lundy to take some speedy and effectual care to prevent it. Whereupon a council of war was held that night, to whom Colonel Lundy imparted his letter (see it in the end). Mr. Cairns's instructions were also read, and he pursuant thereto, represented to them his Majesty's great care and concern for them and that whole kingdom, the great preparations making in England for their relief, and the forces at present hastening to them. He therefore earnestly dissuaded them from deserting the place, and desired, according to his instruction, a particular account of the present condition of the city, as to men, arms, ammunition, &c. This had that effect, that the council drew up the following resolution, which Colonel James Hamilton proposed, and was active to promote:—

"We, the officers hereunto subscribing, pursuant to a resolution taken and agreed upon, at a council of war at Londonderry, held this day, do hereby mutually promise and engage, to stand by each other with our forces against the common enemy, and will not leave the kingdom, nor desert the public service, until our affairs are in a settled and secure posture. And if any of us shall do the contrary, the person so leaving the kingdom, or deserting the service, without consent of a council of war, is to be deemed a coward, and disaffected to their Majesties' service, and the Protestant interest.

"Dated the 10th of April, 1689."

Paulet Phillips.	Jas. Hamilton.
Hugh Magill.	Nich. Atchison.
Richard Crofton.	Hugh Montgomery.
John Hill.	Thomas Whitney.
George Hamilton.	William Ponsonby.
Arthur Upton.	Richard Johnson.
Robert Lundy.	John Forward.
Blaney.	Ger. Squire.
Arthur Rawdon.	J. Blaney.
William Shaw.	John Tubman.
Richard Whaley.	Daniel M'Neill.

This resolution was not only affixed on the Market-house, but read next morning at the head of every battalion, at which the sol-

---

* It was providentially arranged that at this time food was exceedingly cheap and plentiful in the North of Ireland. Thus it happened that Derry was supplied with stores, which sustained the inhabitants during the siege. The following account of the prices of various articles about the time when the Irish army sat down before the city is worthy of record. "A salmon, about two feet long, may be bought for a penny or twopence. Forty-five eggs for one penny. A fat goose for threepence. A fat turkey for sixpence. A fat hen for threehalfpence. A fat lamb or kid for a groat (fourpence)."—*Ireland's Lamentation, being a short but perfect, full, and true account of the situation, nature, constitution, and product of Ireland. Written by an English Protestant that lately narrowly escaped with his life from thence. P. 4. London, 1689.*

diers expressed their great satisfaction with loud acclamations and huzzas. Mr. Cairns, also wrote to several persons of note that were then about going off at Castledoe, to dissuade them, but all in vain. At the same council there were several articles agreed on (see them in the end). The enemy being come over to the Lough, and threatening to come over with their boats, and there being no other vessel in the Lough, but Mr. Cairns's, the Council desired, and obtained his to be used as a privateer against them.

The enemy thus hastening upon them, and some discontents appearing among the soldiers, who murmured especially against Colonel Lundy for taking no more care to put them into a posture of defence, and expressed great readiness to fight the enemy if they were led on, to allay these heats and provide for the common safety, a council of war was held, April the 13th, in which they came to the following resolution :—

Londonderry, April the 13th, 1689.

At a general council of war, resolved unanimously, that on Monday next, by Ten o'clock, all officers and soldiers, horse, dragoons, and foot, and all other armed men whatsoever of our forces and friends, enlisted or not enlisted, that can or will fight for their country and religion against Popery, shall appear on the fittest ground near Cladyford, Lifford, and Longcausey, as shall be nearest to their several and respective quarters, there to draw up in battalions to be ready to fight the enemy, and to preserve our lives and all that is dear to us from them. And all officers and soldiers, of horse, foot, dragoons, and others that are armed, are required to be then there, in order to the purpose aforesaid, and to bring a week's provision at least with them for men, and as much forage as they can for horses.

Robert Lundy.	John Barry.
William Stuart.	C. Fronde.
James Hamilton.	Hugh Magill.
Francis Hamilton.	John Hill.
Nicholas Atchison.	John Hamilton.
Hugh Montgomery.	John Forward.
George Hamilton.	Kilner Brasier.
Francis White.	Walter Dawson.
John Tubman.	Pawlet Phillips.

At this Council Colonel Lundy was chosen to be Commander-in-Chief in the field, which he undertook. This day Major Stroud made some proposals to Governor Lundy, of which no notice was taken. Most of the suburbs on both sides the water were burnt or pulled down.

April the 14th, the body of the enemy's army marched up towards Strabane, part of them within view of the city, whereupon Mr. Cairns went twice to Governor Lundy, pressing him to take some speedy effectual care for securing the passes of Fin Water, lest the enemy should get over before our men could meet. He replied in a careless manner that he had given orders already, but how little was actually done towards the prevention of it the next day gave us a sad demonstration, The same day several others sent word to Governor Lundy, that if he did not march the men that day, the enemy would certainly prevent their getting together in any orderly body, and therefore entreated him to be with the men that night at Clady and Lifford. But their advice was not regarded. Our men had burnt all the corn and forage on the road, so that if those passes had been maintained, the enemy's horse could not have long subsisted there.

This day we had news that a fleet was seen off the coast, near the Lough mouth, but were driven off by the wind to sea again.

Captain Hamill* and Major Crofton, with a party at Lifford, did all this night repulse the enemy (who attempted to come over the ford) with great resolution and success, killing, as we heard, several of them, with their cannon and small shot.

April the 15th, Colonel Cunningham and Colonel Richards, with the English ships and 'forces, arrived in the Lough. They had particular instructions to receive from time to time such orders as Colonel Lundy should give them in all things relating to his Majesty's service, pursuant to which Colonel Cunningham sent three several messages to him. By the first (which was from Greencastle about ten in the morning), he acquainted him with his coming, and desired his orders about landing the two regiments on board. By the second (from Red-Castle about two in the afternoon), having some information of their being gone out to fight the enemy at Clady, he wrote the following letter :—

"From on board the 'Swallow,' near Red Castle, at two in the afternoon, April the 15th, 1689.

"Sir,

"Hearing you have taken the field, in order to fight the enemy, I have thought it fit for their Majesties' service to let you know there are two well disciplined regiments here on board that may join you in

* Captain Hamill was from Lifford. He was the proprietor of an estate then worth about £1,000 per annum.

two days at farthest. I am sure they will be of great use on any occasion, but especially for the encouragement of raw men, as I judge most of yours are : therefore it is my opinion that you only stop the passes at the fords of Finn till I can join you ; and afterwards, if giving battle be necessary, you will be in a much better posture for it than before. I must ask your pardon if I am too free in my advice. According to the remote prospect I have of things, this seems most reasonable to me, but as their Majesties have left the whole direction of matters to you, so you shall find that no man living will more cheerfully obey you than your most humble servant,

"JOHN CUNNINGHAM."

Having no answer to either, he sent a third messenger from Culmore Castle, about nine at night, to desire his orders which he was ready to execute, but he received no answer from Governor Lundy till that evening, of which in its due order.

This day a considerable party of the Irish horse marched from Strabane to Clady, some of their foot being there before them ; our men had the week before broke down some arches of the bridge, and had made a breastwork at the end of it. Our forces at Derry marched about eight or nine in the morning towards Longcausey, Lifford, and Clady ; many troops and companies were gathering from several parts to join them, in all above ten thousand men. A party of the enemy that attempted to ford the river at Castlefin was repulsed by a party of Colonel Skeffington's regiment posted there. Another small party of our men, about thirty dragoons of Colonel Stewart's regiment, commanded by Captain Murray, after most of the few foot posted there were beat off, opposed the enemy's coming over at Cladyford, till all their ammunition was spent. But there was no more ammunition sent them :—nay so strangely had the Governor managed things, that most part of the ammunition was but coming from Derry, about three or four miles out of it, when some part of our forces was fleeing thither upon their retreat. And Major Stroud, who had some horse near the ford was so ill placed, that he could not bring them on, as they were so exposed to the enemy's shot, though he earnestly endeavoured it ; so that they were forced to retire from the bridge. The enemy perceiving this, and observing the scattered condition of our men, several troops of their horse rushed into the river, and swam through (one Major Nangle and another officer were drowned). When they got over, they were, as Gordon O'Neill since told me, in terrible fear lest we should have fallen upon them ; for the waters being high, they had scarce a dry shot left. But Governor Lundy was so far from putting the Protestant forces into any posture to oppose them, that upon notice of their entering the ford, he gave orders to all thereabouts to flee to Derry, himself leading the way ; but sent none to the other parts of the army, which never met in any considerable body. Upon this news of the Irish horse being got over, the foot posted at Lifford, that were shooting at a party of Irish across the river at Strabane, were called off, and retired to the pass at Longcausey. Colonel Francis Hamilton stopped those that fled there, and drew them up in good order behind that pass, expecting the Irish would take that way, and Lundy would come thither from Raphoe ; but the Irish horse chiefly pursued those that took the way to Raphoe, where they did great execution on Colonel Montgomery's regiment of foot, there being no tolerable care taken to bring them off. And they had been all cut off if they had not got into bogs and marshy places to secure themselves from the enemy's horse. The forces at the Longcausey stayed there till towards evening ; but fearing the enemy might come from Raphoe to intercept their passage to Derry, they retired thither. So inexcusable was the conduct of the general, both in abandoning so many passes, and those so easily defensible by a few men, if they had been either supplied with ammunition, or constantly relieved, and in never so much as attempting to draw the forces into a body, when there were in the field above ten thousand men, who, whatever he pretended to the contrary, wanted more care and resolution in their leader, than courage in themselves. But whether this ill conduct must be ascribed to negligence or design, the reader must be left to judge by his following actions.

Governor Lundy, being come into town, ordered the sentinels to shut the gates, so that many officers, soldiers, and private gentlemen were forced that night to lie about the walls ; and the reason that he since publicly gave for it, is not unworthy the reader's notice, viz.:—To preserve the provisions, which he knew to be sufficient for three thousand men for three months, after the rate of four pounds of fish,* three pounds of flesh, and eight quarts of meal, per week, for each man. And though this was very far from being a just account, yet how very dif-

---

* During part of the time of the siege, the inhabitants of Derry were supported, to a considerable extent, on preserved salmon. The cheapness of this article has already been noticed.

ferent a one he gave the officers of the two regiments on board, will appear by what follows.

Governor Lundy this night sent back Major Tiffen, Captain Lyndon, and Captain Cornwall, commander of the "Swallow" frigate, as appears by a certificate annexed at the end, with the following answer to Col. Cunningham's message:—

"To Colonel John Cunningham.

"SIR,

"I am come back much sooner than I expected when I went forth, for having numbers placed on Finwater, as I went to a pass, where a few might oppose a greater number than came to the place, I found them on the run before the enemy, who pursued with great vigour, and I fear march on with their forces, so that I wish your men would march all night in good order, lest they be surprised. Here they shall have all the accommodation the place will afford. In this hurry pardon me for this brevity; the rest the bearer will inform you. I rest, Sir, your faithful servant,

"ROBERT LUNDY.

"Londonderry, April 15, 1689.

"If the men be not landed let them land and march immediately.

"SIR.—Since the writing of this Major Tiffen is come here, and I have given him my opinion fully, which, I believe, when you hear, and see the place, you will both join with me; that without an immediate supply of money and provisions this place must fall very soon into the enemy's hands. If you do not send your men here some time to-morrow it will not be in your power to bring them at all. Till we discourse the matter, I remain, dear Sir, your most faithful servant,

"ROBERT LUNDY."

In the postscript he refers Colonel Cunningham to the account he gave Major Tiffen which was (as himself has since publicly owned), that there was not above ten days provision in town for three thousand men, though all unnecessary months were put out of it, and though what was in the town for private use were taken to the public stores. Accordingly he ordered Colonel Cunningham and Colonel Richards to leave their men still on board their ships, and to come with some of their officers to town, that they might resolve on what was fit to be done.

Accordingly, April 16, Colonel Cunningham and Colonel Richards, with some of their officers, came to town, where Colonel Lundy called a council of war, composed of these sixteen persons:—

Chidley Coote.	Lundy.
James Hamilton.	Blany.
Capts. of Cunning. Reg.	Cunningham.
Cornwall.	Richards.
Echlin.	Hussey.
Traunter.	Tiffen.
Lyndon.	Capts. of Richds.'s Reg
	Pearson.
	Pache.
	Taylor.

The two Colonels, with their officers, were entire strangers to the state of the town, and the rest were in a great measure unacquainted with it, for Colonel Lundy had called none of the inhabitants to it except Mr. Mogridge, the clerk; and when several of the principal officers (who had some suspicion of Colonel Lundy's design), as Colonel Francis Hamilton, Colonel Chichester, Colonel Crofton, Lieutenant-Colonel Ponsonby, &c., desired to be admitted, they were absolutely refused, though at the same council he pretended he had sent for the two first, but said they could not be found, and for Sir Arthur Rawdon, who he said was a-dying.

Colonel Cunningham delivered to Governor Lundy his Majesty's letter and orders, directed to him; but the Governor, who was president of the council, gave them the same account of the state of the town that he had before given to Major Tiffen, and therefore advised them all to quit it, for he said he would do so himself.

Those of the council who came from England, thinking it impossible the Governor should be ignorant of the condition of the town, and observing the account to pass without any contradiction from those there who had been for some time in it, but had not, it seems, informed themselves better, soon agreed in the opinion of returning for England, rather than stay in a place not to be victualled from the country, especially when, as he further said, the enemy were near their gates with twenty-five thousand men; and there was no possibility of a return from England in so short a time. As the Governor affirmed what provision they had must be spent (only Colonel Richards argued against it, because he looked on the deserting that garrison not only as the quitting that city, but the whole kingdom), and accordingly they came to the following resolution :—

"Upon inquiry, it appears that there is not provision in the garrison of Londonderry for the present garrison, and the two regiments on board for above a week, or ten days at most; and it appearing that the place is not tenable against a well appointed army, therefore it is concluded upon, and resolved : that it is not convenient for his Majesty's service, but the contrary, to laud the two regiments under Colonel Cunningham and Colonel Richards' command, now on board in the river of Lough Foyle ; that, considering the present circumstances of affairs, and the likelihood the enemy will soon possess themselves of this place, it is thought most convenient that the principal officers shall privately withdraw themselves, as well for their own preservation, as in hopes that the inhabitants, by a timely capitulation, may make terms the better with the enemy ; and that this we judge most convenient for his Majesty's service, as the present state of affairs now is."

On the result of this council, Colonel Cunningham, and Colonel Richards, with their officers, went down to the ships, which that day fell down below Redcastle. But Colonel Lundy, to delude both the officers and soldiers in town, who were earnestly begging that the English forces might land, that with their assistance they might take the field, and fight the enemy before their cannon were brought over, in order to the preservation of that corner, into which the provisions and wealth of three or four counties was crowded, told them publicly, it was resolved the English forces should immediately land, and when they were in their quarters, the gates should be opened, and all join in defence of the town ; and to cloak the intrigue the better, the sheriffs were ordered to go through the city, to provide quarters for them : who accordingly did so. But all this was mere sham to amuse the town, while they might get away with the greater ease and safety. This order was not publicly known till the 18th ; but one of the officers of this council acquainted Colonel Francis Hamilton, and Captain Hugh Magill with it, and advised them to go off. Captain Magill discovered it to several friends, and particularly to Sir Arthur Rawdon (who then lay extremely weak, and was the only person there by name excepted from mercy in the Lord Tyrconnell's proclamation). This made them look on the town as betrayed, and represented affairs so desperate to them that they thought it madness in them to stay behind, merely to be exposed as a sacrifice to the fury of the Irish ; and therefore many of them got off to the ships the day following.

This day the body of our foot that retreated, by command, from Clady came, in tolerable order, to the gates, but were surprised to find them shut by the Governor's order, who had but the day before commanded them to flee thither. They called to the centries to open them, which they refused : but when one of the captains of Colonel Skeffington's regiment fired at the sentry, and called for fire to burn the gate, that and the other gates were thrown open, and all that had been kept out the night before, now entered the town, which made a considerable body.

There being no forage in the town, the horse went all generally towards Culmore. Some, both officers and soldiers, who had observed Colonel Lundy's ill conduct, and the confused posture their affairs were in, got to the ships : those that stayed gathered to Captain Murray,* and resolved to sell their lives dear, rather than fall into the hands of an enemy from whom they expected no mercy.

Governor Lundy had placed Captain Jemmet Governor of Culmore, who afterwards by his order deserted it, though he had been formerly active in the service of the town A few Irish possessed themselves of it, but it was soon recovered by a small artifice.

April 17.—King James and his army being advanced as far as St. Johnston (five miles from Derry), he, or Lieutenant-General Hamilton, sends one Mr. Whitlow, a clergyman, to Governor Lundy, to know if they in the city would surrender on honourable terms ; which they should have, to prevent the effusion of Christian blood. On this a council was held, who concluded to send to King James, to know what his Majesty's demands were, and what terms he would grant to the city—the messenger himself being allowed to sit and join in debates with them. The same gentleman had on the 16th, told Cornet Nicholson (his old acquaintance), who inquired of him what Colonel Lundy intended, that the town would be delivered up before Saturday following, and therefore advised him to shift for himself. He said the same to Mr. Henry Nicholson. Archdeacon Hamilton, Captain Kinaston, and Captain Neville were sent, who had access to the King, and returned that night, but were refused entrance by the multitude. Only the two former some way got in ; the last (who had before been very active) wrote in a letter the account of their negotiation, and departed.

* Captain (afterwards Colonel) Murray, who so distinguished himself during the siege, is said to have been of noble lineage. He was of the family of Philiphaugh in Scotland. James Murray, Esq., J.P., of Bonds Hill, near Derry, is his descendant.

E

A little before this time Mr. William Blacker and Ensign Twinyo came to town, sent (as was reported, and confirmed by an intercepted letter) by King James, from Charlemont, to amuse the garrison with such accounts of the clemency of the King on the one hand, and the formidable strength of his army on the other, as might incline them to a surrender. This discourse soon exposed them to the suspicion of the garrison, who seized and put them under restraint.—Blacker, while thus confined, writes a letter to the camp (which was intercepted), to this purpose :—That he doubted not they knew he was detained a prisoner in town, but he served their interest as much there as if he were in their camp. They had many friends in town, especially Captain Darcy, Mr. White (Collector of Strabane), &c. There was a council held upon them, but after some time they were both dismissed.

The common soldiers, who knew nothing of the forementioned order of the council, were so enraged at their officers, several of whom (as was before hinted) about this time left them and fled for England, that they could not forbear expressing it with some violence on some of them. One Captain Bell was shot dead, and another officer hurt, who had (as was supposed with that design) got into a boat with several other officers.

CHAP. IV.

THE CHANGE OF GOVERNMENT IN DERRY.

THIS day some in the town sent one Capt. Cole to Colonel Cunningham to offer him the government of it, because they suspected Colonel Lundy's integrity. Colonel Cunningham's answer was, that he being ordered to apply himself to Colonel Lundy for direction in all things relating to their Majesties' service, could receive no application from any that opposed that authority. On the 18th the ships fell down to Greencastle, and on the 19th sailed for England. On the 20th, about one o'clock in the morning, a ship making towards the coast from whence they came, inquired whether they had met the English fleet, upon which Colonel Cunningham, hoping that some part of his Majesty's fleet might be near, from whom they might have provisions, resolved, if he could procure from them provisions for one fortnight, to return to Derry, upon which they gave the signal and made after that ship, but found it to be the Bonadventure frigate, that was conveying some ships with arms and ammunition to Derry, but no provisions. This account I had from Sir Arthur Rawdon and Captain Hugh Magill, who were then on board the same vessel. There was not one of the vessels, but only that wherein Colonel Richards was, that took the signal, and made after the Bonadventure frigate.

This night Major Crofton finding the gates open, and two of the keys wanting, doubled the guard, and changed the word. He was questioned for it the next day by Colonel Lundy, but he thought not fit to insist on it, and so there was no more made of it.

April 18.—What secret assurances were given King James that first induced him to march his army down to the city, or to retire again, in expectation of the multitude being brought to a compliance, those can give the best account that were most active for a surrender, and privy to all the clandestine transactions about it. But it is certain that the Irish army came this day to the Strand above the windmill,* at the South end of

* The position of the windmills, spoken of in the account of the siege, is thus described in the *Londeriad*:

"Near Bishop's gate the fatal windmills lie,
Where cattle feed and criminals do die,
This is the ready passage to Raphoe
And Donegal, from whence their traffics flow."

Derry hill, and there stopped, waiting what answer or salutation the city would give them. The council had, in the meantime, given strict orders that none offer to fire from the walls on severe penalties, and some were sent about the walls to give intimation of it. But how little the council or their orders were valued by the soldiers, the event soon showed. It was at this council that Mr. John Mogridge, who had been clerk to the forementioned council, held by Colonel Lundy, Colonel Cunningham, &c., declared he would conceal no longer the result of that council, viz.:—That Colonel Cunningham should return with the two regiments, and all gentlemen and officers quit the garrison and go with him. He desired Governor Lundy to produce the order—which was a great surprise to this present council, who (though they generally agreed too well with Colonel Lundy about surrendering) yet deeply resented the concealing so material a thing from them.

But our men on the walls paid so little deference to either them or their orders, and so little regarded the secret treaties they were managing with the enemy, that when King James' forces were advancing towards them on the strand, they presently fired their great guns at them, and, as was confidently reported, killed one Captain Troy, near the King's person. This unexpected salutation not only struck a strange terror into the Irish camp, but put the King himself into some disorder, to find himself so roughly and unmannerly treated by those from whom he expected so dutiful a compliance. And those who had encouraged him to try an experiment that proved so dangerous, thought themselves concerned to make some apology for it. The council therefore resolved to to send Archdeacon Hamilton to the King, to excuse themselves for what had passed, and lay all the blame of it on the ungovernableness of the people, whose violent humour they said they could not restrain, while his army continued there ; and therefore begged his patience, till the present tumult was over. And because some of the council, as well as others, could hardly believe that King James was really there, Captain White was sent with the Archdeacon, having often seen the King, to put them out of all doubt about it. Captain White returned to them with assurance of it; but Archdeacon Hamilton took protection (that summer he sickened and died). But King James' being there was an argument that had little force on our men on the walls, who were resolved to defend the Protestant religion and King William's interest against him and his army to the utmost. Nay, they now began to be impatient to see themselves thus betrayed by such as should have been their leaders, and severely threatened both the Governor and his council, for tampering with the enemy.

The Governor and council, though extremely displeased at the boldness and resolution of the soldiers, could not help it, having lost all authority and credit with them, of which this day produced a new instance, as considerable as this: Captain Murray was advanced from Culmore fort to the green field below Pennyburn Mill, with a considerable party of horse, within view of the town, having left fifteen hundred foot below at Brookhill. It was his appearing there had encouraged the men on the walls to accost the Irish army so rudely. The Governor and council perceiving his motion towards the city, despatched one Murray an express to him, with a line to this purport: That he should immediately, upon sight thereof, withdraw with his men to the back of the hill, out of the view of the city. He understood not the meaning of so strange an order; but the messenger, being his relation, explained the mystery to him, that the Governor and his council were about making terms with the enemy for surrendering the town; and added, that several of his friends advised him to hasten to town, if he designed to make any effectual opposition to the enemy; for if he came not, the town would certainly be delivered into their hands. Upon which, he resolved to march with his horse straight to the city, where, with some difficulty from the enemy's dragoons, who fired at him in the way, he came to Ship-Quay gate. Mr. Walker was sent from the council to discourse him, who would have had him alone to be taken up on the walls by a rope,* which he refused with disdain; but Mr. James Morrison, Captain of the guards, without any orders, opened the gates to him and his troops. His presence, when he came, struck a cold damp on the Governor and his council, but inspired the men on the walls with vigour and resolution.

* This fact, which never has been denied, proves that Walker now exhibited very little of that resolution of which he afterwards vaunted. He evidently would have surrendered the city, had not Murray with his friends, at this crisis, appeared in the place.

This same council this day proceeded to conclude a surrender, and drew up a paper to that purpose, which most of them signed, and as far as I could ever learn, all of them —(though many of the signers afterwards heartily joined with us in defence of the place.) But to return to Captain Murray, the multitude having eagerly desired and expected his coming, followed him through the streets with great expressions of their respect and affection. He assured them he would stand by them in defence of their lives and the Protestant interest, and assist them immediately to suppress Lundy and his council, to prevent their design of surrendering the city; desiring all who would concur with him herein, to put a white cloth on their left arm, which they generally did, being also encouraged to it by Captain Bashford, Captain Noble, and others. This greatly alarmed and perplexed the Governor and his council. They conclude to send for him, and try if they can prevail with him to sign the paper for surrendering the city. At their invitation he comes into the council, accompanied with some friends (though dissuaded by others). What passed betwixt him and Governor Lundy being of some importance to the right understanding that strange turn of affairs, on which the preservation of that city depended, I shall give the reader this short account of it. Colonel Lundy desired to know the occasion of his jealousies of him. Captain Murray told him plainly his late actions had declared him either fool or knave; and to make this charge good he insisted on his gross neglect to secure the passes at Strabane, Lifford, and Clady, refusing ammunition when sent for, riding away from an army of ten or twelve thousand men, able and willing to have encountered the enemy, neglecting the advantageous passes of Lougcausey and Carrigins, which a few men might have defended, &c. He urged him to take the field, and fight the enemy, assuring him of the readiness of the soldiers, whom he vindicated from those aspersions of cowardice which Colonel Lundy cast on them; and when Colonel Lundy persuaded him to join with the gentlemen there present, who had signed a paper for surrendering the town, and offered several arguments to that purpose, drawn from their danger; he absolutely refused it, unless it were agreed on in a general council of the officers, which he alleged that could not be, since there were as many absent as present.*

* Walker, in his Account of the Siege, says not a word respecting the spirited conduct of Murray on this occasion, though it was evidently the means of saving the city. He also speaks very

This discourse being ended, the Governor and council go on with their design of surrendering. Captain Murray leaves them, and returns to the soldiers that waited for him. He observed that the council were resolved to give up the city, which, if they should do, it was impossible for him to keep Culmore; and having advised with his friends, he resolves to stay in town, and do his utmost to prevent what he saw the council intended; to which he was the more encouraged by the entire interest he had in the affections of the common soldiers, whom he knew to be generally as averse to a surrender, and as resolute for defending the city, as himself.

The council goes on, after the paper for surrender was subscribed, to consider what methods were fit to be taken for capitulating with the King. They agree to send out twenty men to him for that end, as the King by a messenger had proposed. But the men were not chosen this night; but before the council was dismissed Governor Lundy sent for some of the Non-conformist ministers to come to the council.* None of them went but one, who refused to sit. The reasons of their being sent for were partly to engage them to persuade Captain Murray to comply with the rest for surrendering;† partly that their appearance there to countenance those proceedings of the council might induce the multitude to comply also, who were generally of that persuasion; but they not appearing, this project failed, and this proved the last session of the council.

That these pernicious intentions of the guardedly of the behaviour of Lundy, as if conscious that the ex-governor might have retorted upon him. Walker even acknowledges that, after all his previous misconduct, he and Baker "desired" Lundy "*to continue his government.*"—*True Account,* p. 20.

* Some of the Presbyterian ministers who sought an asylum in Derry, induced a number of stout young men belonging to their congregations to accompany them and assist in the defence. Among those thus influenced by Mr. Crooks, the minister of Ballykelly, were James Wallace and Robert Morrison. The Rev. James Wallace, the missionary of the Irish General Assembly in India, is descended from James Wallace. Robert Morrison had a son named John, who was born in 1702, and who was an elder of Ballykelly congregation. He took a very active part in ejecting Mr. Nelson, a concealed Arian, who was for some time the minister.—*See History of Presbyterian Church in Ireland,* III. 360. The Rev. Hugh Morrison of Killymorris is the great grandson of John Morrison.

† As Captain Murray was a Presbyterian, they tried to bring the influence of ministers of his own communion to bear upon him.

council might be more effectually counteracted, Captain Murray and a party with him went this night to the main guard, took the keys from one Captain Wigston, who then commanded the guard, and appointed guards that night at the gates, and on the walls.

The soldiers and multitude, thus headed by Captain Murray, renew their threats against the Governor and his council, who were so justly apprehensive of their danger from them, that after that time Colonel Lundy kept his chamber till he stole away; and few of his council durst for a while appear in the streets, for fear of the armed multitude.

I have insisted the more largely on the transactions of this day betwixt Captain Murray and the Governor in council, because the opposition he made to their design, both in the council, and especially by his influence on the multitude, was the only thing that prevented the surrender of the city to King James, and altered the whole scene of affairs in it. And I must in justice add that though the body of those that joined with him were called the rabble, yet they were generally men as eminent for their great probity, as for their courage, actuated with a hearty zeal to the Protestant religion, and animated with the hopes of seeing it ere long flourish in that kingdom, under the happy government of King William and Queen Mary. And how much the main stress of the defence of the city lay on them, will appear from the following account of it.

This evening King James with his army went back to St. Johnston, and stayed there till the 20th, waiting for an answer from the city.

April 19.—The multitude having thus broken the authority of the council, would have made Captain Murray both their general and the sole Governor of the town, but he modestly refused it, because he judged himself fitter for action and service in the field, than for conduct or government in the town; and therefore, when several gentlemen invited him to a council, that they might choose a Governor, he very readily agreed to it. At this council, there were at first but about fifteen in all, where all the officers of the garrison ought to have been, as matters then stood. The persons nominated were Major Henry Baker, Major Mitchelburn, and Lieutenant Colonel Richard Johnston; Major Baker had the majority of votes, and was chosen their Governor. Having done this, they immediately considered what regiments might be in town, and concluded on eight.

Governor Baker to be colonel to Sir Arthur Rawdon's dragoons.

Major Walker to be colonel to the Lord Charlemont's regiment, the lieutenant-colonel being gone.

Major Parker to command Colcraine regiment.

Major Mitchelburn to command Mr. Skeffington's regiment.

Captain Hamill to be colonel to a regiment.

Lieutenant-Colonel Whitney to be colonel to Francis Hamilton's regiment.

Major Crofton to be colonel to Colonel Canning's regiment.

Captain Murray to be colonel to the horse.

This being done, the new chosen Governor made a speech to acquaint them that the work they had now laid on him was too much for him to discharge, and therefore desired they would allow him an assistant for the stores and provisions. This he might have done of himself, and therefore they readily agreed to the motion, and desired him to nominate whom he pleased. He named Mr. George Walker, to which they assented.*

The next thing the council fell on (many more being now come into it) was to prosecute and perfect what Lundy had left unfinished the night before, viz.: the choice of twenty men to go out and capitulate with King James. It was proposed to Colonel Murray to be one of them, but he refused, and went to the walls. Colonel Lundy (who kept his chamber) being informed that they had chosen a new Governor, and were proceeding to choose the twenty commissioners, sends Mr. Seth Whittle, parson of Bellaghy, and Mr. George Hamilton to the council, to make all the interest they could there to have friends, as he called them, chosen to go to King James, which they earnestly endeavoured. The twenty are chosen, and ready to go out : the multitude on the walls and at the gates hearing of it, are so enraged that they threatened, that if any of them offered to go out on that errand, they would treat them as betrayers of the town, the

* It is worthy of note, that Dalrymple substantially adopts this account. His words are— " Major Baker was chosen governor; with that modesty which likewise attends true courage, he begged to have *an assistant*. The garrison under the impressions of religion, which danger incites, chose Mr. Walker, a clergyman to assist him."— *Memoirs. Part II. Book II.* Dalrymple thus rejects Walker's statement.

Protestant religion, and King William's interest. Upon which none of them durst offer to go, and so a stop was put to that dangerous capitulation, notwithstanding the orders of the Governor and council. So little did the soldiers regard any commands that seemed to cross their resolutions of defending the city.

Now the soldiers, whom their officers had deserted, chose their captains, and each captain which of the colonels he would serve under, as they pleased themselves.

What the number of men, women, and children in the town might be is uncertain ; some of the aged people, women, and children, with some few others, to the number of near a thousand, left us.

This evening a trumpeter comes to the walls from King James, to know why they sent not out commissioners to treat according to their proposals. The multitude having put a stop to that, Colonel Whitney wrote a few lines to excuse themselves to the King.

April 20.—A party of King James's horse and foot marched down to Culmore, and from thence down through the barony of Innishowen, and there robbed a great number of people, that were waiting for passage to Scotland. They placed guards on the waterside, to stop all passage from this city to Culmore by land, which debarred us of intelligence from that place.

This day the Lord Strabane came to the walls with many proposals, offering honourable terms to the city if they would surrender. Colonel Murray waited on his lordship without the gate, and discoursed long with him.

His lordship earnestly solicited him to come over to their party, offering him a Colonel's place in their army, and a thousand pounds gratuity from the King ; but his offers being rejected, he took his leave, Colonel Murray conveying him through our out-guards.

This evening a party of our horse and foot marched out with a design to attack the enemy, but returned upon an information of some design against them in the town. About the same time Colonel Lundy bribed a sentinel, with whom he stole away, and going to Brookhall, which was then in the enemy's power, he wrote from thence a letter to a lieutenant in town, desiring him to leave the town, and bring off a crop-horse with him.

CHAP. V.

THE SIEGE.

April 21.—THE enemy placed a demiculverin one hundred and eighty perches distant east by north from the town on the other side of the water, and begun early this morning to play upon us, but did little harm, though it was then a little more frightful to our people than afterwards, when they were more familiarized to it. This day our men sallied out, both horse and foot, towards Pennyburn Mill, the horse commanded by Colonel Murray, the foot by several captains, viz.:—Captain Archibald Sanderson, Captain Beatty, Captain Thomas Blair, Lieutenant David Blair, &c., Lieutenant-Colonel John Cairns, and Captain Philip Dunbar, &c., being placed on the hill with a reserve. Colonel Murray divides the horse, which were about three hundred in number, in two parts: with the first of these he charged himself, with great courage; the second squadron was led on by Major Nathaniel Bull, son to Major Samuel Bull, of the County of Meath (who did us very good service by his integrity to the interest of the garrison, and his influence on the soldiers to animate their courage). The rear of that squadron was brought up by Capt. Cochran,* who, when his squadron fled, advanced with a few to the party that was engaged—his horse being shot under him, and himself shot in the leg. The enemy divided their horse into two squadrons also. He that commanded the first party led them on with great bravery. Colonel Murray charged through that brigade, and had that day three personal encounters with their commander, in the last of which he killed him on the spot, whom the enemy themselves confessed to be Lieutenant-General Maumont.† It was also reported that he killed his brother in the same action. In the meantime the rear of our horse fled towards the walls, the enemy's horse being hot in the pursuit of them. Our foot that were at the mill had done great execution on the enemy, but observing the horse were generally fled (except a small party which continued with Colonel Murray), they came down to the Strand side and lined the ditches; and the enemy's horse that pursued ours having no other way to come back but that, our men fired so thick on them at their return that very few of all that party escaped. This day, when this dispute was begun, the enemy in the afternoon brought the cannon they had plied us with down to the point, opposite to our men on the Strand, and played over warmly at them (though without any execution), till one of our guns from the walls disabled their gun, and killed the gunner and others. We could have no certain account how many of the enemy were killed, they were said to be above 200. We lost nine or ten, viz.:—Lieutenant M'Phedris, Cornet Brown,* Mr. M'Kee, one Harkness, and five or six more private soldiers: several were wounded. We got only one standard, but considerable spoil of horse, arms, cloaks, saddles, watches, money, &c. This prey did not a little quicken the appetites, and animate the resolutions of the soldiers in their sallies afterwards, the manner whereof (to suggest that here) was usually this: that when any officer of note, with a few more attending him was about to go out, all that were willing to hazard themselves in the enterprise followed them as volunteers.

The persons of note said to be killed on the enemy's side were, General Maumont,

---

* Captain Cochran was from Armagh.—See *Stuart's Armagh*, p. 418. Among his descendants are several families of the same name, and the family of the late William Thomson, Esq., Fountainville, Belfast.

† Lord Macaulay ascribes the death of the French general to a musket ball shot at random, but the evidence here is quite positive. It is possible that a musket ball disfigured the dead body, and that thus the French report originated. Murray on this day displayed prodigious bodily strength, as well as great courage. He is said to have been six feet five inches high. He died in 1690, leaving behind him a son and daughter.

* Cornet Brown, who fell in the battle of Pennyburn Mill, was the ancestor of the Rev. John Brown, D.D., of Aghadoey. How singular that a Presbyterian minister, lineally descended from one who bought victory so dearly on that bloody day, should be the Trustee of a Presbyterian College erected, one hundred and seventy years afterwards, on a spot overlooking the scene of conflict! Cornet Brown is also said to have been the ancestor of Alexander Brown, who emigrated from Ballymena to the United States towards the close of the last century, and who was the father of the merchant princes of New York and Liverpool.

Major Taaffe, Major Waggon, Major-General Pusignan, Quarter-Master Cassore, Captain Fitzgerald.

April 23.—The enemy planted two cannon in the lower end of Strong's orchard, near eighty perches distant from the town, on the other side the water, over against Ship-Quay Street; these threw balls about ten pounds weight each. With these they played so incessantly on that street, piercing the garrets and walls, that some were hurt, and few dare stay above stairs. The besieged having made a blind in that street to preserve the people, repay them from the walls in the same coin; and killed Lieutenant Fitzpatrick, Lieutenant Con O'Neill, two serjeants, some soldiers, and, as was reported, two lusty friars.

April 25.—Colonel Murray, with some horse, and a good party of foot, sally out and beat the besiegers that had got into the ditches out of them. Some few of our foot had pursued too far: a party of the enemy's horse coming suddenly about the end of the little hill, forced them to retire back to the rest of our party; who, observing the enemy's horse to advance so quick towards them, took themselves to the ditch by the way side, and fired so briskly and continually on them, that they were forced to flee. Our men pursue them down to Pennyburn Mill, and pressed so hard upon them that their dragoons, who were beat from the old mill, near an English mile up the same water that Pennyburn Mill stands on, left their horses, and came down to assist their foot and some horse that were in hazard at Pennyburn Mill. Our men kept them at warm service till towards the evening, and returned, when wearied, without any loss. A party of men that went out late to be a reroguard to our men at the mill, were beat in by a party of horse that were despatched (with each a foot-man behind him) from the enemy's camp, but without loss. This day, Colonel Murray, Captain Nath. Bull, Captain Obrey, Captain John Kennedy, Captain Arch. Saunderson, Capt. Michael Cunningham,* Captain William Beatty, Captain Wm. Moor, and others, behaved themselves with great bravery. The dispute at both the mills was very sharp, and lasted some time. What number of the enemy was killed we could not learn. We lost but two men, and had eight or ten wounded, who recovered.

This night Major Parker left the city, and deserted their Majesties' service here on this occasion. A reroguard of foot had been left to defend our men from a party of the enemy which we on the walls saw coming on them. These Major Parker was too slow and negligent in bringing off, according to his orders, whereby they were exposed to great danger from the enemy. For this misbehaviour he was threatened with a court-martial, which he took this course to avoid.

The enemy planted their mortar-pieces, first in Strong's orchard, on the other side of the water, and threw into town some small bombs, which did not much hurt. Our ammunition was put into several places, as the Church, dry wells, cellars, &c.

At this time, that there might be a good understanding and harmony among the besieged, it was agreed to by Governor Baker, that the Conformists should have the Cathedral Church the one-half of the Lord's-day, during the whole time of the siege, and the Non-conformists the other half;* the latter entering it at twelve, had two sermons there every afternoon, besides two or three other meetings in other parts of the city. In their assemblies there were every Lord's day considerable collections for the relief of the poor people, and the sick and wounded soldiers, who had otherwise perished for any care was taken of them, and they had the use of the Cathedral every Thursday.

Governor Baker, together with Colonel Walker (who was also complimented with the title of Governor, but always understood with reference to the stores, the oversight whereof was, besides his regiment, the only trust committed to him by the gar-

* The *Londeriad* thus describes the religious services during the siege:—

"The Church and Kirk did jointly preach and pray,
In St. Columba's church most lovingly;
Where Doctor Walker, to their great content,
Preach'd stoutly 'gainst a Popish government.
Master Mackenzie preach'd on the same theme,
And taught the army to revere God's name.
The reverend Rowat did confirm us still,
Preaching submission to God's holy will.
He likewise prophesied of our relief,
When it surpassed all rational belief.
The same was taught by learned Mr. Crooks,
And Master Hamilton show'd it from books.
Then Mills, a ruling elder, spoke the same
Of our relief, six weeks before it came!
From sun-rising to sun-setting they taught,
Whilst we against the en'my bravely fought.
Thus heaven assists those actions which proceed
From unity, in greatest time of need."

Mr. Rowat, here mentioned, was the Presbyterian minister of Lifford or Ballindrent; Mr. Crooks, of Ballykelly; and Mr. Hamilton, of Donagheady.

* The *Londeriad* describes Captain Michael Cunningham as coming from Prehen near Derry. There is reason to believe that the second wife of Mitchelburn was the daughter of this gentleman.

rison) examined the stores, and continued the old store-keepers in their several places, till our stores began to fail, and then all was put into one store-house, which was carefully kept by Mr. Joseph Harvey, and his brother Samuel all the time of the siege.* There were persons appointed to search all cellars, and what provisions they found there (which had been plentifully laid in by private gentlemen and others of the country) they brought to the store, and these were the support of the garrison.

Some of the chief officers spoke to the Non-conformist ministers to be chaplains to their regiments, as others to some of the Conformists. Colonel Walker invited myself to be his, the generality of his officers as well as soldiers being Non-conformists; yet the Nonconformist ministers received no allowance out of the stores. Some of them had brought to town a considerable stock of provisions of their own, which was taken to the public store-house, and others of them lived on their own money. The Conformist ministers generally were maintained by the store for some time; and, after that, had 2s. 6d. a-week paid them; while the others had no such allowance—which had like to have been resented to a high degree in the garrison, if some that considered our present circumstances had not been careful to prevent it.

About the 27th of April Captain Darcy (mentioned before, one that was brought from Scotland by Captain Hamilton before the siege, and left prisoner here, having fled from England, where he was one of King James's party) had a pass given him by our Governor to go with horse and arms, which he accordingly did. Lieutenant-Colonel Whitney had sold him some horses, which

* Mr. Harvey is thus distinguished in the Londeriad:—

"Harvey, a tanner, was a leading man,
And John, his son, who now is chamberlain."

The Harveys are said to have been originally from Malden in Essex; and the celebrated physician, who discovered the true theory of the circulation of the blood, belonged to the family. The Harveys of Maliu (perhaps a corruption for Malden) Hall in the county of Donegal are descended from John, the chamberlain. The respectable Harvey family, still resident in Derry, are of the same lineage. One of the Harveys was settled as Presbyterian minister of Glendermot in 1695. His son David was minister, first of Glendermot, and afterwards of Derry Presbyterian Congregation. The sister of the Rev. David Harvey was married to the Rev. Andrew Ferguson, Presbyterian minister of Burt, and the late Sir R. A. Ferguson, so long M.P. for Derry, was her great-grandson.

were said to be none of his own, upon which, and other misdemeanours, Whitney was confined, and afterwards tried by a council of war, and found guilty of being no friend to this garrison, for which he was under confinement during the time of the siege.

About this time Captain Lance is chosen Colonel to Coleraine regiment, which Parker had deserted, and Captain Monro* is chosen Colonel to Whitney's regiment, so that now all the regiments had their Colonels, which continued so during the whole time of the siege.

Governor Baker's regiment of foot, consisting of twenty-six companies.
Colonel Mitchelburn's, of seventeen companies.
Colonel Walker's, of fourteen companies.
Colonel Monro's, of twelve companies.
Colonel Lance's, of thirteen companies.
Colonel Hamill's, of fifteen companies.
Colonel Crofton's, of twelve companies.
Colonel Murray's regiment of Horse, consisting of eight troops.

Besides these men that were regimented, there were several volunteers in town who did good service, as Captain Joseph Johnston who was very careful to have good patrols kept, Captain William Crooke, and Mr. David Kennedy, and many others, who were frequently out upon service, the first of these having his leg broke with a piece of a bomb, whereof he died.

About the beginning of May Colonel Mitchelburn was suspected by Governor Baker and the garrison. The Governor confined him to his chamber, betwixt whom there was some little scuffle when he was apprehended. He continued under the rules of confinement, but was never tried by a council of war. What the grounds of the suspicion were is too tedious to relate, but he was afterwards nominated by Baker Governor during his sickness.

About the same time Governor Baker (fearing lest enemies within the town should work mines in cellars near the walls) took with him Mr. William Mackey, one of the citizens that was very active and industrious for defence of the town, and they two searched all cellars near the walls, under pretence of examining the provisions, but found nothing of what they feared.

Few days passed (while the enemy's camp were coming nearer to us) but Colonel Murray, Captain Noble, Captain Dunbar, Captain Andrew Adams (afterwards Major),

* The *Londeriad* thus speaks of Capt. Monro:—

"He's Major-Gen'ral Monro's brother's son,
Who did oppose the foe in Forty-one."

F

Captain Wilson, Captain Archibald Hamilton, Captain Beatty, Captain Sanderson, jun. (whose father, Captain Alexander Sanderson, was very useful in the garrison ; so were also Major Alexander Stuart, Major John Dobbins, Captain Charles Shaw, Captain Samuel Wright, Captain James M'Cormick), Captain Bashford, Captain Cunningham, Lieutenant Dunlop, Lieutenant Macklin, or some of them, went out with small parties (and sometimes private soldiers only), and they seldom returned without doing some execution on the enemy, or bringing in some small prey.

Captain Noble and others found several letters in the pockets of the slain, giving them some intelligence, particularly about the surrender of Culmore. We were informed that Lundy, as he passed by, sent a message to them that Derry was surrendered. This added to the discouragement they were under (having little ammunition, and eight of the guns being before sent up to town by Captain Jemmet on Lundy's orders), is said to have inclined them to follow the example.

May 5.—About the middle of that night the besiegers under the command of Brigadier Ramsey, came to the Wind-Mill, and beat in our out-guards which were but few, and possessed themselves of that place, and before sunrising had a line drawn from the bog to the water. It was old ditches which they quickly made up.

Early on May the 6th, Governor Baker and other officers were about detaching ten out of every company to attack them, but the men were impatient, and ran out of their own accord, some at Bishop's Gate, others at Ferry-Quay gate. Their numbers being thus increased, they advanced on the enemy, who were come into the ditches and old walls, and beat them from ditch to ditch, till they were got into the line they had made, where they so continually fired on them, that they forced them to quit the line they had drawn, and flee for it. Our men pursued them so close, that they came to club-musket with it. But their foot and dragoons flee in great confusion. Ramsey endeavoured to rally them, but to no purpose ; for he and several other officers were killed on the place. Our men pursued them, beyond all the ditches, to the top of the hill, and drove foot and horse all before them. They returned about twelve o'clock. The enemy lost on the place about two hundred (many of them shot in the face, forehead, and breast, over their own line, as they were firing) ; a great number also died of the wounds they then received.

In this action we got four or five colours, several drums, fire-arms, some ammunition, and good store of spades, shovels, and pickaxes. Of the enemy these persons of note were killed, viz.:—Brigadier-General Ramsey, Captain Barnwell, Captain Fox, Captain Fleming, Lieutenant Kelly, Lieutenant Welsh, Ensign Barnwell, Ensign Kadel ; and the persons following were taken prisoners : Lord Netterville, Sir Gerard Aylmer, Lieut.-Colonel Talbot, Lieutenant Newcomen. We lost but three or four private men, and some wounded, particularly Lieutenant Douglas, who afterwards died.

May 7.—Governor Baker desires the enemy to send some private soldiers and an officer to bury their dead, which they did after a very careless manner.

This week, Governor Baker, with the advice of some officers, resolves on drawing a line across the Wind-Mill hill, from the bog to the water. They set men to work, and soon finished it, and afterwards secured it with redoubts, the better to defend our men from a cannon the enemy planted on the other side the water, directly opposite to the end of the works our men had made there. He also orders every regiment to be by turns on guard night and day at this new line on the Wind-Mill hill ; but afterwards the guard was kept by detachments out of each, occasioned by a suspicion of an officer on that out-guard.

About this time the two captains (Clossos) left us, and took protection.

May 10.—Lieutenant Mitchel went away also (and came again with Major-General Kirke into the Lough). About the same time, Mr. John Brisben, a curate, left the town, and took protection.

A party of our men, about two hundred, under the command of Lieutenant Colonel Blair, were gone out, and were posted among the ditches, doing some execution on the enemy. A great party of the enemy were coming down on them, whom our men in the hollow could not see ; but those on the walls seeing them, Colonel Murray rides along Bog Street, and though a party of the enemy behind a ditch fired incessantly at him, he went on to the place to warn them of the danger, so that they came off safely. Captain Rickaby was shot in the arm.

The besiegers soon after placed a camp at Ballougry, another at Pennyburn Mill, and a third at the orchard beyond the water. They kept the guards so strictly along the water on each side, that we were barred up from all intelligence.

After the placing of these camps they brought their guns to Ballougry, and there successively discharged them all in the dusk of the evening. They also ordered their men in a long range in all their camps, and made them all fire round, with a design (as we supposed) to strike the greater terror into the hearts of the besieged. The enemy were busied in bearing faggots, and making forts or trenches, and in some parts piling up these faggots. Our men sallied out, came to their forts and piles of faggots, and burnt both them and several little houses the enemy had for quarters, with many bridles, saddles, &c., and killed several, both officers and soldiers. The besiegers had built a trench near Pennyburn Mill, on which they planted some of their guns. Our men resolved, in the evening, that next morning early they would attack that fort, and either bring away their guns or nail them up, and accordingly they went out, about two or three thousand men, but effected not their design (which was afterwards thought might have been accomplished, if pursued). Though the enemy discharged their guns at our men, none were hurt, one only was shot through the leg with a small bullet.

About this time our men went out, viz.:— Captain Joseph Cunningham, Captain Noble, Captain Archibald Sanderson, and some others. These Captains, with about one hundred, went too far out in the open fields, where they seized a fort the enemy had made on the heathy hill, and beat the foot out of it. In the meantime a party of the enemy's horse came at full career betwixt our men and the town, took Captain Cunningham prisoner, whom, after quarter given, they perfidiously murdered. (They gave us other instances afterwards how faithless they were to their word. Particularly, they desired one White might come over to some of his friends, engaging their word for his and the boats return; but they detained both him and the boat, to our loss, who had no other, but to their greater reproach and dishonour). Captain Noble and the rest came off, being good footmen. We lost fifteen or sixteen men at that time.

May 21st, being Tuesday, the Non-conformists kept a solemn fast, and had sermons in two places* of the city besides the Cathedral, where there were considerable collections made for the poor, who began to stand in greater need of them. Soon after the Conformists also kept another.

June 4th, being Tuesday.—The enemy approach to our works at the Windmill with a great body of foot and horse. Our men ordered themselves so that in each redoubt there were four, and in some five reliefs, so that they were in a posture of firing continually. The Irish divided their horse in three parties, and their foot in two. The first party of horse was commanded by Captain Butler (the Lord Mountgarret's son), and consisted mostly of gentlemen (who, it is said, had sworn to top our line). They attacked our lines at the water side, and the other parties of horse were to follow the first. The one party of the foot attacked the lines betwixt the Wind-Mill and the water, and the other (being Grenadiers) the lines at the bog side, betwixt the Wind-Mill and the town. Captain James and John Gladstanes, Captain Andrew Adams, Captain Francis Boyd, Captain Robert Wallace, Captain John Macklin, and Captain William Beatty, with their men, had taken their ground near the water. The first party of horse charged furiously, having faggots of wood carried before them. They came on with a huzza, seconded with a huge shout from the Irish camp. They came by the end of the line (it being low water) notwithstanding our firing constantly on them. Our men, viz., Captain James Gladstanes, Captain John Gladstanes, with others next to them, left their redoubts, and took the Strand with their muskets, pikes, and scythes, and fell on them with that vigour that soon spoiled the tune of their huzzas, for few of that party escaped; many of them were driven into the river, and Captain Butler himself taken prisoner by Captain John Gladstanes. The rest of the horse seeing the first party so warmly received, had no great stomach to come on. In the meantime the foot (who had also faggots of wood carried before them) attacked the line betwixt the Wind-Mill and the water. They were as warmly received as the horse. And, whereas, they imagined our men would fire all together, finding that they fired successively, they soon wheeled about, and drew off, only a few came furiously to the back of our works, and were either killed, or hauled over by the hair of their heads. In the meantime the other party of foot, being grenadiers, attack our forts by the bog side, and came on fiercely, but were as vigorously repulsed by our men there. Colonel Monro did there acquit himself very well; Captain Mich. Cunningham, one of the citizens that had been always very active and zealous for the defence of the town, was at the bog side with his company, kept our men to their posts, and opposed the grenadiers with great courage. He narrowly escaped with his life,

* This confirms what has been elsewhere stated. Whilst the Episcopalians had only one place of meeting—the Cathedral, which they could not fill—the Presbyterians kept up services in the Cathedral, which they filled to overflowing, and in two other places, in each of which they met twice on the Sabbath.

a cannon bullet tearing up the ground about him, and he had a small bullet cut out of his back. Lieutenant James Ker, Lieutenant Josias Abernethy, and Lieutenant Clerk did good service, the last being wounded. Mr. Thomas Maxwell was killed about the same time on the walls. This day Governor Baker showed both his conduct and courage in ordering and bringing out frequent reliefs, where the greatest danger appeared. Our women, also, did good service, carrying ammunition, match, bread, and drink, to our men, and assisted to very good purpose at the bog side, in beating off the grenadiers with stones* who came so near to our lines. The enemy lost a considerable number of men. Most of their officers were either killed or taken prisoners. When they retreated, they carried away on their backs many of their dead and mortally wounded with them—as was supposed to shelter themselves the better from the storm of our shot. Those of note killed on the enemy's side were, Lieutenant Colonel Farrell, two French captains, Captain Graham, Lieutenant Burke, Quarter-Master Kelly, Adjutant Fahoy, Ensign Norris, Ensign Arthur. The prisoners were Captain Butler, son to the Lord Mountgarret, Captain Macdonnell, Cornet MacDonaghy, Captain Watson, a French Lieutenant, Lieutenant Eustace, Serjeant Peggot. We lost five or six private men, and one Captain Maxwell had his arm broken by a cannon bullet, whereof he died within three weeks after. He had that day behaved himself with great courage. And one Thomas Gaw had all the flesh shot off the calf of his leg by a cannon bullet, but the bone not being broken, he recovered. There were three of our Colonels out that day, Murray, Monro,† and

* Some of the soldiers performed great feats with the stones supplied by these assistants. Thus the *Londeriad* says:—
"His pike away brave Robert Porter threw,
And with round stones nine Irish soldiers slew."

There is reason to believe that the Robert Porter here mentioned was from Burt, and probably the great-great-grandfather of the Rev. Professor Porter, of Belfast Presbyterian College. Professor Porter's great-grandfather, who was the son of Robert Porter, was born in Derry during the siege.

† Among the officers who distinguished themselves this day, and who were under the command of Colonel Monro during the siege, was Captain Thomas Ash. He kept a Diary of the Siege, first published by his granddaughter in 1792. His father John Ash, one of the Sheriffs of Derry in 1676, was thrice married, and had in all twenty-three children. In consequence of the premature death of her brother, his third wife,

Hamill; the last got a hurt on the cheek with a small bullet. The next day, one Mr. Edmund Stones, in

Elizabeth Holland, became heiress to a considerable property, including a townland called The Heagles, about three miles from Ballymoney. This lady survived him; and Mr. John Cromie, of the County of Antrim, married the rich widow. Her son, Stephen Ash, was married to Mary Edwards, daughter of Edward Edwards, Esq., of Castlegore, and aunt to Hugh Edwards, Esq., the proprietor of a valuable estate at Derg. Their daughter Elizabeth was married to the Rev. John Thomson, Presbyterian minister of Macosquin. In early life Mr. Thompson obtained a commission in the army, but becoming deeply impressed by the truths of the Gospel, he withdrew from the military profession, and entered the Presbyterian ministry. He was minister of Macosquin for nearly 44 years, and died there in 1771. His only child was married to the Rev. James Whiteside, minister of Tobermore; and one of Mr. Whiteside's daughters was married to the Rev. Alex. Martin, minister of Dervock, father of the Rev. Edward Thompson Martin, of Dundonald. Captain Thomas Ash was twice married—first, in 1686, to the only daughter of Mr. Thomas Beck of Magilligan, by whom he had two daughters; and secondly, in 1693, to Elizabeth Rainey, only daughter of Mr. Hugh Rainey, a rich Presbyterian merchant of Magherafelt. Mr. Rainey bequeathed a considerable sum for the establishment of a school in that place under Presbyterian supervision; but, by some management, an act of the Irish Parliament placed the institution under the care of the Primate of Armagh ! Capt. Ash was High Sheriff of the city and county of Derry in 1694. By his marriage with Miss Rainey he had seventeen children, thirteen sons and four daughters. His son Luke Ash, who was born in 1705, after receiving the elements of a classical education at Magherafelt, was placed under the tuition of the Rev. Charles Masterton, Presbyterian minister of Connor. Having subsequently graduated in the University of Edinburgh, and passed through the usual trials before the Presbytery of Tyrone, he was licensed to preach; and, on the 9th of August, 1732, was ordained to the pastoral charge of the Presbyterian Congregation of Sligo, where he remained till his death in 1742. Sarah, the third daughter of Captain Ash by his second marriage, became the wife of Mr. John Jackson, by whom she had three sons, William, Hugh, and Luke. Captain Ash was himself an Episcopalian, but at least some of his children by Elizabeth Rainey adhered to the Church to which their mother belonged. He lived to an advanced age. I have been indebted for much of the information contained in this note to a MS. history of the family drawn up apparently by one of themselves about 1736. A copy of this MS. has been kindly lent me by the Rev. George Hill of Belfast Queen's College. Captain Thomas Ash was ancestor of William H Ash, of Ashbrook, Esq.

time of a parley, went to a little well beyond the bog, having leave from the Irish first. But a French officer came, and putting his one hand to Mr. Stones' cartridge-box, with the other treacherously pulled out his sword to kill him; but he starting back, the sword only pierced his side, and the wound proved not mortal: so meanly base were some of our enemies.

From the 10th of May till near the end of the siege, we had many little parleys with the enemy, sometimes to admit doctors to see the wounded prisoners, the Lord Netterville and Talbot; sometimes to admit provisions to them, which we granted them; sometimes that we might have leave with safety to send messengers to the ships, or abroad for intelligence—but that we could not obtain.

Captain Cole had been among the Irish army for near a month together at the beginning of the siege, and about the 10th or 12th of May came into town again. Governor Baker being suspicious of his being an agent for the enemy, ordered him to be confined till he was satisfied he had no ill design against the city, but had secretly made his escape from the enemy, who had detained him prisoner.

About the end of May, most of the officers having been for some time suspicious of Governor Walker, drew up several articles against him, some of which were to the effect following, according to the account I had of them from the memories of some of the officers then present.

One was that he and others, about the 18th of April, had a secret cabal, wherein they agreed, and privately sent a messenger to King James with proposals about getting the town to be delivered up.

Another was that the said person being on his return confined on suspicion of this, was taken out privately by Mr. Walker's means, and sent over the walls. He went to Culmore, which was soon after surrendered.

Another was that on several days, especially about the latter end of April, Mr. Walker held a consultation with some others in the town, while our men were out against the enemy, to shut the gates upon them, to facilitate a surrender.

Another was for selling or embezzling the stores.

Another was, that he offered to betray the town for £500 in hand, and £700 a-year, which offer was approved by King James, and the money promised.

Another was for abusing officers that went to the stores.

Others of them, relating to personal vices, I shall not mention.

But for a more particular and full account of these matters I refer to the articles themselves, which were lodged in Colonel Hamill's hands.

There were several persons had examined witnesses, and undertook to prove these articles; and Colonel Hamill, Colonel Murray, Colonel Crofton, and Colonel Monro, Lieutenant-Colonel Fortescue, Captain Noble, Captain Dunbar, and above a hundred officers more, subscribed a resolution to prosecute him upon these articles, in order to the removing him from all trust either in the stores or in the army.[*] This occasioned a motion, which Governor Baker readily assented to, viz., that all the government of the stores, as well as the garrison, should be managed by a Council of Fourteen, of which he was to be president, and nothing be done but by them.[†] But the meetings of this Council were soon after, through the difficulty of the siege, especially the danger of the bombs, much interrupted, though the authority of it continued till the end of the siege. This being granted them, Governor Baker earnestly persuaded, and at last prevailed with them to desist at that time from the prosecution of the forementioned articles: yet these articles were revived, and increased to the number of fourteen, soon after Governor Baker's death. Yet all this did not sufficiently caution Mr. Walker from what the garrison looked on as an intruding himself into that part of the government that was never intended him; for after Governor Baker's death he called a court-martial, and appointed Lieutenant-Colonel Campbell to be president of it. The officers, hearing that the court was set, came in, and publicly discharged them from sitting any longer, declaring that he had no power that appointed them, and accordingly they were presently dissolved.

There are but two things relating to the articles forementioned I would take notice of. Those who most suspected the design mentioned in the third article to be real, pri-

---

[*] It is thus evident that Walker was suspected, not merely by the multitude, but by many officers of the highest station and character.

[†] This statement respecting the Council of Fourteen, is exactly corroborated by the *Londeriad*:—

"*Upon some grievances* we chang'd the powers,
And add a council to the governors,
First, all the Colonels, and then four more,
Two for the town, two for the country boor.
Cocken and Squire were chosen for the town,
For country, Dr. Jennings and Gladstane,
Then in this council, this a law was made,
No act should pass unless seven gave their aid."

vately agreed, in all their sallies afterwards, to keep a good reserve in the town for the prevention of it, the care whereof was entrusted by turns to Lieutenant-Colonel Cairns and Captain James Gladstanes (two gentlemen that showed great fidelity and prudence in the council, as well as courage in several sallies for the defence of the city). And the 4th article occasioned an order of council that Mr. Walker's note should not be accepted by the keepers, till signed by the Governor or Major Adams.

June 5.—The besiegers had thrown a great many small bombs before this, but they began about this time with great ones of two hundred and seventy-three pounds weight, each of them being weighed after seventeen pounds of powder had been taken out of it. Some of these (both great and small) did not break, having lost their fire. Those which they threw in the night did not much hurt to people that were able to go to the walls, because they were easily seen and shunned, but several that were sick were killed in their houses. We were in greater hazard by those thrown in the day, it being more difficult to see them. The dread of them forced our people to lie about the walls all night, and to go to the places remotest from houses, some out of Ferry-Quay gate, some to the Ravelin, and others to the Wind-Mill hill; and the cold which the men—especially the women and children—contracted hereby, added to their want of rest and food, occasioned diseases in the garrison, as fevers, flux, &c., of which great numbers died. The bombs, by throwing down some houses, furnished us with fuel, which we then stood in great need of. One of these bombs fell into the house of Captain James Boyd, and broke down the side of it, killing himself; but several officers who were then at dinner escaped the danger, though it fell near the room where they dined. Another bomb killed Mr. Alexander Lindsay, the surgeon, who was very useful to the sick and wounded soldiers; and one Major Breme was killed with a cannon ball; another bomb killed Mr. Henry Thompson, a burgess of this city, who showed great zeal for the defence of it; another killed fourteen men, and fired one or two barrels of powder in a back house; another killed seven, another killed three of our men.

June 7.—There came three ships up to Culmore, and fired at the Castle several days, and one of them running a-ground, or being left by the tide, was much endangered by the enemy's cannon. The enemy called to us from their lines to send down carpenters to mend her. But we soon had the satisfaction of seeing her off again.

After this time, Governor Baker was a little indisposed, and kept his chamber.

June 13.—Major-General Kirke appears with a fleet in the Lough, below Culmore, which gave us at the present the joyful prospect, not only of the siege being soon raised, but of being furnished with provisions which then grew very scarce, as appears by the allowance our men then had from the stores. They were already reduced to such straits, that where they could find a horse a-grazing, near the Wind-Mill, they would kill and eat him. But when we saw them lie in the Lough without any attempt to come up, it cast a cold damp on our too confident hopes, and sunk us as low as we were raised at the first sight of them.

Upon the appearing of the ships, the enemy seemed to be in a mighty consternation. We observed a great motion in their camp of pulling down tents (as we heard), in order to decamping; and many of their common soldiers (as the country people informed us) changed their red coats and ran away. But the terror was soon over, when they saw them make no great attempt to come up, though they had both wind and tide to assist them. And the enemy quickly began to draw down their cannon, and soon after to raise batteries at Charlesfort, where they planted some of their guns to oppose the ships coming up to our relief; and some time after they began to make a boom across the river from that fort to Brookhall directly opposite to it. This first boom was made of oak beams, chained together with iron and great cables twisted about them. For a week together we saw them making some preparation for this boom across the river, as drawing of timber, &c. We afterwards saw several boats on the water busied about it, but (as the country people since informed us) it was not entirely finished, till about a fortnight after the ships appeared in the Lough. But this boom when finished was useless to their design, because it did not float, and it was broke by the great tides. After this they made another of fir beams, chained as the other was: this floated, and served their purpose better; but this latter boom, or what was left of it, the "Mountjoy," of Derry, broke.

June 16.—Colonel Walker had proposed to agree with the enemy to take £500 ransom for Lieutenant-Colonel Talbot. A sort of council was held in Governor Baker's chamber, wherein this was carried; but Governor Baker perceiving it to be ill resented in the garrison, declined it. But Colonel Walker urged it, with some violence and threats against those that opposed it; and ordered the bier that should carry him away to be this day brought to his lodging; at which the multitude were so enraged, that Mr. Walker should take so much on him, that they took the bier, and made a fire of it in the main-guard. They searched for Mr. Walker, who had fled for sanctuary to Baker's chamber in the Bishop's house. Not finding him immediately, they took all the prisoners, that were able to walk, from their several lodgings, and carried them to gaol. They had searched Mr. Walker's own lodging, whence they took the beer, mum,* and butter which they found to the store; and being informed that Mr. Walker was in the Bishop's house, they pursued him, some threatening to shoot him, others to send him to the gaol. Governor Baker, to whom they payed a great deference, came out, though indisposed, to pacify them; engaged there should be no ransom taken for the prisoners; entreated them, for his sake, to pass by what Mr. Walker had done, and suffer the prisoners to go to their own lodgings again—all which they, with some difficulty, consented to, at Governor Baker's entreaty. What construction the multitude put on this practice of Mr. Walker I think not fit to mention.

We afterwards offered to release Lieutenant-Colonel Talbot, on condition they would permit a messenger to go and return from the ships; but this would not be granted, and soon after Talbot died, and put an end to this dispute.

About this time the fever, flux, and other distempers grew rife, and a great mortality spread itself through the garrison, as well as the inhabitants, insomuch as it was observed that fifteen Captains or Lieutenants died in one day; and the garrison being in great strait for want of provisions, some of the citizens and others concerned for the public good, met; called the Captain of the gunners, Alexander Watson, and ordered the gunners (who, for the most part, lived in town) to make diligent search for provisions, which they did to good purpose; for, digging up cellars and other places, they got much provision under the ground, which some that went away, and others during the siege had hid, and many that saw how sincerely concerned they were for the safety of the place, brought forth their provisions of their own accord. By this means the garrison was furnished with bread (though the allowance was little) till the end of the siege.

* This species of beverage was exceedingly nutritive. Hence the poet says:—

" Sedulous and stout
With bowls of fat'ning mum."

Our iron bullet was much spent, but this defect was supplied with lead bullets, made with pieces of brick in the middle of them. Wm. Brown, Adjutant to Governor Baker's regiment, was industrious and dexterous in this piece of service.

There were oats, shilling, and malt in town, which could not be used for want of mills; therefore Captain Gregory and some other workmen took care to have a horse-mill built, as also to have carriages made for the guns—some of which were so out of order that sometimes we could not use them when we wanted them.

About this time, since the enemy had so barred us up from getting any messenger sent to the ships for intelligence, the besieged built a boat (none being here) to go down by water. Lieutenant Crookshanks took care of this, and some of our men in the night attempted to go down in it, but they were beaten back by the enemy's shot from each side of the water.

June 17, or thereabouts, Governor Baker's distemper increases, and he becomes dangerously ill; and Colonel Mitchelburn was deputed by Baker Governor during his sickness.

June 18.—Colonel Murray, Captain Noble, Captain Dunbar, Captain Holmes, two Lieutenants, and about twenty more went up the water in the night in our new boat, it was given out to rob the fish-houses in the isle, but the real design was to land a messenger or two in a wood about four miles up the river, to send to Enniskillen. But the enemy soon took the alarm, and as the boat passed by Evan's Wood they fired a great gun planted there at her, which narrowly missed her. As our men went further up, the enemy fired at them on both sides the shore, but when they came up to Dunnelong Wood, where they designed to land their two messengers, the boys were so terrified that they durst not venture ashore, and it being now early in the morning, our men discovered two large boats behind them, which the enemy had set out and manned with dragoons to cut off their return. Our men made towards them, and soon came to a very sharp engagement, for, after their shot being spent on both sides, one of the enemy's boats came up close to theirs, thinking to have boarded them, but as it happily fell out, they caught a tartar, for our men were as quickly in upon them, beat back some of them into the water, and killed three or four others, besides a Lieutenant in the enemy's boat; whereupon the rest threw down their arms and called for quarter. We took thirteen prisoners in this boat. The enemy in the other boat seeing this ill success of their friends, made off with what haste they could. We carried our prisoners and some small prize towards the city, the enemy still firing at us from the shore; yet in all this adventure not one of our men was hurt (except Colonel Murray, who received some shots in his head-piece, that bruised his head, and for a while indisposed him for service), but one of the prisoners that sat among them was wounded by a shot from the shore. So remarkable was the guard of divine providence about us. Our men, being encouraged by this success, landed their prisoners near the city, delivered them to the guards, and returned to attack a party of the enemy who were at that time drawing off one of their guns; but the enemy perceiving the resolute approach of our men, left her and fled. Our men pursued them to the top of the hill, till they perceived another strong party marching, under covert of the hill, to get betwixt them and their boats, upon which they retreated, and had scarce time to recover her, before the enemy came up.

About the 20th of June, Conrad de Rosen,* Marshal-General of King James's forces, arrived at the enemy's camp, and soon after raised several batteries in the night, and a line on the other side of the bog opposite to the Wind-Mill, brought their camp and trenches near to us, ran a line through the orchard opposite to Butchers' Gate, within some few perches of it, ordered the mortar-pieces to be taken from the orchard on the other side the water, and placed on the side of the hill above the bog, on the west side of the town, and planted their battering guns, which threw a ball of twenty or twenty-one pounds weight, at a convenient distance before the Butcher's Gate. They plied us hard both with their bombs and battering guns. The bombs they threw, some in the night, and some in the day, at uncertain hours, till the 21st of July, after which time they threw no more. Of the number of the bombs, and the time of their throwing, you will find an account annexed. And here began the close siege.

We used all endeavours to get intelligence from the ships, but could have none. We made many signs from the steeple, both by cannon-shot and drawing in our flag, to represent our distressed condition to them. But June 25, one Roche,* a messenger, came to town from Major-General Kirke. When he came to the Waterside, having no expectation of a boat, he swam over, and gave us an account of the ships, men, provisions, and arms that were there for our relief—adding that it was desired if he got safe to town, to give them in the ships notice of it by four guns from the steeple, which was accordingly done. There came another messenger along with him, one Cromie; but because he could not swim, he lay hid a day or two in the bushes, expecting a boat to be sent for him in the night, as the other had promised; but the enemy's guards found him, and being in hazard of his life, they made him promise to give the besieged a discouraging account, and then hung out a flag for a parley, which was granted, and some were sent over the water to discourse him: he (being sworn to do so) repeated to them the words that had been put into his mouth; but when Lieut.-Colonel Blair enquired why he gave a different account from what Roche had done, he replied, he was in the enemy's camp, Roche within the walls of Derry. Roche tried to go to Major-General Kirke again, but was forced to come back because of the enemy's Guards on the Waterside.

This extremely troubled us, that no messenger could get down to give the Major-General an account of our distressed condition. There came one M'Gimpsy to Colonel Murray, and voluntarily offered to swim down the water with intelligence. Colonel Murray acquaints the Deputy-Governor Mitchelburn with it; but he delaying, he resolved to send him down, promised a reward, and wrote him a letter signed by himself, his Lieutenant-Colonel Cairns, and Captain Gladstanes,† representing the great extremity they were reduced to, and with all imaginable earnestness importuning speedy relief.

* Captain Roche, as a reward for his services on this occasion, received a grant of a forfeited estate in the county of Waterford and the profits of several ferries; but various parties claimed an interest in these donations, and he was in consequence involved in much litigation.—*See Harris' Life of William III., p. 209. Dublin, 1749.*

† This document was not signed either by Walker or Mitchelburn. At this time little attention was paid to the rules of official etiquette, though Walker afterwards set up a claim to be chief governor on the ground that his name stood at the head of some letters such as this.

* Lord Macaulay thus speaks of this General: "Rosen was a native of Livonia, who had in early youth become a soldier of fortune, who had fought his way to distinction, and who, though utterly destitute of the graces and accomplishments characteristic of the Court of Versailles, was nevertheless high in favour there. His temper was savage: his manners were coarse: his language was a strange jargon compounded of various dialects of German and French."—*History of England, Chap. XII.*

This letter was close tied in a little bladder, in which were put two musket bullets, that if the enemy should take him, he might break the little string wherewith it was tied about his neck, and so let it sink in the water. Whether this messenger was taken alive by the enemy, or was killed by running himself against the boom (as some reported), is uncertain; but within a day or two they hung up a man on a gallows in the view of the city, on the other side the water, and called over to us to acquaint us it was our messenger.

The enemy work every night to bring their trenches near the walls for mining. Our men were diligent to counterline them, being incited to it every night by Governor Mitchelburn. These works were carried on by the care of Captain Schambroon, and the indefatigable pains and charges of Captain Michael Cunningham and Mr. William Mackey, who both paid some of the soldiers for working out of their own pockets, and gave many of those that wrought meat and drink at their own houses. Hereby the enemy were kept from getting to the near side of the bog, without which they could draw no mines. There was, besides, a blind raised by the persons forementioned before the Butchers' Gate, to defend it from the enemy's battering guns, which had already done some hurt to it. A collection, by way of free-offering, was made among the inhabitants to carry on this work.

June 28.—The Lord Clancarty, with his regiment, comes to the besiegers' camp, and that night attacked our out-works at the Butchers' Gate, and few of our men being out at that time, they soon possessed themselves of them. In the meantime they were throwing their bombs, one of them coming short of the walls, fell among their own men, which discovered them on their march towards the said works. Upon this, the few men that were out retired within the gate. The enemy was led on by their Lieutenant-Colonel Skelton, who had some detachments with him besides Clancarty's regiment. One on horseback comes close to the gate and called for fire to burn it. Captain Noble and Dunbar sally out with our men, some at Bishop's Gate, and some at Butchers' Gate, to the number of sixty or eighty at first; more soon followed. The salliers attack them so briskly, being well assisted from the walls by great and small shot, that they were forced to quit our works, and run to their own lines, to their great dishonour as well as loss. The number of those killed on the place was about thirty; how many were wounded, and afterwards died, we could not tell. Some officers were killed, viz., a French Lieut.-Colonel, Captain O'Brien, a French Captain, an English Captain, an English Lieutenant; Captain Mackartie, Corporal M'Guire, and a private soldier, were taken prisoners.

At this time Governor Baker died, justly lamented by the garrison, in whose affections his prudent and resolute conduct had given a great interest.* After Governor Baker's death there were several meetings appointed for the election of a Governor, but continual action prevented them. However, Colonel Mitchelburn, who had been Deputy-Governor during Baker's sickness, continued to act as Governor, though without any confirmation from the council.

June 30.—Conrad de Rosen, Marshal-General of King James's forces (who was said to swear by the belly of God that he would demolish our town, and bury us in its ashes), sent in this following letter to the Governor and officers :—

" Conrad de Rosen, Marshal-General of all his Majesty's forces,

" Declares, by these presents, to the commanders, officers, soldiers, and inhabitants of the City of Londonderry, that in case they do not, betwixt this and Monday next, at six of the clock in the afternoon, being the first of July, in the year of our Lord, 1689, agree to surrender the said place of Londonderry unto the King, upon such conditions as may be granted them, according to the instructions and power Lieutenant-General Hamilton formerly received from his Majesty, that he will forthwith issue out his orders from the Barony of Innishowen, and the sea-coasts round about as far as Charlemont, for the gathering together of those of their faction, whether protected or not, and cause them immediately to be brought to the walls of Londonderry, where it shall be lawful for those in the same (in case they have any pity of them), to open the gates and receive them into the city, otherwise they will be forced to see their friends and nearest relations all starved for want of food, he having resolved not to leave any of them at home, nor anything to maintain them. He further declares, that in case they refuse to submit, he will forthwith cause all the said country to

---

* The *Londeriad* thus speaks of Baker :—

" He's much lamented and admir'd by all,
Who knew his merits for they were not small.
The town he gov'rn'd with assiduous care,
Was sound in counsel, and expert in war.
Great was his strength of body, but his soul
Did greater actions, which none dare control."

G

be immediately destroyed, that if any succour should be hereafter sent them from England, they may perish with them for want of sustenance ; besides which, he hath a very considerable army, as well for the opposing of them in all places that shall be judged necessary, as for the protection of all the rest of his Majesty's dutiful subjects, whose goods and chattels he promises to secure, destroying all the rest that cannot conveniently be brought into such places as he shall judge fit to be preserved, and burning the houses and mills, not only of those that are in actual rebellion, but also of their friends and adherents, that no hopes of escaping may be left for any man—beginning this very day to send his necessary orders to all Governors, and other commanders of his Majesty's forces, at Coleraine, Antrim, Carrickfergus, Belfast, Dungannon, Charlemont, Belturbet, Sligo, and to Colonel Sarsfield, commanding a flying army beyond Ballyshannon ; Colonel Sutherland, commanding another towards Enniskillen ; and the Duke of Berwick another on the Finwater, to cause all the men, women, and children, who are anywise related to those in Londonderry, or anywhere else in open rebellion, to be forthwith brought to this place, without hopes of withdrawing further into the kingdom. Moreover he declares, that in case before the said Monday, the first day of July, in the year of our Lord 1689, be expired, they do not send us hostages, and other deputies with a full and sufficient power to treat with us for the surrender of the said city of Londonderry, on reasonable conditions, they shall not, after that time, be admitted into any treaty whatsoever ; and the army which shall continue the siege, and will, with the assistance of God, soon reduce it, shall have order to give no quarter, or spare either age or sex, in case it is taken by force. But if they return to the obedience due to their natural Prince, he promises them that the conditions granted to them in his Majesty's name shall be inviolably observed by all his Majesty's subjects, and that he himself will have a care to protect them on all occasions, even to take their part if any injury contrary to agreement should be done them, making himself responsible for the performance of the conditions on which they shall agree to surrender the said place of Londonderry to the King. Given under my hand, this 30th day of June, in the year of our Lord 1689.

"Le Marshal de Rosen.

"Per Monseigneur Fetart."

Lieutenant General Hamilton had also a little before this letter sent into town the following proposals :—

"Lieut.-General Hamilton's Proposals.

"1. That Colonel O'Neill has a power to discourse with the Governor of Derry from General Hamilton, as appears by his sending this.

"2. That the General has full power does appear by his commission.

"3. That General Rosen has no power from the King to intermeddle with what Lieutenant-General Hamilton does as to the siege, being only sent to oppose the English succours, and that all conditions and parleys are left to the said Lieutenant-General Hamilton, that as to what articles shall be agreed on, they may see by the King's warrant he has full power to confirm them. Notwithstanding, if they do not think this sufficient, he will give what other reasonable security they can demand. As to the English landing, such as had commissions from the Prince of Orange need not be apprehensive, since it will be the King's interest to take as much care of his Protestant subjects as of any other, he making no distinction of religion.

"4. As to what concerns the Enniskillen people, they shall have the same terms as those of Derry on their submission—the King being willing to show mercy to all his subjects, and quiet his kingdom.

"5. That the Lieutenant-General desires no better than having it communicated to all the garrison—he being willing to employ such as will freely swear to serve his Majesty faithfully ; and all such as have a desire to live in town, shall have protection, and free liberty of goods and religion.

"As to the last point, such as have a mind to return to their homes, shall have a necessary guard with them to their respective habitations, and victuals to supply them, where they shall be restored to all they possessed formerly, not only by the sheriffs and justices of the peace, but also by governors and officers of the army, who from time to time will do them right, and give them reprisals of cattle from such as have taken them to the mountains.

"Richard Hamilton.

"At the Camp at Derry,
June 27, 1689."

Lest these proposals should be kept up from the garrison (they weakly imagining the soldiers more inclinable to comply than the Governor or officers) they threw them into us in a dead bomb, the better to disperse them.

These proposals not being accepted, the

French general issued out his orders, as he had threatened in his letter, and drove in all the Protestants for near ten miles round, protected as well as unprotected, men, women, and children, the 2nd of July. Many tender people, and some women with child, died by the rude and barbarous usage they met with on the road (being most stripped, and guarded in dirty pounds and rotten houses, &c.). When they first appeared, we took them for a body of the enemy, and the guns were discharged at them; but the shot (being directed by an unerring hand) touched none of our friends, but, as we afterwards heard, killed some of those merciless soldiers that were pushing them on. But it was dismal to us to hear their cries when we perceived who they were, and saw the enemy driving them with their drawn swords down to the walls. Our men resolved to put them without our lines at the Wind-Mill, and in the night many of them were brought within our lines. It moved our compassion the more when these poor people so earnestly entreated us not to surrender out of pity to them, adding that they knew they would save neither us nor them alive after it. This put the Governor and officers on making the following experiment :—They immediately ordered a gallows to be erected on the bastion next the camp, on which they threaten to hang all the prisoners (now put into jail) if these people have not leave to go to their several habitations. Lieutenant-Colonel Campbell, and Captain Jenny, a clergyman (two gentlemen that were very faithful and active in the garrison), are sent to remind them of preparing for death, upon which they wrote this following letter, and have leave to send a messenger to carry it, and bring back an answer :—

"MY LORD,
"Upon the hard dealing the protected (as well as other Protestants) have met withal, in being sent under the walls, you have so incensed the Governors and others of this garrison, that we are all condemned by court-martial to die to-morrow, unless these poor people be withdrawn. We have made application to Marshal-General de Rosen, but having received no answer, we make it our request to you (as knowing you are a person that does not delight in shedding innocent blood), that you will represent our condition to the Marshal-General. The lives of twenty prisoners lie at stake, and therefore require your diligence and care. We are all willing to die (with our swords in our hands) for his Majesty, but to suffer like malefactors is hard; nor can we lay our blood to the charge of the garrison, the Governors and the rest having used and treated us with all civility imaginable. We remain, your most dutiful and dying friends,

"NETTERVILLE, E. BUTLER,
"G. AYLMOR, M'DONNELL,
"(In the name of all the rest).
"To Lieutenant-General Hamilton."

The Lieutenant-General returns to them this following answer :—

"GENTLEMEN,
"In answer to yours, what these poor people are like to suffer, they may thank themselves for, being their own fault, which they in town may prevent by accepting the conditions that have been offered them; and if you suffer in this, it cannot be helped, but shall be revenged on many thousand of these people (as well innocent as others), within or without the city.
"RICHARD HAMILTON."

But, notwithstanding this answer, we supposed the regard they had to their imprisoned friends prevailed with them, for the poor people had liberty to return to their dwellings on the 3rd of July, and many of our weak people and women got away among them, though they sent many back, knowing them by their colour. We got some able men among them, which were driven in, who stayed with us to the end of the siege.* The enemy soon saw their error in this treatment of the poor people. The garrison had here a convincing instance before their eyes, how little trust there was to be reposed in their promises, for many of these people had protections under the King's or Lieutenant-General's own hands. And this could not fail of making them obstinate against all proposals of surrendering, whilst it was possible to hold out. The people being sent away, the gallows was taken down, and the prisoners sent to their several lodgings. About this time Mr. Andrew Robinson left us, but the enemy stript and sent him back, because of some imprudent expressions.

* Among those now taken into the town was an ancestor of the Rev Dr. Cooke, of Belfast. During the remainder of the siege he did good service as an artilleryman. "An ancestor of mine," says Dr. Cooke, "was driven at the point of the bayonet to Derry: all his family were murdered save one little boy. His father carried him with him, and when he arrived at Derry, he had no cover for his child, but placed him beside him at the embrasure of the walls beside the guns. It pleased God to protect the boy—and here am I, the humble individual who addresses you, a descendant of that child."—*Speech at Belfast in January*, 1841.

Captain Beatty* also went away, and took protection, and lived at Moneymore ; but the reason of it was because he had a violent flux, which rendered him useless to the garrison, and he went to try if he could recover his health, for he had been at all the encounters and skirmishes with the enemy before, and ever behaved himself with great integrity and valour.

About the 6th or 7th of July we observed few men about their camps. Governor Mitchelburn, by advice, draws out the body of our men beyond our lines at the Wind-Mill, that we might know what body of men would appear to oppose them. Some of our men go down to the old ditches and fire at theirs in their lines. The enemy fired at them. Colonel Barker, with about a dozen horse came to the Strand, and stood at a distance. Few of their foot—not above two companies—appear marching down to the rest that were in the lines ; but it growing dark, our men, by mistaking the word of command, came within our own lines again in some confusion. Colonel Barker received a shot in his hand, which put him into a high fever, whereof he was reported to have died.

About this time we heard a loud huzza in all the camps of the enemy round the city, which, when we inquired the reason of it, they told us it was for joy of Enniskillen being taken.†

July 11.—The enemy calls for a parley, and sends one to know if we would treat with them for surrendering the city. We considered that most of the ships were gone, we knew not whither ; provisions grew extremely scarce ; and therefore to gain time, it was thought advisable to agree to it. They desired that if we agree to treat, there may be six commissioners chosen on each side ; that we send the names of the six we would choose, and the terms we would demand, with some person the next day, being the 12th ; and they would send the names of their six the same day, that they might have time to consider our terms. And Saturday, 13, was appointed the day of treaty ; all which was agreed to.

The names of the Commissioners and the terms you will find in the Commission and articles annexed in the end.‡

* He was ancestor of the late Archdeacon Beatty of Moydow, in the county of Longford.
† This was a mere sham, as Enniskillen made a successful defence ; but the Irish army hoped thus to dishearten the besieged.
‡ The reader will find, on reference to the document in the Appendix, that the Rev. John Mackenzie, the author of this Narrative, was one of the six Commissioners chosen on this occasion. He here modestly declines to record this

These articles were sent to the enemy, with the names of the commissioners for the city, on the 12th of July, and on the 13th, the six commissioners went out, being empowered to treat with the enemy.

About their commission there was a great debate : some of the Council of Fourteen would have had the commission run in their name, because they had the power. Mitchelburn and Walker laid some claim to it (though Mr. Walker had only his first post, and Mitchelburn was only deputed Governor by Baker during his sickness, but never confirmed Governor by a council). The Colonels and other officers would have had it run in theirs, because the interest was chiefly theirs. But at last the name of Governors in general, without any particular application of it was (though not without great opposition) thought fit to be used, for this reason, that the enemy might not look upon us as a confused multitude without any government.

July 13.—Our commissioners went out to the enemy's camp, and had a long debate till night with the commissioners on their side. The enemy consented to all things material demanded in the aforesaid articles, except three, viz.:—1. The time for surrendering : they would grant no longer time than till Monday, the 15th, at twelve o'clock. 2. The securing of hostages : they would allow they should be kept in Derry, but not put into the ships that Major-General Kirke brought. 3. The manner of marching out : they would allow no arms to our soldiers, but only to the officers and gentlemen in town. Our commissioners returned, and with great difficulty obtained time till next day at twelve o'clock to return an answer.

That night after the return of the commissioners there was a council, where the commissioners gave an account of their negotiation that day, and a council was appointed at eight o'clock the next morning, to consider what answer they should return.

While our commissioners were out on the treaty, Colonel Walker received a letter from Lieutenant David Mitchell out of the ships by a little boy, and transcribed it, with some additions of his own ; for whereas the letter mentioned Major-General Kirke's having sent some to encamp at Inch, he wrote it four thousand horse and nine thousand foot. This humour was the more unaccountable, because upon the return of the commis-

fact. As he was the only clerical member of this important deputation, his appointment is a signal proof of the confidence reposed in him as a man of wisdom and integrity.

sioners, he earnestly urged a compliance with the enemy's demands for surrendering the town the next day;—and therefore when the contents of his letter from Lieutenant Mitchel were objected to him as a strong argument against surrendering—especially the numbers that were landed—he confessed that part of the letter to have been framed by himself: which indiscretion, joined with his ill advice, had like to have proved of as dangerous consequence to himself, as the advice had been to the garrison, if they had complied with it.*

July 14.—The Council met, and had some debate about the answer to be returned, and the following answer was resolved upon (not without renewed opposition from Colonel Walker):—that unless the enemy would give us time till the 26th of July, and secure the hostages in the ships, we would not surrender. And for the manner of marching out, that was left to the commissioners to debate. The commissioners went out, and delivered this answer; but the enemy refusing absolutely to grant these terms, the treaty was ended. So evidently did that gracious God (who had determined our deliverance, and to whose all-comprehending eye that particular season of it that would most illustrate His own glory was obvious) infatuate the counsels and harden the hearts of our enemies. Had they accepted the proposals, the city had been unavoidably surrendered, and we could not have held out three or four days longer than the time we desired.

July 16.—About ten o'clock, a small party of the enemy suddenly attacked our works without Butchers' Gate (none of our men being out), and soon possessed themselves of them; but from the walls they were warmly repulsed, and beat off again. Our men beat them with stones out of the old walls. Some few were killed, and one taken prisoner in this action.

Two regiments of the enemy marched down from their camp in order towards the works on the Wind-Mill. Our men go out cheerfully to the works in considerable numbers, encouraged thereto by Governor Mitchelburn. The enemy when they came to the middle of the hill stopped, and wheeled about, and marched back again up the other side of the park. Our men raised an huzza from one end of the line to the other, waving their hats to them to come down, but they marched off.

* The facts here stated speak for themselves. Walker afterwards winced exceedingly under these statements, and yet he knew it was in vain to attempt to disprove them.

This day Colonel Murray, and about twelve more with him, went down to flank the enemy's trench before Butchers' Gate, and continued firing till their ammunition was spent. One of his men was killed, viz., James Murray, and himself shot through both the thighs up near his body, which proved so dangerous to him that he did not fully recover of it till near November.* A few days after he was wounded there fell out a sad accident in his chamber. Lieutenant Ross came there to search, as he pretended, for some of Sir Arthur Rawdon's saddles, &c. His unexpected rudeness occasioned some heat betwixt him and one of Colonel Murray's regiment, and the Lieutenant striking several times at him with his sword, the other took up a carbine and shot him dead.

The enemy had played very smartly at the town and gate with their battering guns, and about this time they took them away in the night down to Brookhall, where the boom was, and planted them there.

There was no action of note from this time to the 25th of July. The enemy had several cows feeding behind their lines very near us. Our men resolve they will try to get so welcome a prey into their own hands, and accordingly, July 25, early in the morning, they go out at Ship Quay, Bishop's, and Butchers' Gates, surprised Sir John Fitzgerald's regiment, who were in those lines, made havoc of them, beat them from their trenches, killed Lieutenant-Colonel Fitzgerald, and Captain Francis Wilson; took Captain Nugent prisoner. A party of the enemy's from the nearest camp came quickly down, which forced our men (being then enfeebled with the scarcity of provision) to retire without their desired prey. There was a considerable number of the enemy killed. We lost one Lieutenant Fisher, who was killed by a shot from the enemy's drake, as he was going out. We afterwards tried another experiment of tying a cow to a stake, and setting fire to her, in hope of drawing in some of theirs; but she breaking loose, that project failed.

About the 20th of this month, provisions growing extremely scarce, one Mr. James Cunningham, merchant,† found out a way of supplying the garrison for six or seven days. He showed them where there was a good

* Walker never mentions the sufferings of this brave officer. As Murray was one of the colonels, and the most distinguished soldier in the garrison, such an omission cannot be ascribed to forgetfulness.
† James Cunningham was one of the Presbyterian burgesses of Derry.—See *Presbyterian Loyalty*, p. 120

quantity of starch in the town, which they mixed with tallow, and made pancakes of—which proved not only good food, but physic too to many of those whom weariness and ill diet had cast into a flux.

July 28.—This morning Captain Charleton left us, and went to the enemy. Mr. Walker about this time had preached a discouraging sermon; and indeed the desperate necessities that were growing upon us had almost sunk us all into a despair of relief. But the hour of our extremity was the fit season for Divine Providence to interpose, and render itself the more observable in our deliverance, for this evening, about seven o'clock, we perceived three ships (viz., the Mountjoy, of Derry, the Phœnix, of Coleraine, and the Dartmouth frigate) coming up the Lough of Culmore, betwixt whom and those in the fort there was desperate firing; but when we perceived they had passed the fort our expectations of speedy succour raised us to a strange transport of joy.* The enemy plied

* In the *History of the Presbyterian Church in Ireland* (Vol. II., 366—8), the following explanation relative to the breaking of the boom is supplied by Dr. Reid:—" The unaccountable inactivity of Kirke, who had the command of the squadron in Lough Foyle, specially despatched from England for the relief of Derry, is well known, and has been ascribed to various motives,—sometimes to treachery, and at other times to cowardice. What ultimately induced him to determine to move his ships towards the city has never been stated or even conjectured; but the true cause is now at length ascertained. It was owing to the local knowledge and the warm remonstrances of an Irish Presbyterian minister, who, at the hazard of his life, had sailed from Greenock, where he had taken temporary refuge, to Lough Foyle, and who urged the General to make the attempt which proved so successful, and which, had it been delayed for even a few days longer, would have been too late! This interesting fact has been preserved by the truly indefatigable Wodrow, in the collection of miscellaneous historical materials which he entitled 'Analecta.' The minister referred to was the Rev. James Gordon, who was minister of the Presbyterian Church at Glendermot, nigh Derry, from about the year 1680. At the first appearance of danger from the Popish faction, he took an active part against their machinations; and he it was, according to Mackenzie's 'Narrative' (p. 9), who first ventured to propose the bold measure of shutting the gates against the Irish regiment sent by the lord-lieutenant to garrison Derry; and, in opposition to the strenuous advice of the Bishop of Derry, he succeeded in effecting this object, on which so much ultimately depended. He was afterwards obliged to leave the country, and sojourned for a time at Greenock. After the deliverance of the city, to which

them with cannon and small shot from both sides the river, and the ships made them good returns; but when the foremost vessel he had contributed so materially, he returned to Scotland, and became minister of the parish of Cardross, on the Clyde, near Dumbarton, whence, by letter to the Presbytery of Lagan, in January, 1692, he demitted the charge of the congregation of Glendermot. He died at Cardross not long after. The following is the account preserved by Wodrow :—

"'Mr. John Smith gives me this further account of Mr. James Gordon, which he had from his successor, Mr. A. Wallace. That Mr. Gordon, in the time of the siege of Derry, was at Greenock, and fell under great impressions of the hazard and danger they were in, and resolves to go and see; he gets a boat and goes to Derry Lough, where Major Kirke was lying with provisions, but either would not (as many say) or could not get up for the cross-boom or chain the besiegers had fixed. He goes aboard one of the English ships, Captain Brourey—(this was the Mountjoy, Captain Browning)—whether he was acquainted with him or not the relator knew not, and abused him for not venturing up the lough when the city was so much in strait. The captain laid the fault on Kirke, and desired Mr. Gordon to be silent, for Kirke stormed extraordinarily, and said he would hang Mr. Gordon. He went straight to him, and Kirke made him very welcome, and asked how he was. Mr. Gordon told him he heard he said he would hang him! Kirke took him to the cabin, and challenged him for his opprobrious language, and for his calling them cowards. Mr. Gordon told him he had said so, for the design (or plan for relieving the city) was easy. Kirke said it was impossible! Mr. Gordon called for paper and said he would draught it for him (which he was able to do from having been, as minister of Glendermot, personally acquainted with the locality). When Kirke saw Mr. Gordon's skill, he said—" Aye, but who will venture?" "I will venture for one," says Mr. Gordon, "and Captain Bronrey said he would venture, and another." And so Kirke yielded and commissioned them. The captain's ship went up first and broke the boom in the lough, and the captain was killed; yet the ship got through and came up to the town, and was the means of relief to it. This account Mr. Gordon gave to several of the elders of Cardross, from whom Mr. Wallace had it.'

"A few years after Wodrow had received this account, he heard the same incident related by another person, and he also inserts it among his collections. As it varies in some particulars from the preceding statement, it is here subjoined :—

"'Mr. John Richy confirms to me all the accounts before set down anent Mr. James Gordon. He came to Mr. A. Gordon, and told him he behoved to go to Derry, and would not be put off; that the commander of the ship to which he went was one Brown, who entertained him as a chaplain under the notion of a Protestant minister; that he allowed him to pray and expound Scrip-

came (as it is supposed) to the boom, she made some stop, the little wind they had while they passed the fort entirely failing, and a dead calm succeeding. The smoke of the shot, both from the land and from the ships, clouded her from our sight, and she was (as we afterwards learned) unhappily run aground; and when the enemy, who gathered in swarms to the water side, raised a loud huzza along the shore, telling us our ships were taken, and we perceived them both firing their guns at them, and preparing boats to board them, this struck such a sudden terror into our hearts, as appeared in the very blackness of our countenances. Our spirits sunk, and our hopes were expiring. But this did not continue long, for the Mountjoy, by firing a broad-side, with the help of the increasing tide, got off from the

ture some days in his ship; that in his doctrine he reproved them for lying idle and feasting, while their brethren were perishing; that Kirke had hanged some for making a mutiny some days before; that he came aboard Brown's ship, and called for that schoolmaster he heard was reflecting on his management; that Mr. Gordon briskly told him he was a minister and knew the country, laid down the scheme, directed a fort to be keeped in play with one ship till another broke the boom, and Brown was shot just as the boom was broke; however the ship got through, and came up to Derry; that Mr. Gordon stayed with Kirke in his ship, as a hostage till the experiment was tried, and was willing to undergo any punishment he pleased, if it did not succeed.'

"There can be no hesitation in receiving this account as substantially correct and perfectly authentic. Mackenzie's 'Narrative' evinces the deep interest which the minister of Glendermot took in the early defence of the city; and from the other anecdotes of him recorded by Wodrow, he was obviously of that ardent and zealous temperament which would lead him to return to Lough Foyle, in hopes of benefitting his besieged brethren. The collateral facts contained in this statement are all correctly given; and the death of Captain Browning, who alone knew of Mr. Gordon's interference (with the exception of Kirke, who was not likely to divulge it), may account for this anecdote not having found its way into any of the contemporary narratives of the siege of Derry. It has now been disinterred from the oblivion in which it was so long shrouded. Let it never be forgotten, then, that while the maiden city was heroically defended from within by a garrison, of which above nine-tenths were Presbyterians, its relief from without, at that most critical moment, when its gallant defenders were reduced to the last extremity, and when, to all human appearance, the pressure of the famine must have forced them to a speedy surrender, was owing to the intrepidity, the local knowledge, and the courageous interference of a Presbyterian minister!"

shore; and we soon perceived the ships firing at them, and advancing towards us, though but slowly, which made the enemy draw their guns from place to place after them; but at last they came up to the Quay, to the inexpressible joy of our garrison, that was at this time reduced to that distress, that it was scarce possible for them to subsist above two or three days longer. The first that broke or passed the boom was the Mountjoy, of Derry, commanded by Captain Micaiah Browning,* who was, to our great regret, killed by the enemy's shot—a gentleman whose memory should never be forgotten by the garrison and inhabitants of Derry, who generously sacrificed his own life for the preservation of theirs, and had freely offered to make this attempt sooner, if the Major-General would have permitted him. But the Phœnix, of Coleraine, came first to the Quay, Captain Andrew Douglas master, laden with eight hundred bolls of meal, from Scotland. The ships came in late, and that we might the better secure the people employed in bringing in the provisions to the stores, there was a blind made along the Quay, of casks and hogsheads filled with earth. The enemy continued to fire at us from their trenches as before, till the 31st of July. That day we perceived them firing several parts of the country about. In the night they burnt all the tents and huts of their camp round the city, and before the daylight had gone off towards Lifford and Strabane, keeping a strong rere-guard of horse. We had no horse left to pursue them, and our foot were in no condition to make such an attempt. They encamped at Lifford and Strabane, till they heard the unwelcome news of their forces, under the command of Major-General Macarthy, being routed by the Enniskillen men.†

* The widow of Captain Browning, on whom King William conferred a pension, is said to have been sister-in-law to Captain Thomas Ash, mentioned in a preceding note. He left behind him only one child—a daughter, who died young. The statement here made—that he had offered to make the attempt sooner—exactly accords with the account already given relative to the Rev. James Gordon.

† At the battle of Newtonbutler—"the greatest and most remarkable victory over the Irish," says Hamilton, "obtained in this or any former age. They were reckoned six thousand, and we not much above two: we killed that day in the morning and the afternoon about two thousand; brought to Enniskillen about four hundred prisoners, with their General (Macarthy), and a great many other officers. There were drowned in several places of Lough Erne, as was computed, about five hundred . . . . . . We took seven cannon, fourteen barrels of powder, a great quantity of

This so alarmed them, that, for haste, they burst some of their big guns, threw waggons of arms into the river, and left many of their army that were sick behind them. Some few of our men went out, and brought in some grenadiers prisoners, that were firing houses at six or seven miles distance from the city. Others of them went to Inch, where Colonel Steward having received orders to ship all his men, and come off, had called a council of his officers, and by their advice delayed the execution of them till he had sent to acquaint the Major General with the condition of the Protestants there, and should receive his further orders, as being loath to expose so considerable a body of them

cannon and musket balls, all their drums, and what colours they had. . . . . The action of this day made the Irish, through the whole kingdom, take new measures: it put them in a very great consternation; and, had we followed our blow, we might, in all human reckoning, have marched to Dublin."—*The Actions of the Enniskillen Men, pp.* 44, 45. This battle took place on Wednesday, the 31st of July.

as had come in to him to the merciless fury of an enraged enemy.

And thus was the siege of Derry raised, to the admiration of our friends who had given us over for lost, and to the disappointment of our enemies, who were no less confident they should soon make themselves masters of so weak and indefensible a place. The glory of it being entirely due to the Almighty who inspired a garrison, for the most part made up of a few raw and untrained men, and those labouring under all possible discouragements, with that resolution that enabled them to defeat all the attempts of a numerous army to reduce them, their zeal and affection for the just cause they had undertaken supplying all the defects of military discipline. So singular has been the favour of God to that city, as well as Enniskillen, in making it once more* a sanctuary to the distressed Protestants of the province of Ulster.

* It had already in 1641 afforded them protection.

CHAP. VI.

THE NEW ESTABLISHMENT BY MAJOR-GENERAL KIRKE.

Aug. 4.—CAPT. WHITE, Captain Dobbin, Captain J. Hamilton, Captain Jenny, and Mr. Knox were sent to the Major-General who had that day come to town. Col. Crofton had waited on him at Inch, and desired leave to draw out two or three hundred men, to go out into the county at large, to preserve the houses of the Protestants from being burnt, promising also to bring in a vast quantity of cattle; but his proposal was rejected. And near a week after that, some small parties of Irish, that stayed behind, burnt Newtownlimavady, and several gentlemen's houses in the county. The Major-General put out several proclamations: one —That all persons not in arms, who had fled to that place, should leave the city, the country being now clear, and repair to their respective habitations, without taking any of their goods with them, unless they had a particular order. Hereby the bedding of many was detained from them. Another was—that no person dying should be buried within the walls. Great droves of the country people's cattle were brought near the town, upon pretence of their belonging to the enemy; and so few could recover their own again, that many families were deprived thereby of the only considerable means of their subsistence. Colonel Mitchelburn was made Governor* by the Major-General, in whose hands the cattle were left, who sold them, according to the Major-General's orders, for good rates to the butchers and others.

An address was prepared to be presented to the King; and Colonel Walker was appointed by the Major-General to go with it. Many of those that signed it neither knew of the bearer, nor were well pleased with the great compliment passed on the Major-General in it, but were not willing at that time to make any disturbance by any public opposition to it.

The men were all drawn out to the field, and every colonel's regiment by itself. The soldiers went out the more cheerfully because it was reported the Major-General would that day distribute two thousand pounds amongst them. But they soon found themselves mistaken, not only in that, but in their hopes of continuing in their present posts. Colonel Mitchelburn's and Colonel Crofton's regiments were joined, and Crofton reduced. Colonel Walker's and Colonel Hamill's were joined, Walker demitted, and Hamill reduced, Captain White being made Colonel to it (who died September following). Colonel Monro's and Colonel Lance's regiments joined, Colonel Monro reduced, Lance made colonel (who died September following). Colonel Baker's and Colonel Murray's regiments were designed to be joined; but all of Colonel Murray's, except a very few, refused, and went off into the country with their carbines and pistols, and the Major-General seized their saddles, as he also did Colonel Murray's horse which he had preserved with great care during all the siege. St. Johns was made colonel of Baker's regiment. This being done, the Major-General named new captains to most of the companies, leaving them to choose their lieutenants and ensigns, so that a great many of those captains, who had not only raised and armed their companies almost wholly at their own charge, but had done the greatest service in the defence of the town, were either disbanded or reduced, and their companies were given to others, that had neither expended anything of their fortunes, nor hazarded their lives in that cause.* This was ill resented in the garrison; but when one of these captains took the liberty to complain of it, instead of any redress, he was (as himself informed several of us) threatened with the new gallows, which was ordered to be set up without the Ravelin. There were orders also given to the sentries at the gates, that none should be suffered to go out with

---

* Colonel Mitchelburn lost his wife and all his children during the siege. Though thrown into prison for debt in 1700, he died in 1721 possessed of considerable property. Tradition describes him as tall and of a fine military appearance. He was married a second time, and resided for several years before his death in the neighbourhood of Derry. He died in the seventy-sixth year of his age, leaving a widow, but no children.

* The conduct of Kirke was so tyrannical, and his injustice so odious, that Walker himself, on his arrival in London, endeavoured to obtain redress for the garrison. He was, to some extent, successful; but, in the end, many of the brave defenders of Derry and Enniskillen were reduced to beggary, in consequence of the non-payment of the arrears due to them.

any arms, and some that were walking out at the gates had their arms seized by the guards placed there. This unexpected treatment seemed very harsh and strange to them, that they could not be trusted to bear those arms about them which they had so lately employed in the vigorous defence of their country. The weak and sick soldiers had nothing allowed them to subsist on out of the stores, whereby they were forced to travel, and beg their bread in the country, which, being extremely depopulated, many of them perished for want. The lieutenants and ensigns fared no better than the captains, many of them being turned out, and others, who had at least never been in the siege, put in their places: nay, some that continued captains had detachments of fifteen men taken out of their companies, and put into the regiments of such as could not raise men, and then the captains were threatened to be turned out if they made not up their companies; nay, some of them were turned off, after they had been made use of to do that piece of service for such as were intended to succeed them. And even the new modelled regiments of Derry, that were received into the General's army, had only the following subsistence:—

Colonel	£0	5	0	per diem.
Lieutenant-Colonel	0	3	0	,,
Major	0	2	6	,,
Captain	0	2	0	,,
Lieutenant	0	1	0	,,
Ensign	0	0	8	,,

Serjeants, corporals, drummers, and private men, 2d. per diem each, besides bread; and, without bread, 3d.

The Enniskillen foot had the same allowance, and their horse had only 9d. a day for every private trooper, and 6d. a day for each of the dragoons.

But however they have been used by the Major-General's influence, they have always had a deep and grateful sense of his Majesty's extraordinary care and concern for their preservation; and the honourable character which he was graciously pleased to give of them and their services in his letter to them, was itself thought a valuable reward; and resented with the highest affections that subjects can pay to a prince who has an entire sovereignty in their hearts, and from whose generous goodness they still expect all the favour and encouragement that may put them into a capacity of giving more evident proofs to the world of their zeal for the Protestant religion, and affection to his Majesty's government.

APPENDIX.

The Letter to my Lord Mountjoy, from the inhabitants of Derry.

RIGHT HONOURABLE,
 The last post carried up to his Excellency the news of what our rabble had done in the town, how they had shut the gates against some of the Earl of Antrim's regiment, which we then blamed them for, though we could not restrain them; but yesterday and this day, being on all hands informed that a general massacre was determined, at least in Ulster, to be executed on the British Protestants: and having certain intelligence that the priests and friars of late bought up great numbers and quantities of horses, and arms, and other habiliments of war, as chain-bridles (whereof Dean Cahan for his part bought up twelve): recollecting further many dark speeches in ordinary conversation of late, and very odd sermons by the priests and friars preached in this neighbourhood: and hearing that the very soldiers that were to quarter there had been overheard to utter terrible threats against us, as to burn houses, &c.: and several outrages being committed by some of them on several persons, particularly one of them, without any provocation, cut one of the ferry-men, almost to the loss of his hand; some of them broke open houses, and took provisions thence by force, &c.: and when we were certainly informed that under pretence of eight companies, consisting of four hundred men, that were to come to this town, there were at least twelve hundred on the road to this place, besides great numbers of women and boys (which the Ultoghs always carry along with them, when they expect spoil): and lastly, when we caused the potent to be inspected, and found that it referred in the body thereof to the names of the captains underneath, and yet not one named, we cannot but think it a most wonderful providence of God to stir up the mobile for our safety, and preservation of the peace of the kingdom against such bloody attempts of the Northern people had formed against us, which we doubt not but his Excellency will look upon as a great and very acceptable service to his Majesty, to whom we resolve always to bear true faith and allegiance against all disturbers of his government whatsoever, and only to act in our own defence, without the least disturbance or prejudice to any that will live peaceably with us. And we doubt not but that all that are alarmed and terrified with the like danger in this and adjacent counties, and hereupon have put themselves also upon their defence, to the number, as we are informed from several parts, of near twenty thousand horse and foot, will do the same, if they be not assaulted. The rabble in their heat found means to get into the magazine, and thence took some arms and ammunition; but we have caused it to be locked up, and a guard set thereon, and an account taken of what is taken thence, and what left therein. Our request is, that your lordship will represent our danger to his Excellency, the necessity we are under, and obtain from him his allowance and countenance for securing ourselves from these Ulster enemies, that will never be obedient when they have power in their hand. Your lordship's kindness herein will be a perpetual obligation on the inhabitants of this city and neighbourhood, and very much tend to his Majesty's service in preserving the lives of thousands of his good and innocent subjects, that were designed for slaughter. We remain, your lordship's most obedient humble servants,

JOHN CAMPSIE.
SAMUEL NORMAN, &c.

Londonderry, Dec. 9, 1688.

The Letter to the Society at London, sent from Derry by Mr. Cairns.

RIGHT WORSHIPFUL,
 IN our sad calamity, and under the greatest apprehension of our total excision by the Irish in these parts of the kingdom which border upon us, we thought it necessary for us immediately to despatch David Cairns, Esq., a very worthy citizen of this city, and lately a member of this corporation, into England, to report our case to you, and to use his endeavours by all just means for our speedy relief. And we have eternal obligations laid on us to bless God, whose mercy and providence rescued us from the designs of wicked men, that conspired our ruin, without any provocation on our parts, whose inclination, as well as interest, it was to live peaceably with all men.

On Friday, the 7th instant, several intimations came to several hands hereabouts, that on the Sunday following a massacre was designed by the Irish in Ulster; and although it caused great thoughts of heart to the most assured amongst us, yet none of the more aged or grave came to any other resolution than to submit to the Divine Providence, whatever the event might be; and just at that juncture, whilst the younger and more inconsiderate were consulting their own safety (and, it seems, had resolved on the means), a part of the Earl of Antrim's regiment newly levied, and all composed of Highlanders and Ulster Papists, came to the river side, and their officers came over into the city to the sheriffs, for quarters and lodgings for them. We confess our fears on the occasion became more pungent, but we still remained silent, except our prayers and devotions. But just as the soldiers were approaching the gates, the youthhood, by a strange impulse, ran in one body and shut the gates, and put themselves in the best posture of defence they could. We blamed, but could not guide or persuade them to any less resolution that night: and so the soldiers retired, and were quartered in the neighbourhood, where, although they did not murder or destroy any, yet many threats they uttered, and outrages they committed. The next day we hoped to prevail with those that assumed the power of the city to open the gates and receive the garrison; but the news and intimations of the general design came so fast—so full from all quarters, that we then blessed God for our present escape, effected by means unforeseen, and against our wills. In the general hurry and consternation of not us only, but all the neighbouring counties, when we have but scarce time to hear the repeated informations of our danger, it is not possible for us to furnish the bearer with all requisite testimonials to evince this sad truth, nor will it consist with our safety to protract his stay till it can be done, the vessel that carries him being just ready to sail. We must refer you to his report, and copies of papers carried over by him (signed by us), for your further satisfaction in particulars; but do most humbly and heartily beseech you, as you are men of bowels and charity, to assist this gentleman how best you can, to secure us from the common danger, and that we may peaceably live, obeying his Majesty and the laws, doing injury to no man, nor wishing it to any. Your interest here is now no argument worthy to engage you, the lives of thousands of innocent men, women, and children are at stake. If you can, and will not now afford your help to the utmost, we shall never be able to use a motive to induce you, or to prevail upon you. May the Lord send deliverance to us, and preserve you all in peace and tranquillity, is the hearty prayer of, gentlemen, your most obedient servants,

GEORGE PHILIPS.*
JOHN CAMPSIE.
SAMUEL NORMAN.
ALEXANDER TOMKINS.
MATTHEW COCKEN, &c.

Londonderry, Dec. 10, 1688."

* Walker in *The True Account* asserts that Col. Philips, on the approach of Antrim's regiment to Derry, sent an Express, designed for "the sober people of the town," to Alderman Norman, "*advising him to cause the gates of the city to be shut,*" and assured them he would be with them with his friends the day following, and would stand by them, and

A Letter from Enniskillen, directed to David Cairns, Esq., or the other officers commanding in chief now in Londonderry.

GENTLEMEN,

The frequent intelligence we have from all parts of this kingdom of a general massacre of the Protestants, and two companies of foot, of Sir Thomas Newcom's regiment, viz., Captain Nugent's and Captain Shurloe's, being upon their march to garrison here, and now within ten miles, hath put us upon a resolution of refusing them entrance, our desire being only to preserve our own lives and the lives of our neighbours, this place being the most considerable pass between Connaught and Ulster, and hearing of your resolutions, we thought it convenient to impart this to you, as likewise to beg your assistance both in your advice and relief, especially in helping us with some powder, and in carrying on a correspondence with us hereafter, as we shall, with God's assistance, do with you, which is all at present from, gentlemen, your faithful friends and fellow-Christians,

THE INHABITANTS OF ENNISKILLEN.

We are not now in a condition to spare men for a guard, therefore must entreat your assistance in that.

ALLAN CATHCART.	WILLIAM SMYTH.
WM. BROWNING.	ARCHIBALD HAMILTON.
THOMAS SHORE.	MALCOLM CATHCART.
	JAMES EWART.
	ROBERT CLARKE.

The Declaration of the inhabitants of Derry.

To all Christian people to whom these presents shall come, the mayor, sheriffs, and citizens of the city of Londonderry, send greeting. Having received intimation from several credible persons, that an insurrection of the Irish was intended, and by them a general massacre of the Protestants in this kingdom, and the same to be acted and perpetrated on or about the 9th day of this instant December; and being confirmed in our fear and jealousy of so horrible a design, by many palpable insinuations, dubious expressions, monitory letters, and positive informations, all conducing and concurring to beget in us a trembling expectation of a sudden and inevitable ruin and destruction, we disposed ourselves to a patient and tame resignation to the Divine Providence, quietly hoping for some deliverance and diversion of this impending misery, or to receive from the hand of God such measure of constancy and courage as might enable us to possess our souls in patience, and

serve them to the hazard of his life and fortune." In this document, signed by Colonel Philips himself, the statement is shown to be incorrect. Philips, as he here acknowledges, was not all prepared for so bold a movement as the shutting of the gates.

submissively to wait the issue of so severe a trial. Accordingly, when on the 7th instant, part of the Earl of Antrim's forces advanced to take possession of this place, though we looked on ourselves as sheep appointed for slaughter, and on them as the executioners of vengeance upon us, yet we contrived no other means of escape than by flight, and with all precipitation to hurry away our families into other places and counties. But it pleased the Lord who watcheth over us so to order things, that when they were ready to enter the city, a great number of the younger and some of the meaner sort of the inhabitants ran hastily to the gates, and shut them, loudly denying entrance to such guests, and obstinately refusing obedience to us. At first we were amazed at the enterprise, and apprehensive of the many ill consequences which might result from so rash an undertaking; but since that, having received repeated advertisement of the general design, and particular informations which may rationally induce us to believe it; and being credibly assured that under the pretence of six companies to quarter among us, a vast swarm of Highland and Irish Papists were on the ways and roads approaching to us; that some of the Popish clergy in our neighbourhood had bought up arms, and provided an unusual furniture of iron chains for bridles (whereof sixty were bespoke in one place, and some of them seized, and now in our custody), we began to consider it an especial instance of God's mercy to us, that we were not delivered over as a prey unto them, and that it pleased Him to stir up the spirits of the people so unexpectedly, to provide for their and our common safety and preservation. Wherefore we do declare and remonstrate to the world that, as we have resolved to stand upon our guard, and defend our walls, and not to admit of any Papists whatsoever to quarter among us, so we have firmly and sincerely determined to persevere in our duty and loyalty to our sovereign Lord the King, without the least umbrage of mutiny or seditious opposition to his royal commands. And since no other motives have prompted us to this resolution, but the preservation of our lives, and to prevent the plots and machinations of the enemies of the Protestant religion, we are encouraged to hope that the Government will vouchsafe a candid and favourable interpretation of our proceedings, and that all his Majesty's Protestant subjects will interpose with their prayers to God, their solicitations to the King, and their advice and assistance to us on this so extraordinary and emergent an occasion, which may not only have an influence on the rest of the kingdom, but may have a probable aspect towards the interest of the Protestant religion, and may deserve a favourable regard from all the professors thereof within his Majesty's dominions.

GOD SAVE THE KING.

The Lord Mountjoy's Articles, with the City of Derry, 21st December, 1688.

Articles of agreement indented, made, and concluded by and between the Right Honourable Lord Viscount Mountjoy, Master of the Ordinance, and one of his Majesty's Most Honourable Privy Council, of one part, and the Mayor and Sheriffs of the City of Londonderry, in behalf of themselves and the inhabitants of the said City, and their adherents, of the other part, at Londonderry, this 21st of December, 1688.

1. That the said Lord Mountjoy shall with all possible expedition, and at furthest within fifteen days after the date hereof, procure a free and general pardon to all and every the inhabitants of the city, suburbs, and liberties of the city of Londonderry, and to all and every person and persons within the province of Ulster, that have abetted and adhered unto them, for all matters and things relating to the late commotion and revolution in the said city; and for all offences done against the law, murder excepted, and all penalties thereby incident and incurred; the same to be perfected under the great seal, and delivered to the sheriffs of the said city, or their order, within the time before limited, and published by proclamation.

2. That until the said pardon be so perfected and delivered, no more or other soldiers shall be garrisoned in the said city, or quartered in the liberties thereof, except the two companies commanded by Lieutenant-Colonel Robert Lundy, and Captain William Stewart; and that whatsoever companies shall after that time, and until the first day of March next, be quartered in the said city and liberties, shall consist of one-half Protestants at the least.

2. That until the pardon be delivered as aforesaid, the inhabitants of the said city shall not be disturbed in keeping their guards and watches, and that no stranger or unknown person shall be permitted to come within the city with fire-arms or swords, or to lodge within the gates all night, unless he be allowed by Colonel Lundy and the two sheriffs.

4. That if at any time before the first of March next, the soldiers of the Lord Mountjoy's regiment shall, by potents or other order, be required to remove, the said Lord, or his officer commanding-in-chief, shall leave the said city free to their guards and watches.

5. That if at any time any inhabitant or inhabitants of the said city and suburbs, shall desire to remove with his or their family and goods, he or they shall be freely permitted; and that the ships now in the harbour, or which shall be hereafter loaded, shall not be stopped by any embargo; and if any ship or ships which have sailed from this port since the 7th day of this instant December, shall be arrested or stopped in any port or harbour within this kingdom, on account of the late commotion, the said ship or ships shall be immediately released.

6. That until the 26th day of March next no soldiers of the Earl of Antrim's regiment shall be quartered in the city or liberties of Londonderry, to prevent all animosities and disorders that may arise between them and the people.

7. That the Lord Mountjoy shall interpose with the Commissioners of his Majesty's revenue on behalf of Warham Jemmet, Esq., and other officers of the customs, that no imputation or blame may remain on them, for the involuntary compliance with the people of Derry in the late commotion, and that his lordship may be pleased to pardon William Hemsworth, clerk of the stores, and Alexander Watson, gunner, for the like offences.

8. That the two sons of the Lord Mountjoy, now resident in Londonderry, shall remain in the said city, as pledges for the full and final performance of these articles.

9. That the said two companies commanded by Colonel Lundy and Captain Stewart shall be permitted to enter the city, and be quartered therein by the Sheriffs of the said city, whensoever the Lord Mountjoy shall appoint it, and the keys of the gates and magazines delivered to his order.

10. That in the meantime all arms taken out of his Majesty's stores shall be gathered, and after the pardon delivered as aforesaid, shall be returned to the clerk of the stores, fixed, and in good order, the inhabitants of the said city nowise doubting or mistrusting, that since their undertaking and late actions took their rise from self-preservation, and to avoid imminent danger, they shall be absolved before God and the world from all tincture of rebellion, perverseness, and wilful disobedience to the King's authority, and the established laws of the land.

The Antrim Association.

It being notoriously known, not only to the Protestant inhabitants of the northern counties, but to those throughout this whole kingdom of Ireland, that the peace and quiet of this nation is now in great and imminent danger, and that it is absolutely necessary for all Protestants to agree within their several counties upon some speedy and effectual methods for their own defence, and for securing (as much as in them lies) the Protestant religion, their lives, liberties, and properties, and the peace of this kingdom, which are so much endeavoured to be disturbed by Popish and illegal counsellors, and their abettors; and inasmuch as union and despatch are necessary for effecting the same, we, the nobility and gentry of the county of Antrim, do associate together, firmly resolving to adhere to the laws of this kingdom and the Protestant religion, and to act in subordination to the Government of England, and the promoting of a free Parliament. And we do declare, if we be forced to take up arms, as it will be contrary to our inclination, so it shall be only defensive, not in the least to invade the lives, liberties, or estates of any of our fellow-subjects, no not of the Popish persuasion, whilst they demean themselves peaceably with us. The reasons which induce us to put ourselves in some necessary posture of defence, are so obvious and urgent upon us, when we consider of the great levies daily made of Popish soldiers, and at this time especially, when the King is retired, and their arming can in nowise be serviceable to his Majesty's interest. It were inconsistent with common prudence not to suspect their designs to be such as will tend, if not to the destruction, yet to the great endangering of the lives, liberties, and properties of the Protestant subjects of this kingdom, if not prevented. And we do declare that at present we will admit none but Protestants into our association, yet we will to our power protect even Papists from violence, whilst their behaviour amongst us is peaceable and quiet; and we doubt not but all good Protestants in this kingdom will, in their several stations, join with us in the same public defence, and that God will bless these our just, innocent, and necessary undertakings, for our lives, laws, and religion. And, whereas, it will be necessary, for the more effectual and successful carrying on these mutual endeavours for the preservation of our religion and properties, and to avoid confusions and distractions, which in such cases may otherwise happen, to appoint some eminent person or persons, to whose conduct we may entirely submit ourselves in this undertaking; we do therefore, by these presents, unanimously elect and appoint the Right Honourable Hugh Earl of Mount-Alexander, and the Honourable Clotworthy Skeffington, Esq., or either of them, jointly or severally, as they shall think fit, to be our commander or commanders-in-chief of all the forces in the said county of Antrim, and do hereby oblige ourselves to serve under their or either of their command, in such manner, place, and station as they or one of them, in their discretion and judgment shall direct; and that we will, from time to time, observe and obey all such orders and methods, for the better carrying on this enterprise, and procuring of horse and foot, and such numbers of men, arms, and ammunition as our County Council of five shall think fit; and that we will with all expedition immediately be arrayed, and formed into troops and companies, and be disposed of from time to time according to their or either of their orders, they or one of them acting with the advice and consent of the said County Council of five, or the major part thereof.

Massareene.	William Shaw.
William Franklin.	Henry M'Cullough.
Arthur Upton.	John Guest.
Robert Adair.	George Buttle.
William Leslie.	George Johnston.
Charles Stewart.	Henry Clements.
Edward Harrison.	Edward Clements.
Patrick Shaw.	Richard Dobbs, jun.

John Donalson.
Wm. Cunningham.
Wm. Shaw.
James Macartney.

William Shaw.
Mich. Harrison.
James Shaw.*

The King's Letter to Ireland, by Capt. Leighton.

Having received an account from Captain Leighton of what he was entrusted to represent to us, in relation to the condition of the Protestants in Ireland, we have directed him to assure you in our name, how sensibly we are affected with the hazards you are exposed to, by the illegal power the Papists have of late usurped in that kingdom, and that we are resolved to employ the most speedy and effectual means in our power, to rescue you from the oppressions and terrors you lie under; that in the meantime we do well approve of the endeavours we understand you are using to put yourselves into a posture of defence, that you may not be surprised—wherein you may expect all the encouragements and assistance that can be given you from hence. And because we are persuaded that there are even of the Romish Communion many who are desirous to live peaceably, and do not approve of the violent and arbitrary proceedings of some who pretend to be in authority; and we thinking it just to make distinctions of persons, according to their behaviour and deserts, do hereby authorise you to promise in our name to all such who shall demean themselves hereafter peaceably and inoffensively, our protection, and exemption from those pains and forfeitures, which those only shall incur who are the maintainers and abettors of the said illegal authority, assumed and continued contrary to law, or who shall act anything to the prejudice of the Protestant interest, or the disturbance of the public peace in that kingdom. And for further particulars we refer you to the report you shall receive from Captain Leighton (who hath acquitted himself with fidelity and diligence in your concerns), of the sincerity of our intentions towards you. And so we recommend you to the protection of Almighty God.
Given at St. James's,
the 10th day of Feb., 1688.

WM. H. ORANGE.

To the Earl of Mount-Alexander, to be communicated to the Protestant nobility and gentry in the North of Ireland.
By his Highness's command.

WILLIAM JEPHSON.

* James Shaw was appointed one of the Burgesses of Belfast at the time of the Revolution. He was a Presbyterian.—See *Presbyterian Loyalty*, p. 424. The first William Shaw appearing in this list resided at Bush, near Antrim, and had shortly before been High Sheriff of the county. He also was a Presbyterian. Another William Shaw here named resided at Gemeway; and Patrick Shaw was the proprietor of the small estate of Ballygelly in Cairncastle, near Larne. The Ballygelly family, which always adhered to the Presbyterian Church, became extinct several years ago by the death of the last male heir. The estate of Ballygelly, with its picturesque old castle, was sold by Mr. Shaw in the early part of the present century to one of the Agnews of Kilwaughter for about £15,000. Charles Stewart, another of the subscribers to this document, resided at Ballintoy; Edward Harrison was one of the Burgesses of Belfast; Richard Dobbs was of Ballynure; and John Guest was a solicitor who appears to have resided in Belfast.—See *Presbyterian Loyalty*, p. 417.

The Declaration of the Protestants of Sligo, January the 4th, 1688-9.

We, the Protestants of the county of Sligo, at present assembled for our common safety, do hereby declare the occasions and motives of this our association, and what is intended by it.

1. We resolve to adhere to the laws of the land and the Protestant religion.
2. We shall, as we ought, unite ourselves accordingly with England, and hold to the lawful Government thereof, and to a free Parliament.
3. We declare that our taking up arms is only defensive, and not in the least to invade the lives, liberties, and estates of any of our fellow-subjects, whether Roman Catholics or others, while they demean themselves in peaceable manner to us.
4. Our reasons for thus doing are so urgent, that we could no longer with prudence forbear putting ourselves in some necessary posture of defence, for the Roman Catholics arming in such vast numbers throughout all the kingdom, do give us just apprehensions of ill designs in them, they pretending the King's commission for what they do, whereas we are assured that the King has commanded all Roman Catholics to lay down their arms, which we conceive should as well extend to Ireland as England; and therefore we doubt that the leaders of this Irish army do act from their own heads, upon designs of their own, which we may justly fear will be prejudicial to the lives, liberties, and properties of the Protestant subjects of this kingdom, if not prevented.

Lastly, we declare that, as we will assault none that molest not us, so we will to our powers protect all from violence, even Roman Catholics themselves, whilst they behave themselves peaceably and neighbourly amongst us (though we will admit none but Protestants into our association), until we be ascertained from the lawful authority and Government of England what further orders we are to obey; and we doubt not but that all good Protestants in this kingdom will, where they are able, join with us in the same public defence, and that God will bless this so just, innocent, and necessary undertaking, for our lives, laws, and religion.

And, whereas, it will be necessary, for the more effectual and successful carrying on of these our mutual endeavours, for the preservation of our laws, religion, and country, and the security of our lives and properties, and to avoid confusion and distractions, which in such cases might otherwise happen, to appoint some eminent person or persons to whose conduct we may entirely submit ourselves in this our undertaking:

We do therefore, by these presents, unanimously nominate, elect, and appoint the Right Honourable Robert Lord Baron of Kingston, and the Honourable Chidley Coote, Esq., or either of them, or both of them, jointly and severally, as they shall think fit, to be commander or commanders in-chief of all the forces in the said county of Sligo:

And do hereby oblige ourselves to serve under his or their command, in such manner, and in such place and station as they or one of them, in their discretion and judgment, shall direct:

And that we will procure such horse and foot, and such a number of men, arms, and ammunition as we or any of us can possibly provide, and that with all expedition, immediately to be arrayed and formed into troops and companies, and to be disposed of from time to time according to their, or either of their orders. In witness whereof we have hereunto subscribed our hands.

At Sligo, this 4th of January, 1688-9.

Colonel Lundy's Instructions.

Instructions to our trusty and well-beloved Lieutenant-Colonel Lundy, Commander-in-Chief of the town and garrison of Londonderry, or in his absence to the Commander-in-Chief there.

Having taken into our consideration the danger that at present threatens the Protestant interest in that kingdom, and how much it concerns the good of our subjects that all our garrisons there be in as good a posture of defence as may be, we, therefore, reposing trust and confidence in your good affection and courage, have thought fit hereby to direct you:

1. That you do, upon receipt hereof, buy and furnish that garrison with such necessary provisions and ammunition as may enable it to subsist and make defence for some time, in case of any attack.

2. That, for its better defence, you do break down such bridges, and cut up such dikes and sluices as, in your judgment, shall be thought necessary.

3. That you take special care in preserving the gates of the town, the guns with their carriages, as well as the fortifications of the place, in good order and repair, and that you add such works as you shall find necessary.

4. That, on prospect of any more imminent danger, you do pull down such houses, and fell and cut down such trees, as may prove in the least a prejudice to its defence.

5. That you put and set up pallisades in such places as shall be thought necessary, and that you do and provide for the defence of that place what else you shall upon due consideration judge requisite.

6. And to that end you are to receive and dispose of the thousand pounds which shall be remitted to you, to the best advantage of our service, and the safety of that garrison, and to transmit an account thereof hither.

7. That you also send hither from time to time, as opportunities offer, a true and particular account of the condition of that place to one of our principal Secretaries of State.

8. That you shall also cause the oath herewith sent you, to be taken by all the officers, both civil and military, in that town and garrison.

Given, &c., 21st Feb., 1688.

Mr. Hamilton's Instruction.

Instruction to our trusty and well-beloved Jas. Hamilton, Esquire, appointed by us to carry arms and other provisions of war to the town of Londonderry, in our kingdom of Ireland.

WILLIAM R.

You are to receive into your charge, as soon as they shall be put on ship board, the arms, ammunition, and stores of war, which we have directed to be sent to Ireland, with a commission and instructions to Lieutenant-Colonel Lundy, and the sum of one thousand pounds, which we have ordered the officers of the Customs and Excise at Chester to pay unto you, to be delivered by you to the said Lieutenant-Colonel Lundy, who is to dispose thereof for the necessary occasions of that garrison. And you are to take care that the ships on which the said arms and stores shall be laden, do not leave the English coast without the convoy of a frigate which we have appointed to accompany the said ships to the said town of Londonderry; and at your arrival with the said ships upon or near the coasts of Ireland, you are, if you see convenient, to deliver fifty barrels of powder to any officer commissioned by us within the county of Down, or thereabouts, in order to the better defence of those parts, taking the receipt of the said officer for the same. And you are, as soon as may be, to inform yourself in the best manner at what distance the enemy shall be at that time from Londonderry, and with what safety the said arms and provisions of war may be put on shore, at or near that place, and secured within the said town, for the use and defence of the Protestants against the Papists, according to your directions in that behalf; and in case the same may be done without apparent danger, you are to proceed accordingly in the execution thereof, and to deliver the said commission and instructions, money, arms, and stores to the said Lieutenant-Colonel Lundy, or to the commander-in-chief of the said town, taking his receipt for the same; provided, nevertheless, that before you deliver the said commission, instructions, money, arms, and stores of war to the said Lieutenant-Colonel Lundy, or the commander-in-chief of the said town, you first cause him to take the oaths herewith sent, on board the ship wherein you shall arrive there, in the presence of the mayor, or chief civil magistrate of Londonderry. But if he shall refuse the said oaths, or any one of them, or that you shall find the approach to the said town difficult, and the landing or delivery of the said arms and stores insecure, you are then not to land the said stores, or part with the said commission, instructions, and money; but to cause them to be brought back on board the said ship, under the same convoy, to some port in England; whereupon notice thereof being given to us, we shall signify our further orders thereupon, and for so doing, &c.

Given, &c., Whitehall,
the 22nd of February, 1688.
By his Majesty's command,
SHREWSBURY.

The King's Letter to Colonel Lundy by Mr. Cairns.

Whitehall, 8th March, 1688.

SIR,

I am commanded by the King to acquaint you that his Majesty's greatest concern hath been for Ireland, and particularly for the province of Ulster, which he looks upon as most capable to defend itself against the common enemy. And that they might be the better enabled to do it, there are two regiments already at the sea side ready to embark, in order to their transportation into the province, with which will be sent a good quantity of arms and ammunition, and they will be speedily followed by so considerable a body, as (by the blessing of God) may be able to rescue the whole kingdom, and resettle the Protestant interest there. His Majesty does very much rely upon your fidelity and resolution, not only that you should acquit yourself according to the character he has received of you, but that you should encourage and influence others in this difficult conjuncture to discharge their duty to their country, their religion, and their property, all which call upon them for a more than ordinary vigour, to keep out that deluge of Popery and slavery which so nearly threatens them.

And you may assure them, that besides his Majesty's care for their preservation, who hath a due tenderness and regard for them (as well in consideration that they are his subjects, as that they are now exposed for the sake of that religion which he himself professes), the whole bent of this nation inclines them to employ their utmost endeavours for their deliverance; and it was but this very morning that his Majesty hath most effectually recommended the case of Ireland to the two Houses of Parliament, and I do not doubt but they will thereupon immediately come to such resolutions as will show to all the world that they espouse their interest as their own.

As to your own particular, you will always find the King graciously disposed to own and reward the services you shall do him in such a time of trial.

And for my part, wherever I can contribute either to the general service of that kingdom, or to your own particular satisfaction, I shall never be wanting in, Sir, your very humble servant,

SHREWSBURY.

Subscribed for Colonel Lundy, Governor of Londonderry.

Instructions to Mr. David Cairns.

You are, with what convenient speed you can, forthwith to repair to Londonderry, in the kingdom of Ireland.

At your arrival there you are to acquaint the Governor and magistrates of the said city, of his Majesty's great care and concern for their security, which he hath shown not only in sending thither at this time men, arms, and ammunition, but in the further great preparations he is making, as well for the particular defence of that place, as for the safety and protection of that whole kingdom.

You are particularly to inform yourself of the present condition of Londonderry, both as to men, arms, and ammunition, and whether the country thereabout can be able to furnish provisions for a greater force intended to be sent thither, without carrying provisions from England; an exact account whereof you are to bring yourself with the best speed you can, or to send it with the first conveniency to me, or to the committee of council appointed for Irish affairs.

You are to get the best informations you can what force the enemy has, as well horse as foot; in what condition the troops are, and how armed, and what care is taken for their subsistence, whether by providing magazines and stores, or by trusting to the provisions they shall find where they march.

You are to inquire what new levies have been made, of horse, foot, or dragoons, by those colonels who had their commissions sent them some time since by Captain Layton, of what numbers they are, and how disposed of.

Given at the Court of Whitehall,
this 11th day of March, 1688-9.

SHREWSBURY.

Mr. Cairns's Certificate.

Charles Earl of Shrewbury, Waterford and Wexford, &c., one of the Lords of his Majesty's most honourable Privy Council, and principal Secretary of State.

Mr. David Cairns, the bearer hereof, being appointed by the committee for Irish affairs forthwith to repair to Londonderry, these are to certify whom it may concern, that the said Mr. Cairns hath, for these two months last past, attended constantly his Majesty and the council in behalf of the said city, and that he hath behaved himself with prudence, diligence and faithfulness.

Given at the Court at Whitehall, this 11th day of March, 1688-9.

SHREWSBURY.

Articles at a Council of War, at Derry, April 10, 1689.

At a Council of War at Londonderry, present—

Colonel Robert Lundy.   Lord Blayney.
Colonel J. Hamilton.   Sir Nicholas Atchison.
Col. Hugh Montgomery.   Col. Francis Hamilton.
Lieut.-Col. Whitney.   Lieut.-Col. Ponsonby.
Lieut.-Col. White.   Major Crofton.
Lieut.-Col. Johnston.   Major Hill.
Lieut.-Col. Shaw.   Major Phillips.
Major Barry.   Captain Hugh Magill.
Major Tubman.

Resolved.—1. That a mutual engagement be made between all the officers of this garrison and the forces adjoining, and to be signed by every man. That none shall desert or forsake the service, or depart the kingdom, without leave of a council of war. If any do, they will be looked upon as cowards, and disaffected to the service.

2. That a thousand men shall be chosen to be part of this garrison, and joined with the soldiers already herein, to defend the city; the officers of which thousand, and the garrison officers, are to enter into the engagement aforesaid.

3. That all officers and soldiers of any of our forces in the neighbourhood, not of this garrison, shall forthwith repair to their respective quarters and commands.

4. That all colonels and commanders of every regiment, or independent troop or company, be now armed and fitted, that so we may take up resolutions for field service accordingly, the lists to be sent hither by Saturday next.

5. That the several officers in their respective quarters shall take care to send provisions to the magazines of this garrison for supply thereof, and take care that they leave with the owner thereof some of their victuals and provisions for their own supports, and to send in spades, shovels, and pick-axes.

6. That the thousand men to be taken into this garrison shall have the old houses about the walls and ditches without the gates divided among them, to be levelled with all possible speed.

7. That the several battalions and companies in the city shall have their several stations and posts assigned them, to which they shall repair upon any sudden alarm.

8. That all persons of this garrison, upon beating of the retreat every night, shall repair to their several quarters and lodgings.

9. That a pair of gallows shall be erected in one of the bastions upon the south-west of ▓ city, whereupon all mutinous or treach▓ persons of this garrison shall be executed, shall be condemned thereunto by a court-martial.

10. That the articles of war shall be read at the head of every battalion, troop, or company, and that all soldiers shall be punished for their transgressing them, according to the said articles.

11. That every soldier of the garrison, and noncommissioned officers shall be weekly allowed out of the magazines eight quarts of meal, four pound of fish,* and three pounds of flesh, for his weekly subsistence.

12. That every soldier and noncommissioned officer shall be allowed a quart of small beer per diem, as soon as the same can be provided, until some money shall come to allow them pay.

Agreed upon at the said Council of War, and ordered to be copied.

WILLIAM R.

Orders and Instructions to our trusty and well-beloved John Cunningham, Esquire, Colonel of our regiment of foot, and upon his death or absence, to Colonel Solomon Richards, or the officer-in-chief with the regiments whereof they are colonels.

You are without delay to repair to the quarters of the regiment under your command, and take care that it be in a readiness to march to Liverpool at such time as you shall appoint.

Whereupon you are to go to Liverpool, and to enquire what ships there are in that port appointed to carry over the two regiments, whereof you and Solomon Richards are Colonels, to the town of Londonderry, and whether the frigate ordered for their convoy be arrived there. And as soon as the said ships and frigate shall be in readiness to sail, and fitted with all provisions necessary for the sustenance of the said regiments, in their passage to the said town, and for their return from thence if there be occasion, you are to cause Colonel Richards' regiment to go on board, and at the same time to order the regiment whereof you are colonel to march to Liverpool, and to embark with all speed.

And whereas we have ordered a thousand arms to be carried to Liverpool, you are to cause such a number of the said arms as shall be wanting in the said regiments to be delivered unto them, and the residue of the said arms and stores, now there, to be put on ship-

---

* It is stated, in a pamphlet published at this time, that about the commencement of the siege, the Protestants shut up in Derry obtained possession of about sixty tons of salmon belonging to Lord Massareene.—See *A True and Impartial Account of the most material passages in Ireland*, p. 22. London. 1689.

board, and carried to Londonderry, to be there employed for our service, as the government of the said town and you shall think fit.

And we have also directed the sum of two thousand pounds sterling to be paid unto you at Chester, by Matthew Anderton, Esq., collector of our customs there : you are hereby authorized and required to receive the same, and to dispose of the said sum towards the necessary subsistence of the said regiments, and for the defence of the said place, in preparing and providing what shall be defective therein, and to such other uses as you, with the Governor of the said city, with whom you are to entertain a good correspondence and friendship, shall find necessary for our service, of all which expenses you are to give us an account the first opportunity.

When the particulars necessary for the voyage shall be fully complied with, you are then, wind and weather permitting, with the regiments under your command, to make the best of your way to Londonderry; and being arrived there, or near that place, you are to make inquiry whether the said city be yet in the hands of the Protestants, and whether you may with safety put our said regiments into the same; and in that case you are immediately to acquaint Lieutenant-Colonel Robert Lundy, our Governor thereof, or the commander-in-chief for the time being, with our care in sending those regiments and stores for the further relief of our Protestant subjects in those parts; and delivering him our letter and orders to him directed, you are to land the said regiments and stores, and to take care that they be well quartered and disposed of in the said city, following such directions as you shall receive during your stay there, from our said Governor Lieut.-Colonel Robert Lundy, in all things relating to our service.

You are to assure the Governor and inhabitants of Londonderry of further and greater succours of men, arms, money, and provisions of war coming speedily from England for their relief, and the security of those parts: and in the meantime you are to make the best defence you can against all persons that shall attempt to besiege the said city, or to annoy our Protestant subjects within the same.

You are to give us an account soon after your arrival (and so from time to time) of the condition of the place, the fortifications, number, quality, and affection of the people, soldiers, and others therein, or in the country thereabouts; and what quantity of provisions of all sorts, for horse, foot, and dragoons, shall or may be bought up or secured in those parts for our service, without the necessity of bringing any from England, upon sending more forces thither.

You are to inform us whether Captain James Hamilton be arrived at Londonderry, and how he has disposed of the money and stores committed to his charge: and in general you are to return to us an account of everything, which you in your discretion shall think requisite for our service.

In case you shall find it unsafe to land the regiments at or near Londonderry, so as to put them into the town, which you are to endeavour by all reasonable and prudent means; you are not to expose them to extraordinary hazard in so doing, but to take care that they be carried in the same ships, and under the same convoy, with the arms, stores, money, and provisions above-mentioned to Carrickfergus, and to endeavour the landing of them there, or the same may be done with safety, or otherwise to Strangford, at both or either of which places you are to use the same caution, and to follow as near as may be the like directions as are now given you in relation to Londonderry; but in case you do not find it for our service to land the said regiments at any of the said places, you are then to take care that they be brought back to the port of Liverpool, giving us speedy notice for our further orders.

Given at our Court at Whitehall, this 12th day of March, 1688-9.

By his Majesty's command,

SHREWSBURY.

In the first year of our reign.

WILLIAM R.

Additional Instructions for our trusty and well-beloved Colonel John Cunningham, or the officer-in-chief with our two regiments of foot, whereof he and Colonel Richards are Colonels.

Whereas we have ordered £2000 sterling to be paid unto you by several bills of exchange, over and above the £2000 you shall receive from our collector in the port of Chester; you are accordingly to receive the same; and upon your arrival at our city of Londonderry, to pay £500 thereof to our trusty and well-beloved Robert Lundy, Esquire, Governor thereof, as of our royal bounty, in part of the reward we intend him for his faithful services, and the residue of the said £2000, you are to employ towards the defraying the contingent charges which our said Governor, yourself, and Colonel Richards, shall find requisite for the security of the garrison, or of such other place where our said regiments shall arrive, or be put on shore; provided always that you do not in any manner put off or delay the departure of our said two regiments from Liverpool to Londonderry, in case the said sum be not immediately paid unto you by the respective persons from whom it is to be received.

Given at our Court at Whitehall, the 14th of March, 1688-9, in the first year of our reign.

By his Majesty's command,

SHREWSBURY.

Colonel Tiffin's and Captain Lyndon's Certificate to Colonel Cunningham.

This is to certify whom it may concern that we, Zechariah Tiffin, Colonel of one of their

Majesties' regiments of foot, and John Lyndon, Captain in one Colonel Stuart's regiment, together with Captain Wolfranc Cornwall, commander of the "Swallow" frigate, were sent by Colonel Cunningham on the 15th day of April last, from Culmore Castle to Londonderry, with a letter he then wrote to Colonel Lundy, to desire his orders and directions, for the best and securest way of putting into the town the two regiments then on board the fleet at anchor near the Castle, where the tide had failed so as they could not sail up that night. We accordingly went to Londonderry, where Colonel Lundy, having read the letter, told us affairs were in great confusion, and in a much worse posture than could be imagined; therefore desired Colonel Cunningham would leave the fleet, with the soldiers on board, still at anchor, and come next morning to town with Colonel Richards, and what other officers they thought fit, where he intended to call a council of war, and give further account of the condition of the garrison. With these orders we returned that night to Colonel Cunningham, who, in pursuance thereto, with Colonel Richards, and several of their officers went up next morning to the town. All which we certify under our hands, the 30th day of September, 1680.

ZECHARIAH TIFFIN.
JOHN LYNDON.

From the English Camp,
near Dundalk, in Ireland.

I do also testify this certificate to be true. Dated the 26th of October, 1689.

WOLFRANC CORNWALL.

Instructions for our trusty and well-beloved Robt. Lundy, Esquire, Governor of our City and Garrison of Londonderry, in our Kingdom of Ireland.

Whereas we have thought fit to send two of our regiments of foot, under the command of Colonel Cunningham, and Colonel Solomon Richards, for the relief of our city of Londonderry; we do hereby authorise and empower you to admit the said regiments into our said city, and to give such orders concerning their quarters, duty, and service, during their stay in those parts, as you shall think fit for the security of the said city and country thereabouts.

And whereas we are sending to the said city of Londonderry, further succours of money, men, arms, and provisions of war; we do expect from your courage, prudence, and conduct, that in the meantime you make the best defence you can against all persons that shall attempt to besiege the said city, or to annoy our Protestant subjects, within the same, or within the neighbouring parts, and that you hinder the enemy from possessing themselves of any passes near or leading to the said city; giving all aid and assistance you may with safety to such as shall desire it, and receiving into the said town such Protestant officers and men able and fit to bear arms as you may confide in, whom you are to form into companies, and to cause to be well exercised and disciplined, taking care withal that you do not take in more unuseful people, women, and children into the said city than there shall be a provision sufficient to maintain, besides the garrison. You are to give us an account as soon as may be, and so from time to time, of the condition of our city of Londonderry, the fortifications, number, quality, and affections of the people, soldiers, and others therein, or in the country thereabouts; and what quantity of provisions, of all sorts, for horse, foot, and dragoons, shall or may be bought up or secured in those parts for our service, without the necessity of bringing the same from England, upon sending of more forces thither.

Lastly, we do recommend unto you, that you entertain good correspondence and friendship with the officers of the said regiments, and more especially with the respective colonels of the same; not doubting but by your joint counsels, and by your known courage, as well as your affection to the Protestant religion, which we shall not fail to reward with our royal favour and bounty, the said city will continue under our obedience, until, upon the arrival of an army, which we are sending from England, all things shall be in such a posture as that we may there, with the blessing of God, restore in a short time our kingdom of Ireland to its former peace and tranquillity.

Given at our Court at Whitehall, the 12th day of March, 1688-9, in the first year of our reign.

By his Majesty's command.

Proposals of Articles to be made to the Right Honourable Lieutenant-General Hamilton, by the Governors, Commanders, Officers, Soldiers, and Citizens of the City and Garrison of Londonderry, the 11th of July, 1689.

Imprimis, that all persons, as well officers and soldiers, clergymen and laymen, as others, that now are in the said city, or have been in the same since the 7th of December last, or that have borne arms against his Majesty, King James the Second, in the provinces of Ulster or Connaught, or either of them, or that have been aiding, abetting, counselling, advising, or in any ways assisting to them, or any of them, or any way deemed of that party, shall be pardoned and forgiven until the 26th day of July instant, of and from all treasons, rebellions, robberies, felonies, and other offences whatsoever, by them or any of them, committed against his said Majesty, or any person or persons whatsoever: and that such of the said persons now alive, or which shall be alive the said 26th day of July, and the heirs, executors, administrators, or assigns of such of them that are dead, or shall before that time be killed or die, shall be immediately restored to all their personal and real estates, as if they or any of them had never taken up arms, or committed any offence against his said Majesty, or any other person or persons whatsoever: and that they and every one of them shall, and may have, hold, and enjoy their said estates, with other their rights, liberties, and privileges, notwithstanding any act or acts by them committed or done, or to be committed or done, against his said Majesty, or any other person or persons whatsoever, until the 26th of July instant: and that they, their heirs, executors, administrators, or assigns, shall have their estates, personal and real, put in their actual possession immediately after the said 26th of July instant: and that from the date hereof there shall no waste or harm be committed, suffered, or done on any of their lands, inheritances, possessions, woods, farms, houses, mills, barns, kilns, stables, or other houses, or on any of their corns, and other goods and chattels.

2. That all ecclesiastical persons of the Protestant religion within the said provinces shall immediately have the possession of their several churches, chapels, tithes, and other ecclesiastical dues, and enjoy the same as they did before the 7th day of December last: and that all other Protestants, as well ministers as others, shall, from the said 26th of July instant, have the full and free benefit and exercise of their religion, as they had before the said 7th of December.

3. That all persons whatsoever now in Londonderry shall have free liberty to depart this kingdom for England or Scotland: and those that are willing to remain in this kingdom shall have safe conducts to Dublin, or any other part in Ireland, with their goods and chattels: and those that have a mind to transport themselves by the shipping under the power of the said King, or by other English or Scottish ships, shall have passports from time to time allowed them, and liberty of boats from England or Scotland to transport them.

4. That all persons to be pardoned that please shall transport and carry with them their goods and chattels, unless they have a mind to sell them here, and that then they may have liberty to dispose of them to the best advantage; and likewise those that depart the kingdom shall be put in possession of their goods and chattels, lands and tenements, by their attorneys which they formerly enjoyed, and reprisals of goods and chattels, if not to be found in specie.

5. That such persons, men, women, and children, as are not able to travel to their respective habitations, shall have a sufficient competency of provisions to maintain them, until they be able to depart, and get to their several dwellings; and that all officers and soldiers that are sick or wounded, now in the garrison of Londonderry, or shall be there the 26th of July instant, shall have the same allowance and provision, and as great care taken for their recovery as those of the said King's army; and that from time to time they shall be sent into England, or Scotland, or to any part in Ireland as they shall think fit, and conveniency shall offer, with provisions and safe passes.

6. That all persons here designed to be pardoned, shall have reprisals of their goods and chattels immediately after the said 26th of July instant, given them by the said Lieutenant-General; and until they shall be so reprised, they shall have sufficient provisions of meat, drink, and bedding allowed and given them.

7. That no person or persons hereby designed to be pardoned, shall be forced to take any oath to his Majesty, but those that voluntarily enter into his service in the army, or shall take on him some office or place of trust, nor shall they be compelled to enter into his Majesty's service.

8. That if any prince or state shall land an army in this kingdom against the said king, the persons hereby designed to be pardoned, and which shall remain in the same, shall not be molested anyways in body, goods, or estate, they not taking up arms against his Majesty.

9. That no person or persons hereby designed to be pardoned, shall hereafter be sued, arrested, impleaded, or imprisoned, at the suit of the King, for any debt due to his Majesty before the date hereof. And that none of the persons aforesaid hereafter shall be sued, arrested, impleaded, or imprisoned, for any wounding, maiming, trespassing, taking of goods or chattels, or for any other cause whatsoever accrued, or that shall accrue, before the said 26th of July, by any party or person whatsoever, other than for debt, and not for debt for twelve months from the date hereof; and that his Majesty shall not call for, or receive any of his crown rents, quit rents, hearth-money, excise, or license of wine, ale, beer, strong waters due, or which shall fall due unto him by any of the persons aforesaid, before the said 26th of July.

10. That no interest of money shall be allowed or paid, from the first of May, 1688, until the 1st of November, 1690, and then but a moderate interest, and not according to the rate of ten pound, per cent., per annum.

11. That the officers and gentlemen hereby designed to be pardoned shall all remain in this kingdom, and each one of them with a servant, shall have liberty to keep and wear pistols and swords, and keep their fuzees, without molestation, and the citizens and townsmen to have the like liberty; and that the rest of the people may keep their swords, and wear them.*

12. That the said half-pike men, and rabble of the mere Irish in the said provinces, be disarmed, and care taken that they kill not, rob, or spoil the Protestants in the said provinces;

---

* At this time ordinary citizens were in the habit of wearing offensive weapons. Hence Mackenzie speaks of the apprentice boys "drawing their swords" when they ran to shut the gates.

and that they be sent to their habitations, and not suffered to cotter and wander in the country, or use reproachful language to the Protestants.

13. That all troops and companies now in the city of Londonderry, which please, shall have liberty to depart either by land or water, to Culmore, or any part near the same, for conveniency of shipping; and that with their arms, colours flying, drums beating, lighted matches, and a suitable quantity of ammunition, and there to ship or embark; and shall before their departure, deliver up to the said Lieutenant-General, or to such whom he shall appoint, for his Majesty's use, the possession of the said city, with all stores, ammunition, artillery, and other habiliments of war, other than the arms hereinbefore excepted.

14. That all and every person and persons whatsoever, that have taken the possession of the lands, houses, farms, of the persons hereby designed to be pardoned, shall immediately quit the possession of the same, and restore them to the owners, or their agents and assigns, with their goods and chattels now in their possession, and that the said owners, their agents and assigns, may cut and carry home their corn and hay.

15. That all the said articles and conditions, or such of them as shall be thought needful by those that are designed to be pardoned, shall, within

be confirmed by Act of Parliament, to be passed in this kingdom, or by the King, under the great Seal of Ireland.

Provided always that no person or persons now in arms against the King, in or about Enniskillen, Ballyshannon, Donegall, or Killybeggs, that will accept of these or the like articles, before the said 20th day of July, shall have the benefit of them, they or their chief commanders having eight days notice of these articles before the said 20th of July, by having delivered to them copies of them, which are to be sent them by the said Lieutenant-General, by some of his party, and some of this garrison.

16. That a convenient number of persons be appointed as commissioners in this city, and in each county of the said provinces, before the 26th of July, by the said Lieutenant-General, and the Governors, commanders, officers, and soldiers of this garrison, with sufficient authority to see these articles made good and performed.

17. The hostages be given by the said Lieut.- General to the garrison of Derry, to be kept there, or on board the English ships now in the river Foyle, viz.,

and for the garrison of Derry

to be given as hostages, and kept in their camp, or at Strabane, Lifford, or Raphoe.

18. That during the time of treaty, and until the said 26th day of July (if, in the meantime, no army shall come to relieve the city), there shall be a cessation of arms between the besiegers and the besieged, and that no acts of hostility shall be committed by either side, provided that none of either party (but such as shall have licenses) shall come within the lines of the other.

19. That as well the persons that are in this garrison, or shall be there the 26th of July, as shall embark or ship for England or Scotland, as those that go to the country, shall, at their departure hence, have horses and boats allowed them, for carrying the officers, sick men, women, and children home to their several habitations, or places whither they have a mind to resort.

Provided always that these articles shall not be binding on either party in case the said city shall be relieved by the English, or some other army, before the said 26th day of July; and if it shall be so relieved, that then the said hostages delivered on both sides shall be delivered to each other in safety.

The Commission.

To all Christian people to whom these presents shall come, know ye, that we, the governors, commanders, officers, soldiers, and citizens, now in the city and garrison of Londonderry, have nominated, constituted, appointed, and authorised, and by these presents do nominate, constitute, appoint, and authorise Colonel Hugh Hamill, Colonel Thomas Lance, Captain Robert White, Captain Wm. Dobbin, Matthew Cockins, Esq., and Mr. John Mackenzie, as commissioners for us, and in our name to repair to, and treat with the Right Honourable Lieutenant-General Richard Hamilton, now encamped against Londonderry, with an army of his Majesty's, King James the Second, besieging the said city or garrison, or to somewhere near the said camp and city, or to Colonel Dominick Sheldon, Colonel Gordon O'Neal, Sir Neal O'Neal, Sir Edward Vaudry, Lieutenant-Colonel Skelton, and Captain Francis Marow, commissioners nominated, constituted, appointed, and authorised by the said Lieut.-General Hamilton, and there to treat with him or them, concerning the rendering up of the said city and garrison to the said Lieutenant-General, for his Majesty's use, with all the stores, ammunition, artillery, arms, implements, and habiliments of war, according to the annexed instructions and articles, and such other instructions and articles as you shall from time to time have from us; and on such other articles, matters, and things as shall be proposed to you, our said commissioners, by the said Lieutenant-General, or by his said commissioners; and on such treaty to conclude on such articles, matters, and things, for the delivering up of the said city, to the said Lieutenant-General, or whom he shall appoint, with the said stores, ammunition, artillery, arms, implements and habiliments of war, for his majesty's use; and for the giving and receiving of hostages, for the performance of what shall be stipulated and agreed upon; and the same to reduce into writing, and sign and seal, and to receive the same signed and sealed by the said Lieutenant-General or the said Commissioners for us and in our behalf. And what articles, matters, and things you shall agree upon, and reduce into writing, and sign and seal for us and on our behalf, we by these presents bind and oblige ourselves to observe, keep, and perform entirely; in witness whereof, we hereunto put our hands and seals, at Londonderry, the 12th day of July, 1689.

Signed and delivered in the presence of

Francis Hamilton.
Robert Cochrane.

James Young,	*George Walker.
Stephen Herd.	John Mitchelburn.
David Ross.	Richard Crofton.
Robert Wallace.	Adam Murray.
Christophilus Jenny.	Henry Monro.
Arthur Noble.	Stephen Miller.
Adam Downey.	Alexander Stewart.
Arch. Hamilton.	John Crooks.
Henry Arkwright.	William Campbell.
Thomas Ash.	William Draper.
Theophilus Morrison.	James Graham.
William Ragston.	John Cochrane.
William Hamilton.	Francis Obrey.
Warren Godfrey.	John Crofton.
George Holmes.	John Thompson.
John Henderson.	William Mure.
Hercules Burleigh.	Richard Alpin.

* I should not take notice of so trivial a thing as Mr. Walker's signing first, if it had not been improved into an argument of his being Governor of the garrison as well as the stores; but as the forementioned debates about this very commission, as well as the whole story of the siege, evidently show the contrary, so to obviate this objection against the truth of those passages, I am obliged to add that Mr. Walker's signing first in some papers during the siege was partly owing to the modesty and complaisance of Governor Baker, and afterwards Governor Mitchelburn, but much more to the forward temper of Colonel Walker, who, when Governor Baker or Mitchelburn signed first, seldom failed to crowd in his name before them, of which I could produce several notorious instances, but shall only mention a late one: Several certificates were signed by Mitchelburn in November last, to some officers of Baker's regiment, which, when brought here, he not only thrust in his name above him, but blotted out of each of these certificates these words—Colonel Baker [Governor of the said city.]—Thus:

"These are to certify all whom it may concern that the bearer hereof Robert Louther, served during the late siege of Londonderry, in the station or post of a Lieutenant, in Captain Nicholas Holme's company, under the command and regiment of Colonel Henry Baker; [late Governor of the foresaid city] : and also after under the command of Colonel St. John, and continued in the said regiment, till the 9th day of October; during which siege he behaved himself with good conduct and courage, both in the sallies that were made against the enemy, and the preservation of the said city. Given under my hand,* at Londonderry, the 27th day of November, 1689.

"George Walker.
"J. MITCHELBURN."

And how far he was from being esteemed as Governor of the garrison, even after Governor Baker's death, may appear by the following testimony of one of Major-General Kirke's officers, (who commanded the soldiers in the "Phœnix," when Derry was relieved, and showed great resolution in that eminent piece of service;) and I insert it the rather because it cannot be reasonably suspected of the least partiality.

"As I was commanded in person with my detachments by Colonel Mitchelburn, Governor of Derry, so during my stay there, I observed in every particular, and upon all occasions, he not only was, but acted as, sole Governor, and was the only person that application was made to as such.

"FIENNES TWISTLETON."

The same gentleman confirms the account given before, concerning the boom: and even when the ships came up to our relief, they saw boats working at it to repair it, for some days before they made the attempt.

An account of Officers killed and taken by the besieged in Derry, during the Siege.

April 18—
Captain Troy killed, as was confidently reported.
Killed at Pennyburn-Mill, April 21—
General Maumont.
Major Taaffe.
Major Waggon.
Major-General Pusignan.
Quartermaster Cassore.
Captain Fitzgerald.
Killed at the Wind-Mill, May 6—
Brigadier-General Ramsey.
Captain Barnwell.
Captain Fox.
Captain Fleming.
Lieutenant Kelly.

* This certificate shows clearly that Mitchelburn ignored the governorship of Walker, and we surely could not desire a more competent witness. It also illustrates the paltry officiousness of the reverend gentleman. He does not seem to have observed that the paper was intended only for one signature. In the grant of a pension of £300 per annum to Baker's widow, dated November 2nd, 1689, *no mention is made of the fact that her husband was Governor of Derry.* The document was obviously drawn up under the direction of Walker, as he was the sole trustee, and the omission of so important a circumstance is thus easily explained.—See *Harris's History of the Life and Reign of William III., Appendix,* p. 28.

Lieutenant Welsh.
Ensign Barnwell.
Ensign Kadel.
Prisoners taken—
  Lord Netterville.
  Sir Gerard Aylmer.
  Lieutenant-Colonel Talbot.
  Lieutenant Newcomen.
Killed at the Wind-Mill, June 4—
  Lieutenant-Colonel Farrel.
  Two French Captains.
  Captain Graham.
  Lieutenant Burke.
  Quartermaster Kelly.
  Adjutant Fahoy.
  Ensign Norris.
  Ensign Arthur.
Prisoners taken at the same time—
  Captain Butler, son to my Lord Mountgarret.
  Captain M'Donnel.
  Captain M'Donaghy.
  Captain Watson.
  A French Lieutenant.
  Lieutenant Eustace.
  Serjeant Peggot.
Killed at the Butcher's Gate, June 28—
  A French Lieutenant-Colonel.
  Captain O'Bryan.
  A French Captain.
  An English Captain.
  An English Lieutenant.
  Captain Macarthy.
Taken Prisoners—
  One Corporal M'Guire.
  And one Private Soldier.
Officers killed in several places about the town—
  Lieutenant Fitzpatrick, in the orchard on the other side the water.
  Lieutenant-General O'Neal.
  Ensign Connelly, killed in the boat.
  Two friars, killed in their habits.
  Ensign Ambrose, on the mountains.
  Lieutenant Talbot had his arm shot off at Culmore, from the ships.
Drowned coming over to Clady—
  Major Nangle, and one Ensign, as was reported.

An Account of all the Enemy's Officers killed during the Siege.

Generals	1	Ensigns	1
Brig.-Generals	1	Serjeants	1
Major-Generals	1	Corporals	5
Lieut.-Colonels	3	Cornets	1
Majors	5	Quartermasters	2
Captains	16	Adjutants	1
Lieutenants	9		

In all 49, and 2 Friars.

An Account of the Bombs.

	Big.	Small.
April 24.	—	3
25.	—	3
27.	—	11
From the 27th till the 6th of May, at several times.	—	6
June 2.	3	1
3.	28	—
4.	37	—
5.	22	—
6.	30	—
7.	6	—
8.	36	—
11.	—	28
13.	26	—
21.	—	11
24.	6	—
27.	13	—
28.	22	—
29.	10	—
July 2.	—	22
3.	—	28
4.	14	—
5.	3	6
6.	5	10
7.	—	18
8 & 10.	—	24
11.	—	4
14.	—	18
15 & 16.	—	40
17 & 18.	—	26
19.	—	22
21.	—	28
	261	326

Total, 587, till the 22nd of July.

Memorandum.—That one of the great bombs being brought to the scale, did weigh two hundred and seventy-two pounds, after seventeen pounds of powder was emptied out of it; and that one of the smallest being emptied did weigh thirty-four pounds.

July 22—Forty-two cannon balls thrown into the city, about twenty pounds weight a-piece, before nine of the clock in the morning; more at six the same evening.

July 23—Twenty more before noon.

An Account of the Subsistence delivered out of the Stores to the Soldiers, by the Store-keepers.

April 20.—To each company a barrel of beef and a boll of meal.

27.—To each man four pounds of beef, four quarts of meal, and three pounds of salmon.

May 4.—To each company a barrel of beef, one hundred and twenty pounds of meal, and half a hundred weight of butter.

21.—Six pounds of meal for each private man.

18.—Two pounds of wheat to each man.

24.—Half a barrel of beef to each company, one hundred and twenty pounds of meal, half a barrel of barley.

June 1.—To each regiment five barrels of Wheat, and five barrels of shilling, to be divided proportionably, according to the number of companies in each regiment.

8.—One pound and a-half of meal to each

man, and half a barrel of barley to each company.
15. Half a barrel of barley to each company, and a pound of meal to each man.
19.—One pound of meal, and one pound and a-half of wheat to each man.
21.—One pound and a-half of wheat to each man.
25.—One pound of tallow to each man, one pound of meal, and half a pound of beef, the army consisting of 6,185 men.
July 4.—To each man one pound of meal, one pound of French butter, and two pounds of ginger, the army being 5,709 men.
8.—To each man one pound of meal, one pound of French butter, two pounds of anniseeds to each company, and one quarter of a pound of tobacco, the army being reduced by death to 5,529 men.
13.—To each man half a pound of meal, half a pound of shilling, half a pound of beef, the army consisting of 5,334.
17.—To each man half a pound of meal, half a pound of shilling, half a pound of tallow, three pounds of salt hides, the army being 5,114.
22.—To each man half a pound of starch, a quarter of a pound of tallow, one pound of anniseeds to a company, the army being 4,973.
26.—To each man half a pound of tallow, half a pound of shilling, three-quarters of a pound of dry hides, the army being 4,892 men.
27.—To each man half a pound of meal, one pound and a-half of beef, with two pecks of bay salt to each company, the army being 4,456 men.
30.—To each man three pound of meal, two pound of Beef, one pint of peas, the army being 4,508 men.

There was subsistence delivered out to the officers beside, though the allowance was but very small.

The Names of the Clergy that stayed in Londonderry in the time of the Siege.

CONFORMISTS.

Mr. George Walker, of Donoughmore, near Dungannon.
Mr. Christopher Finny, of Mullabroak.
Mr. Moses Davis, of Donaghendrie.
Mr. John Knox, of Glasslough.
Mr. Bartholemew Black, of Aghalow.
Mr. Thomas Sempell, of Donoughmore, near Cladyford.
Mr. Robert Morgan, of Cappy.
Mr. John Campbell, of Sego.
Mr. Andrew Robertson, of Derryloran.
Mr. Michael M'Clenahan, of Derry.
Mr. Christy, of Monaghan.
Mr. Seth Whittle, of Bellaghy. Dead.
Mr. Wm. Cunningham, of Killeshandra. Dead.
Mr. Richard Crowther, of Comber. Dead.
Mr. James Watmough, of Arigal. Dead.
Mr. John Rowan, Balteagh. Dead.
Mr. —— Elingsworth, near Newry. Dead.

NON-CONFORMISTS.

Mr. Thomas Boyd, of Aghadoey.
Mr. William Crooks, of Ballykelly.
Mr. John Rowat, of Lifford.
Mr. John Mackenzie, of Derryloran.*
Mr. John Hamilton, of Donagheady. Dead.
Mr. Robert Wilson, of Strabane. Dead.
Mr. David Brown, of Urney. Dead.
Mr. William Gilchrist, of Kilrea. Dead.†

* *i.e.*, Cookstown. The town was so called from Allan Cooke, who founded it in the seventeenth century. The parish is still called Derryloran.
† In a preceding note (p. 4)) a passage is quoted from the *Londeriad*, indicating that a ruling elder, named Mills, was distinguished during the siege. This elder resided at Ballougry, near Derry, and was probably a member of the Derry Session. Mr. Robert Mills, his great-great-grandson, now resides on the farm held by his pious ancestor. A part of it, still known as the *Camp field*, is said to have derived its designation from the circumstance that it was occupied during the siege by a section of the Irish army. The Rev. William Scott, of Newtoncunningham, is maternally descended from the same Presbyterian patriarch.

SUPPLEMENT.

OSBORNE'S VINDICATION.

IN Walker's *True Account of the Siege of Londonderry* the following passage occurs :—
"There were eighteen clergymen in the town of the communion of *the Church*, who, in their turns, when they were not in action, had prayers and sermon every day. The seven Non-conforming ministers were equally careful of their people, and kept them very obedient and quiet, *much different from the behaviour of their brother, Mr. Osborne, who was a spy upon the whole North, employed by my Lord Tyrconnell*, and Mr. Houston, who was very troublesome, and would admit none to fight for the Protestant religion till they had first taken the covenant."

K

This passage gave great offence in many quarters, as it was considered altogether disingenuous and partially untrue. It concealed from the English public the important fact that, during the siege, the Non-conformists had the use of the Cathedral; and, instead of giving them due credit as the most resolute defenders of the place, it spoke of them as if they had been an inferior class, who were entitled to no higher praise than that of remaining "obedient and quiet." It cast a foul reflection on the Rev. Alexander Osborne, of Dublin, representing him as the "spy" of the infamous Tyrconnell, when he had, in fact, signalised himself as one of the most faithful guardians of the Protestant interest in Ireland: and it tried to fasten on the Presbyterians the odium of the proceedings of David Houston, a misguided man, who had long before been deposed by them from the ministry. The Rev. Joseph Boyse, a young Presbyterian minister settled in the Irish metropolis, immediately took up his pen in defence of his aged colleague, Mr. Osborne, and it has been thought right to insert in the present publication some of the most important passages of his now very scarce pamphlet. As this pamphlet is not found in the folio edition of his works, it is all the more necessary that at least a part of it should be thus preserved. It is entitled—
"A Vindication of the Reverend Mr. Alexander Osborne, in reference to the affairs of the North of Ireland, in which some mistakes concerning him in the printed account of the Siege of Derry, the Observations on it, and Mr. Walker's Vindication of it, are rectified, and a brief relation of these affairs is given, as far as Mr. Osborne and other Non-conformist ministers in the North were concerned in them. Written at Mr. Osborne's request, by his friend, Mr. J. Boyse. Licensed November 22, 1689, and entered according to order." London, 1690.

The noise of the preparations made in the north, by raising of regiments, &c., as well as of the revolutions in England, extremely alarmed the Government in Ireland, and though the Lord Tyrconnell went on vigorously with the completing of his new levies, yet he was so apprehensive of the strength of the northern forces, that he deferred the sending down his army twenty days after it had been first resolved on in council; but when Friar O'Haggerty (who was unhappily suffered to bring up the capitulation betwixt those of the north and the garrison of Carrickfergus) gave him a full account from his own observations of the posture of the British in the north, [viz., that they were untrained, and had few experienced officers; that the most part were without arms, and such as had them, their arms were unfixed and unfit for service; that they were very much scattered, and their number not near what had been written, and was confidently reported in Dublin; that they wanted all ammunition and necessary provisions for appearing in the field,] he resolved immediately to dispatch the most considerable and best trained part of his army, under the command of Lieutenant-General Hamilton. I am here obliged to omit some material passages, for a reason too obvious to be named; but as to Mr. Osborne, shall add—that as he perceived by his letters from the north, that their too great confidence of their own strength, of aids from England, and of Tyrconnell's fears, made them so secure that they looked on all the threatenings of an Irish army as only big words, so he began to fear they would be perfectly ruined for want of such timely notice of their danger as might enable them to put themselves into any good posture for their own defence. He found all way of communicating intelligence to them by sea or land entirely stopped. He had been, without his knowledge, mentioned to the Lord Tyrconnel as a person very fit to communicate any message he pleased to send to them; and his deep concern to prevent their threatened ruin brought him at last (though with great reluctancy) to yield to the urgent advice given him, not to refuse so fair an opportunity of conveying to his friends in the north, the best information and advice that could be given them. And that this wisdom of the serpent may appear fully consistent with the innocence of the dove, I shall transcribe all the discourses that passed between them, as transmitted to me in his own letter.

Lord Tyrconnel.—"I am informed you are well acquainted in Ulster with several of the nobility, gentry, and ministry living therein, having had your residence there for many years,* to which parts I am a great

* Mr. Osborne appears to have been a native of the north of Ireland. He had for a considerable number of years been minister of Brigh, and had removed to Dublin only in the early part of the year 1688.

stranger, and cannot but admire at the rebellious carriage and actions of some hot and rash spirited men who have incited the people to leave their labour, and run out into rebellion : yet I pity the poor people, and am willing to pardon them, upon the delivery of their serviceable horses and arms, and giving up six of their chief leaders."

To this Mr. Osborne replied, he "knew the Protestant nobility and gentry in the north in former times to have carried it loyally and soberly; but having had his residence chiefly in Dublin for twelve months by-past, he could not give a distinct account of the present irregularities among them."

The Lord Tyrconnell upon mention of "irregularities," grew hot, and said, "What, Sir, do you call them but irregularities ?—they are guilty of the very height of rebellion." To this Mr. Osborne, considering his circumstances, thought not fit to make any answer, but proceeded to put this question to him, "What, if the people in the north should incline to deliver up six of their chief leaders —and those six, discovering their inclinations, should withdraw or transport themselves to England or Scotland—whether he would send down his army to destroy the poor people, whom he judged to be drawn to take up arms by their persuasion ?" To which he answered, "If they did withdraw and leave the kingdom, he would have done with them:" and added, "that to show his lenity, he would be content with three of their chief leaders." Mr. Osborne proposed again "If those three would not be clear to accept what offers were made to them in his Excellency's discourse to him, but should rather incline to come and discourse with himself, he granting them safe conduct for coming to him ; and, if they agreed not—for returning again—to be in the same circumstances as before." To which he condescended, with a solemn attestation ; adding, "Though the Earl of Mount - Alexander, and Sir Arthur Rawdon should come to him, whom he judged the most active in that affair, he would grant what was demanded." The third person Mr. Osborne could not learn from him. Mr. Osborne proposed again to the Lord Tyrconnell's consideration (with a design to gain time for the assistance expected from England, and procrastinate the march of the Irish army), that Ulster was a large province, consisting of nine counties, and therefore begged his Excellency would allow him a considerable and convenient time for travelling through those counties, that he might discourse what he had heard from his Excellency's own mouth with the nobility, gentry, and ministry scattered in them, and chiefly concerned in the Ulster Association : to which he replied—that he would not stop the march of his army for one day or hour, but would give directions to Lieutenant-General Hamilton to treat with any that should be sent to him from the Protestants in arms there ; and then he showed him a paper, which he said was a copy of the declaration he would send along with Lieutenant-General Hamilton, and published before he entered into war, as containing the best terms they might expect if they accepted not those proposed to them by Mr. Osborne ; and he added here that passage concerning the Irish rabble, mentioned in Mr. Osborne's letter, and added further, that had he been sooner ready with his army he would sooner have resented their rebellious actions, and the indignity offered to his proclamation of clemency ; and being now ready, would delay no longer, and would not be afraid to go through all Ulster with five thousand men, and would be at Newry against the 11th of March, and go on (as in the letter), being confident he would meet with no resistance till he came to the walls of Derry ; that he knew well the case they were in, and that their expectations from England made them so violent, but they would find themselves disappointed, for no help would come so soon as they expected.

This is (as near as Mr. Osborne can remember) the whole of that discourse that passed between them, which the reader had not been troubled with at this length, were it not requisite to obviate their reproaches, who, rather than fail of something to criminate Mr. Osborne with, are pleased to argue, that if Mr. Osborne was true to the interest of the North he must be false to his promises to the Lord Tyrconnell : for he made him none, nor gave him ground to expect any more from him, than that he would relate what he heard ; which accordingly he did in the printed letter.* So unexceptionably clean and innocent was this negotiation of his. And indeed the Lord Tyrconnell was as much overseen in permitting Mr. Osborne to go down to the North, as they were in suffering Friar O'Haggarty to come up to Dublin. And that the success was so different was not, as will now appear, Mr. Osborne's fault.

Mr. Osborne having obtained the Lord Tyrconnell's pass, left Dublin, March the 7th, came to Newry, March the 8th, and the next

---

* Walker reprinted this letter in the appendix to the *True Account*. It merely states the proposals of Tyrconnell without expressing any opinion respecting them.—See note to this edition of Mackenzie's *Narrative*, p. 20.

day he and his two guards were pursued by the Rapparees, but got safe to Loughbrickland. Here he wrote the forementioned letter to my Lord Massareene,* and going on to Hillsborough, he wrote the same letter to Sir Arthur Rawdon, not finding him there as he expected—in which letter it was as needless as it was unavoidable, to give his own opinion of the Lord Tyrconnell's proposals, since the design of it was to draw the nobility and gentry to meet, and consult their common safety; and he knew not what necessity there might be of his going back with any message from them, or about his own affairs, to Dublin. But to those of the nobility and gentry that were there on the 9th and 10th, he delivered in a paper containing many particulars, by way of information and advice, of which these that follow were a part.

1. That for the Irish army, though their horses were good, yet their riders were but contemptible fellows, many of them having been lately cow-herds, &c.

2. That their provisions of ammunition were not plentiful.

3. That should tho' 7 of the North comply with the offers made to them, they had no reason to expect any true performance; the Lord Tyrconnell having broken all such capitulations as he had lately made in the like case with the Protestants in the South and West of Ireland, and thereby reduced them to poverty and slavery.

4. That the eyes of all Protestants were upon them. A great interest depended on their carriage; and it were better to die honourably, than live miserably under Popery and slavery: that their self-defence might be of great consequence to Britain as well as Ireland, either to their advantage or disadvantage, as their part should be well or ill acted.

5. It was advised that they should instantly gather all the forces they could from all parts, and choose out of their best armed and trained men, to engage the enemy, and have the rest ready to fall on their wings and outskirts.

6. It was advised also, that the conduct of their military affairs should be committed to their best known and experienced officers.

7. That they should debate with them from pass to pass, and so weary out their men, horses, and provisions, in expectation of relief from England.

These, with many other things, he suggested.

The Irish army being come to Newry on the 11th, he was, on the 12th, called for by such as were in the Consult, and his own advice desired. He insisted on the advice forementioned, and with all modest importunity urged them to defend themselves, and not to trust any Irish promises; and, accordingly, he was ordered by them to send back the following answer to the message he brought:—

"We declare the utter abhorrence of the effusion of blood, and that we will use all proper means to avoid it, but cannot consent to lay down our arms, which we were forced to take up for our own defence, nor to part with our goods by any other than legal means; and that we are ready to appoint persons to treat on such heads as are consistent with the safety of our religion, lives, and liberties."

* * * * * *

---

* Shortly after this period this nobleman sustained great damage from the Irish army. One of his servants, for a bribe of ten guineas, discovered to the plunderers money and plate, to the amount of between £3,000 and £4,000, concealed at Antrim Castle, which was also stripped of all its valuable furniture.—*History of the Presbyterian Church in Ireland*, II., 349, note. About the same time his lordship's chaplain, the Rev. Elias Travers, was seized and carried to Dublin, where he was kept prisoner for six or seven weeks. The history of this gentleman is remarkable. He was the nephew of the Earl of Radnor, better known as Lord Robarts, and when that nobleman came to Ireland in 1669 as Lord Lieutenant, Travers, then about twenty years of age, was appointed to a situation in the Secretary's office. Leaving Ireland shortly afterwards, when his relative relinquished the viceroyalty, he studied for some time at the University of Cambridge; and, as he had good talents and powerful connexions, he was urged to become a minister of the English Establishment. But he could not conscientiously conform, and he eventually became a Dissenting pastor. He succeeded the celebrated John Howe as chaplain to Lord Massareene; and his removal to Dublin by the partizans of James led to his settlement among the Presbyterians in the Irish capital. Happening to preach shortly after his liberation to the congregation of Cook Street, he received a call from them, which he accepted. He officiated as one of the Presbyterian ministers of Dublin till his death in 1705. Mr. Boyse preached his funeral sermon.—See *Boyse's Works*, I., 430. London, 1628. "He had," says Boyse, "a very intimate acquaintance with the Holy Scriptures, and well deserved the honourable character that he was a *walking Bible*. His gift of prayer was very eminent and edifying. There was an air of solemnity and reverence that appeared in all his ministrations, and carried convincing evidence into the conscience of all that attended them that he felt himself what he delivered to them, and that out of the abundance of his heart his mouth spake."

But these measures came too late: for the Irish army pressing on them with unexpected haste, and their leaders neither agreeing about entrenching themselves, nor about the choice of any pass in those parts which they thought defensible, and some of them leaving the kingdom: this uncertainty in their counsels, joined with the discouragement which the delay of expected succours from England gave them (with other things not fit for me to insist on), prevented their appointed rendezvous, and obliged them to retire in great confusion towards Coleraine and Derry.

But this should not be forgotten, that though these northern forces so unhappily failed in their design of defending those parts; yet many of those regiments raised there made up the chief strength of Derry; Mr. Walker's own regiment was raised for the Lord Charlemont, Captain Chichester, being the designed lieutenant-colonel, but afterwards made colonel of it; and the behaviour of such of them as stayed in that garrison, has, as Mr. Walker justly observes in his Narrative, "set them above apologies for miscarriage."

This being a true relation of matters of fact (of which undeniable evidence will be produced, if desired), every one that reflects on them, must needs think this worthy gentlemen deserved some other character than that of Tyrconnell's spy; nor can there be a greater wrong done to him than to impute those mischiefs and calamities which befel that part of the kingdom of Ireland to his management and advices, by which he did all that was possible to prevent them. These reproaches are but a sorry requital of those services which wanted nothing but that success which is not in human disposal, to render them as considerable as any of his profession was capable of, and were not a little expensive as well as hazardous to himself. How different the apprehensions which the Consult in the North had of Mr. Osborne were from these Mr. Walker had received from idle reports, will appear in the following testimonial, subscribed by several, of whom all but one were members of it, and two of them are the very persons to whom the letter so much talked of was directed:—

"We, whose names are hereunto subscribed, do, at the request of Mr. Alexander Osborne, a Presbyterian minister late of Dublin, hereby certify that the said Mr. Osborne was, to the certain knowledge of some of us, and as others have credibly heard and believe, for divers months before his coming down to the north of Ireland in March last, entrusted and employed by divers Protestants of credit in the North, as a person of known integrity and zeal to the Protestant interest, under a private method to correspond by letter, and give intelligence from time to time of affairs in Dublin, especially of the Lord Tyrconnel's proceedings there, in reference to the army, and his designs upon the north of Ireland, which, with other matters of no mean importance to the Protestant interest, he (as we have ground to believe) transacted with great care and fidelity; and that, about the beginning of March last, when all correspondence between Protestants from Dublin to the North was cut off, the said Mr. Osborne perceiving the Lord Tyrconnell immediately about to march down his army to the North against the Protestants there, whereof they could in all likelihood have no notice, but were in manifest danger of being surprised and destroyed thereby: he then (as we have credibly heard and believe), in order to prevent the same so far as in him lay, by timely information, found means of procuring the Lord Tyrconnell's pass for himself to the north, where he had his former abode, the Lord Tyrconnell first telling him that he might acquaint the Protestants there, especially some of the chief, with what his lordship then expressed; whereupon he came down to the north, running a considerable hazard of his life by the way, being, notwithstanding his pass, pursued by some of the Irish on that road (as we were credibly informed and believe). Being come to the North, he, by his letters, acquainted some of us, and others, with the purport of the Lord Tyrconnell's discourse to him as he left Dublin; but in the same letters desired, if we thought fit, some personal conference, that he might have opportunity of discoursing more fully with us touching the matters therein contained, as by those his letters of March 9, 1688-9, may appear; whereupon divers of us and other Protestants meeting with him at Hillsborough, received from him a more particular and full account thereof; he, the said Mr. Osborne, at the same time advising us, as his own private judgment, and as we valued our lives and interests, not to put confidence in the Lord Tyrconnell or any of his promises, but if we possibly could to defend ourselves to the utmost, or words to that effect; and as for his letters, containing the substance of Tyrconnell's discourses and threats against the Protestants, some of us ordered by common consent, copies of the same to be sent and dispersed through the country, that they might the better prepare themselves against the dangers that threatened them.* We likewise directed what answer the said Mr. Osborne should make, and committed the same to his discretion and care. Now in regard some of late, unacquainted (as we presume) with the proceedings then in that part of the country, or at least with what passed on that occasion, have represented the said Mr. Osborne in a public manner, in respect of his being so concerned, as an ill man, and " spy upon the whole north, employed by the Lord Tyrconnell, and so serving two masters, the British and the Irish," and the like to his great disadvantage, we cannot but own that we, who had, as we suppose, good reason to understand him herein, had, and still have, better thoughts of him, and are so far from looking on him as guilty of any such matters, that we are well assured of his having intended, and done therein the best service he could to the Protestant interest there, and that he was very faithful to that same to his utmost ; all which, at his desire by letter, in order to his just vindication, we do hereby certify this 19th day of November, 1689.

" Massareene.
" Arthur Rawdon.
" Arthur Upton, Esq.
" Wm. Cunningham, Esq.
" Hugh Magill, Esq.
" William Shaw, Esq."

This testimonial is so full, that had I received it sooner, it had spared me a great part of my labour. And I hope Mr. Walker himself will pay too great deference to the testimonies of persons who knew these affairs, and whose reputation is above all exception, to persist in those mistakes concerning Mr. Osborne, which the little stories of some ignorant people had imposed on him. And the very same character of his integrity and zeal has been given, both by the Earl of Mount-Alexander, and by other gentlemen of the north, who have left this town, as Jas. Hamilton, of Tullymore, and Jas. Hamilton, of Bangor, Esqrs., and John Hawkins, Esq. The principal members of the Consult were so well satisfied with his services that they judged them worthy of a public reward ; as indeed they must be thought by all that take their estimate of worthy actions from the sincerity and prudence of the actor,

* Mr. Walker, as has been stated, had printed this letter, in the Appendix to his *True Account*, with a view to create a prejudice against Mr. Osborne. These gentlemen here testify that they had previously circulated it themselves for the purpose of serving the Protestant interest.

rather than the success, which was not in his own power. For my part, though Mr. Osborne cannot but think this usage very hard, yet I think him not a little obliged to Mr. Walker for laying on him such an absolute necessity of exposing his own, as well as his brethren's exemplary zeal for the Protestant interest, to public view—which their modesty would else have suppressed the notice of ; and doubt not but the Government will, in due time, take it into consideration.

For Mr. Houston, whom Mr. Walker joins with Mr. Osborne, I suppose he is not ignorant that he was some years before publicly discarded by the Non-conformist ministers in the North,* for his scandalous and turbulent carriage ; and therefore they do no more than right to themselves, in disowning him. His narrow zeal, that would suffer none to fight for the Protestant religion but such as would take the Covenant, was certainly very unseasonable, as well as foolish bigotry ; and I hope, as Mr. Walker spied this mote in Mr. Houston's eye, he will not overlook the beam in theirs, who are as zealous to exclude all from fighting for the same cause who comply not with their Sacrament Test ; for they equally sacrifice the common interest of the Protestant religion to that of a party, and deprive their Majesties of the service of one part of their subjects, as firm and steady to the Protestant religion and the present Government as any whatsoever.†

Having done this right to Mr. Osborne, I think myself concerned also to do the same justice to the dissenters in Derry. I confess I think it would become both parties more to join in their thankful acknowledgments to God for such a series of wonders in their deliverance, than to quarrel about their share in being only the instruments of it. But as Mr. Walker gave the first public occasion to these debates, by that passage in his Preface, which (as explained by himself) ascribes the chief, not to say the sole glory of it, to the

* David Houston was at one time a probationer in connexion with the Presbyterian Church in Ireland, but in consequence of various irregularities, his license had been withdrawn in February, 1672. After a suspension of a year and a half, he was restored to the office of a licentiate, when his folly again brought him under ecclesiastical discipline, and in February, 1687, he was finally deposed. He was not in Derry, either at the shutting of the gates or during the siege; and yet Walker found it convenient to mention him, as his proceedings had brought discredit on the Presbyterian name.

† According to the Test Act, those who declined to partake of the Lord's Supper were excluded from all public offices, civil and military.

Church of England;* so he is chiefly accountable for the ill consequences of them. And what I shall here suggest is only to rectify what, if I mistake not, Mr. Walker has misrepresented. As the Dissenters of Derry do not dispute with Mr. Walker most of the principal and experienced officers in the garrison being Conformists (for it could not be otherwise, while none else but such had access to military employments, till some raised regiments in this juncture), so on the other hand Mr. Walker should as little dispute with them, their numbers in Derry being more considerable. By the modestest account of such officers in the garrison as were Conformists, the Dissenters in the garrison itself, as well as those that stayed in town, were near five to one; nay many of them make the disproportion much greater. Nor are the arguments employed in Mr. Walker's Questions, in his " Vindication," p. 15, of any force to prove the contrary; for as a Governor, Colonel Baker had those advantages to recommend him, that would easily set him above any competitor in their choice; and he had too great an interest in the hearts of Dissenters, on the account of his known affections to them, to be excepted against by them. All that can be inferred from his being a Conformist, on supposition of the Dissenters being more numerous, is only this —that they were too zealous for their common interest, to prefer their affection to a party before the safety of it, and regarded more in that excellent person the qualities that fitted him for that station than the distinguishing name he bore. Nor had any other been chosen, if Colonel Baker had not desired an assistant to be joined with him, on the civil part to take care of the stores; and it was on his recommendation that the garrison assented to the Rev. Mr. Walker's being his assistant,† which may still consist with the supposition fore-mentioned, if we but allow the Dissenters the good temper which Mr. Walker himself elsewhere attributes to them. And they paid too great respect to

* In the Dedication to William and Mary, prefixed by Walker to the *True Account*, the following words occur :—" God, ... by making use of a poor minister, the unworthiest of the whole communion of which he is a member, would intimate to the world by what hand He will defend and maintain your Majesties' interest, and the religion you have delivered."

† It is to be observed that this Vindication appeared *before* the publication of Mackenzie's *Narrative*, and that Boyse had means of knowing the truth apart from any information communicated by the minister of Cookstown. His testimony is thus of special value.

the laws to desire such a share in the church as they then had, on any other occasion; and were too modest to go about to engross it. But I would humbly offer to Mr. Walker's memory a much surer way of computing their numbers than this that he has offered. In the Cathedral, in the forenoon, when the Conformists preached, there was but comparatively a thin auditory; in the afternoon it was very full, and there were four or five meetings of Dissenters in the town besides;* and how any man will reconcile this with the number of Conformists being more considerable, or indeed near equal to that of their brethren, I cannot well imagine : and for the Non-conformist ministers (and the same may be justly said of the Conformists), they not only kept their people quiet and obedient, but, by their exhortations, constantly animated their courage in their many bold and resolute sallies; and, therefore, so very slender a commendation of them as the former needed not have been allayed, by adding the misbehaviours of their brother, Mr. Osborne, which are but feigned, and the real ones of Mr. Houston, wherein they are not concerned. Nor are Mr. Walker's reflections on their brethren here in England (to whom he supposes the temper of their brethren in Derry a reproach) any better grounded than those on Mr. Osborne; but being only general, no man is concerned to go about to disprove them. I must also add, as to those ministers in Derry, that there was some real ground to suspect the ingenuity of Mr. Walker's ama-

* There is every reason to believe that, during the siege, a number of Episcopalians felt it a privilege to attend the Presbyterian services. The Presbyterian ministers could adapt their prayers to the emergency; but candid and intelligent members of the Establishment must have felt that their Liturgy was ill suited to their condition, and that some of the petitions it supplied were peculiarly unseasonable. They had just thrown off the yoke of a sovereign whom they had obeyed for years, and whom, according to the doctrine of their own bishop, they were still bound to serve; so that there was something extremely awkward in the prayer—" From *all* sedition, privy conspiracy, and rebellion, . . . Good Lord, deliver us!" They were frequently required to sally out against the enemy, and yet they were expected to say after the minister— " Grant that this day we fall into no sin, *neither run into any kind of danger.*" At this season of terrible endurance the Book of Common Prayer afforded no vent to crowds of emotions struggling for expression. It furnished no appropriate reference to the increasing severity of the famine —to the horrors of civil war—to the menaces of the Romanists—or to the threatened extinction of civil and religious liberty.

nuensis in the omission of their names (all being willing to excuse Mr. Walker himself from so mean a thing). For not to insist on other things, a minister here received a letter from two of his brethren in Scotland, bearing date Edinburgh, August, 15, 1689, wherein are these words—"This account we have confirmed by Mr. Walker, &c., on whom we waited yesterday at the Abbey, in Dr. Hamilton's lodgings, &c., to inquire concerning the condition of our brethren there. The account he gave us of our brethren is indeed afflicting, there being three besides Mr. Gilchrist removed (by death), viz., Mr. William Crooks, Mr. Robert Wilson, and (as we took it) Mr. John Rowat. The rest of them, viz., Mr. Thomas Boyd, Mr. John Hamilton, Mr. John Mackenzie, and another, whose name he could not remember, were in health, &c.* This general hint is all we judged needful for the present, but you may have a more full account from Mr. Walker, who hath taken his journey this day for London."

* Mr. Walker here makes some mistakes as to those who survived and those who died—a circumstance not strange, as the greatest mortality prevailed towards the end of the siege—but otherwise he repeats the names and surnames correctly. He omits Mr. David Brown, of Urney, who died during the siege.

DR. WALKER'S
INVISIBLE CHAMPION FOILED:
OR, AN
Appendix to the late Narrative of the Siege of Derry;

Wherein all the Arguments offered in a late Pamphlet, to prove it a False Libel, are Examined and Refuted.

BY JOHN MACKENZIE,

Publisher of the said Narrative.

LONDON: *Printed for the Author, and Sold by the Booksellers of London.* 1690.

DR. WALKER'S INVISIBLE CHAMPION FOILED.

I AM sorry to find Dr. Walker's reputation sunk so low, that his friend who undertakes his defence, dare not publish his name.* For since he dare not, and yet makes so bold with other men's reputations, he looks much more like a libeller than one who, by owning what he writes, renders himself accountable to the public for the truth of it. And if I make any conjecture about my accuser, either from this disingenuous practice, or from his admirable style and humour (which are all of a piece with it), it is the same gentleman that wrote "Remarks on Mr. Osborne's Vindication;" but I fear he will have as little success in disproving what he calls a libel against Dr. Walker, as he had in justifying, or rather palliating the Doctor's real libel against Mr. Osborne. And as Mr. Boyse was better employed than to throw away his time in refuting such a heap of falsehoods as his former scribble contained, dressed up in a medley of Grub Street and Billingsgate, so should I have served this, if he had not endeavoured to amuse the world with some show of proof for the few things he has to say against my Narrative.

It is no inconsiderable argument of the truth of that relation, that one whose inclination and interest led him to take so much pains to blast the credit of it, has produced no greater objections against it. There being not above two or three passages, and only one of any moment, in the Narrative itself that he ventures to nibble at; for the greater part of his powder and shot is spent against a passage or two in the Preface, where he tells us the venom lies. But how little execution he has done either on the Preface or the Narrative will appear by a particular examination of all that is material in his certificates about them. For the scurrilous humour which he will needs, without any occasion given him, vent against religion, I think unworthy of my notice.

* This defence is entitled "Mr. John Mackenzie's Narrative of the Siege of Londonderry, a false libel; in defence of Dr. George Walker. Written by his friend in his absence." London, 1690. There is no doubt that all Walker's influence was exerted to get up the certificates contained in this pamphlet, and reviewed in the present rejoinder.

I have said in the Preface to my Narrative that that part of it which gives an account of the siege of Derry itself, was offered by me to be reviewed by such of the officers of Derry as are now in town; several of whom, as Colonel Crofton, Colonel Murray, Lieut.-Colonel Blair, Captain Alexander Sanderson, &c., having heard it read in the presence of Sir Arthur Rawdon,* Sir Arthur Langford,† Colonel Upton, and several other gentlemen, and being desired, upon every material paragraph, to object against anything either misrepresented or omitted in that relation, freely professed their assent to it.

Here are two things asserted—that that part of the narrative was offered to be re-

* As Sir Arthur Rawdon was an Episcopalian, his testimony on this occasion is all the more valuable. He was married to the granddaughter of Archbishop Bramhall. He died in 1695, on the very day on which he completed his thirty-third year. He is represented by contemporaries as a person of the strictest integrity.

† Sir Arthur Langford, Bart., was a member of the Presbyterian congregation of Wood Street, Dublin, but he occasionally resided at Summerhill, in Meath, where there was a small flock of Protestant Non-conformists. He died unmarried in 1716, and the Rev. J. Boyse, in his funeral sermon, thus speaks of him:—"He was strict and constant in keeping up the exercises of family religion, and thought it not beneath his character to officiate himself, when ministers were not present. His religious, his just and sober conversation rendered him an exemplary ornament to his profession, and his extensive charity an eminent support to it. . . . . During his long-continued disorders, he would, in his audible prayers, be much enlarged in begging of God the restoration of the oppressed Reformed churches abroad, and the general enlargement of the interest of the Reformed religion, as well as the revival of practical piety in these lands. . . . . . As he was blessed with a plentiful estate, so he had an heart and head open and enlarged in doing good. . . . . . I cannot easily forget the last words I heard him utter. Being told that our Lord Jesus had promised to come quickly, and to bring his reward with him, and that it should be the language of our believing souls—'Amen; even so come Lord Jesus;' he replied with an earnest emotion—'I go to Him—I go to Him!'"—*Boyse's Works*, I., 300.

viewed by such of the officers of Derry as were then in town, and that several of them, particularly those named, had heard it read, and freely professed their assent to it.

Against which, after abundance of such language as is suitable to his breeding, he produces three certificates, and I doubt not but he may obtain many more of the same kind from the like persons.

Against the former assertion he brings a certificate of seventeen, called Derry officers, then in town, who declare they never saw my narrative before it was printed, and do not now approve of it, p. 3, 4.

Now, if he please to put on his spectacles, and compare the words of the preface with those of this certificate a little better, he may, perhaps, be able to discern that the contradiction betwixt them lay only in his imagination. That it might be offered to be reviewed by those who had not leisure or inclination to be present at the reading of it ; and that it was actually offered to be reviewed by the chief officers of the regiments he mentions, and that they were desired to bring any others with them that they thought capable of giving me any information, appears by the following certificate:—

"We, whose names are subscribed, do hereby certify that on the 28th of February last past, we consented and agreed with Colonel Murray, Colonel Hamill, Lieutenant-Colonel Blair, and Captain Sanderson, to meet at the Fountain Tavern, in the Strand, on the next day, being the first of March, to peruse that part of Mr. Mackenzie's Narrative which related to the siege of Londonderry, and desired the said gentlemen to inform Colonel Crofton, and any other officers that they knew in London that were capable to give any account of the said siege, all which persons might have liberty to hear the said account, and be admitted to make any objections thereto before it was printed. Witness our hands, this 22nd of May, 1690.

"Arthur Langford.
"Wm. Cunningham."

And now let the reader judge, whether the everlasting shame with which he would charitably brand me on this ceasion, be not much more due to his ignorance or malice, or both. I would here only add, that whether these seventeen persons mentioned in this certificate approve the Narrative or no, I think myself little concerned, unless they had shown me any mistakes in it. Some of them, it may be, did very good service ; but for others of them, perhaps they may dislike it, because it makes no more mention of themselves. But that was not any defect of mine, but their misfortune, in having done nothing more memorable. Besides some of them are not in the list of officers which I had from the only store-keeper ; but it is fit to return them as such, that they may do some service.

Against the latter assertion he produces two certificates, one of Colonel Crofton's, that I did not read all that part that related to Derry (he should have said the Siege of Derry), and that he objected several things against it, and does not assent to or approve of it ; another of Captain Sanderson's, that he did not assent to two particulars, viz.:—the articles against Dr. Walker, and the discouraging sermon, not knowing anything of them.

For Captain Sanderson's certificate, it is no way contradictory to the true intent of the Preface, which in asserting their assent to the Narrative, cannot be reasonably thought to imply they personally knew the truth of every particular related in it. It is sufficient that there was no passage they could object against the truth of. But how little regard is due to either of these certificates, so far as they contradict what is said in the Preface to the Narrative, will appear by the testimony of the following gentlemen then present, whose credit must be allowed by all that know them sufficient to overpoise theirs in this matter :—

"We, whose names are subscribed, do certify that that part of Mr. John Mackenzie's Narrative which relates to the siege of Londonderry (particularly the passages now controverted in the pamphlet, entitled "Mr. Mackenzie's Narrative a False Libel,") was before the printing of it, on the first of March last, at the Fountain Tavern in the Strand, read in our presence and hearing, before Colonel Murray, Colonel Crofton, Lieutenant-Colonel Blair, Captain Alexander Sanderson, and Captain Samuel Murray, late officers at Derry, who, being frequently desired and urged while it was a reading to object freely against anything either misrepresented or omitted in that relation, and to that purpose several stops and pauses being made at the end of material paragraphs, told us that where they made no objection, we might take it for their assent to what was read; and accordingly there were but two or three passages about which any doubt was raised ; and even as to those, the objectors, upon hearing the debates about them, acquiesced in the evidence given by others for the truth of them, particularly Colonel Crofton and Captain Sanderson owned the change of the government to be truly expressed, the former also owned that there were such articles against Dr. Walker, and the latter denied not his having heard frequently of them. Given under our hands, this 8th of May, 1690.

"Jno. Cunningham
"Arthur Rawdon.
"Arthur Langford.
"Arthur Upton.
"David Cairns.
"Samuel Bull.
"Wm. Cunningham.
"John Abernethy.*
"J. Boyse."†

I must add that this certificate from Colonel Crofton is the more strange, because he not only

* The following character of Mr. Abernethy is given by a contemporary:—" The Rev. Mr. Abernethy was well known to have been adorned with the happy conjunction of three rare qualities, which seldom meet in one man—viz.: a sprightly quickness of apprehension, a great depth of solid judgment, and a vast memory, justly admired for singular celerity and long retention; and these rich intellectual endowments were replenished with a large stock of acquired knowledge, and accompanied with a generous public spirit, great piety, and remarkable candour and integrity: he was a man of polite address, and of that peculiar felicity in conversation as made him fit to be a companion to men of all stations and persuasions; from whom, the amiable beauties of his mind set off with a countenance made venerable with majestic gravity and humble sweetness, did at once command both awful respect and endearing love."—Kirkpatrick's *Presbyterian Loyalty*, p. 408. See also note at page 17 of this volume.

† The Rev. Joseph Boyse, so often mentioned in this volume, was one of the most eminent ministers of his generation. When comparatively young we find him corresponding with such men as John Howe and Matthew Henry, the Commentator. One of his contemporaries thus speaks of him:—"Mr. Boyse now living in Dublin is a great scholar and a very smart disputant, and the world has seen a specimen of his talent that way in his 'Answer to Bishop King.' He is now preaching on 'The Four Last Things.' His subject was 'Heaven' when I heard him; and he preached in such an extraordinary manner on that subject as if he had been in the third heaven himself, and was returned to relate what he had seen."—See Dunton's *Life and Errors*. London, 1818. Mr. Boyse died in 1728 in the sixty-eighth year of his age. His discourse "of a Scriptural Bishop" had the honour of being burned by order of the Irish House of Lords; a proof that the spiritual peers, who then generally constituted the majority of that section of the Legislature, could furnish no more luminous answer to it.—See *History of the Presbyterian Church in Ireland*, III., 69, note.

confirmed what is said of Col. Lundy, Mr. Walker, and Major-Gen. Kirke, which he has also since owned before Serjeant Osborne, and other gentlemen, but acquainted us with some passages that, on his information, were inserted. Nor do any then present remember any material objections he made, except one, which was against the meeting (which, at Colonel Lundy's persuasions, signed a paper of surrender) being called a Council; but he could not deny what is said of them to be true; and whatever names he would now assign them, they then called themselves a Council. And now for the civil language, of a spirit of lying, brassy impudence, bold asseverations, gross prevarication, studied and deliberate lie, &c., which this pamphleteer uses on this occasion; the reader will better understand where to apply it.

For the articles against Dr. Walker I need no other instance of this gentleman's extraordinary confidence, than his saying they were never exhibited but in my narrative. It is a sign he is an entire stranger to Derry that has the face to deny what was so publicly known there, and there are yet so many living witnesses of. But as this advocate of Dr. Walker's has said nothing to disprove the articles themselves, so his big words about them do not much affright me. Dr. Walker will, I suppose, be wiser than to offer himself to a fair trial upon them; and whether in such a trial he be cleared or cast, concerns not the truth of my Narrative, which only affirms such articles were drawn up, and a considerable number of officers engaged to prosecute him upon them, till Governor Baker diverted them by offering to put the government into the hands of the Council of Fourteen, whereof he was made president; and it is not probable they would undertake to bring such a charge against him without strong presumptions of the truth of it.*

The next thing which this pamphleteer falls upon, is to prove Dr. Walker Governor of the garrison as well as the stores. That he was Governor of the stores, and therein assistant to Governor Baker, is asserted in the Narrative, and no way denied in the Preface: but that the care of the military affairs of the garrison was committed to him, or that he showed himself a hero in the management of them, is not asserted in the Narrative, because it is not true, and therefore the Preface does but justly expose his pretensions to it.

* Walker was not permitted to preside in the Council of Fourteen, which really constituted the governing body. It is thus evident that he was guilty of great presumption when he described himself as *the* Governor.

Now to prove Dr. Walker Governor of the garrison, as to the military affairs of it, as well as Governor of the stores—here are three certificates produced, one signed by seventeen, called Derry officers, another by Captain Bennet, and a third by Mr. Squire, (whom he calls the present Mayor,)

On which I need only make the following reflections to show the insufficiency of them to the end for which they are brought :—

1. He has not (though great pains were taken to that purpose) produced the testimony of one officer for what he asserts concerning Dr. Walker being chosen Governor, that was present to vote at the election of Governor Baker on the 19th of April. As for Colonel Crofton, I can show him a paper, under his own hand, wherein he affirms that Colonel Baker was sole Governor of the garrison. What Lieutenant-Colonel Blair has said of that matter will appear in its due place. And for Colonel Murray, he did, to the doctor's face, deny him to have been Governor of the garrison, before the committee of his Majesty's Privy Council, Col. Hamill and Lieutenant-Colonel Blair being then present, and not offering to contradict what he said, though the Doctor made his appeal to them. And sure these gentlemen that sign this certificate cannot pretend to know that matter better than those who were present when it was transacted. And even some of these very persons have frequently declared the quite contrary to what they here certify, as Captain Macullogh, Captain Watson, &c. ; so little regard is due to their assertions, who are so little constant to themselves.

2. It is strange that neither these seventeen persons, nor the pamphleteer for them, should offer the least syllable to invalidate the truth of those matters of fact, which plainly overthrow what they here certify.

I might, upon a little more leisure, have produced the testimonies of more of those present at Governor Baker's election, for the truth of what is there related, but I need them not while the matters of fact there mentioned stand uncontradicted. It is strange that Dr. Walker should be chosen Governor of the garrison, and the military affairs of it, when he did not so much as stand a candidate with Colonel Baker and the other two competitors, nay, when he was not so much as present till after Colonel Baker was elected Governor, and the regiments were concluded on. And as it is in itself a most improbable thing that they should, in their circumstances, while their safety entirely depended on their union, set up two Governors entrusted with equal power ; and much more, that they should commit the military affairs to one who they knew could not pretend to the least skill or conduct in them ; so the falsehood of it is evident from the very reason alleged by Col. Baker for desiring an assistant, and from what he spoke on that occasion, and from the nomination of his assistant being left to himself. Besides the frequent attempts of Dr. Walker to assume more to himself, and the vehement opposition he still met with in all of them (See Narrative, p. 45, 47, 52) plainly show the vanity of his pretensions ; for if he was Governor of the garrison, he was such a one whose authority was so very insignificant and contemptible in it, that were it not for the liberal reward that name has so luckily produced him, he had better never laid any claim to it. But with the good leave of the writer of the Epistle, annexed to the end of that pamphlet,* these passages do not merely prove that his government was opposed, as he would now gladly colour the matter, but that his pretensions to the military part of it were rejected with disdain by the major part of the garrison, who were forced by such rude treatment to check his busy, confident humour, in intermeddling with more than belonged to his province.

3. Yet it is more strange that these seventeen persons should never acquaint us with the manner of his being chosen Governor as to the military affairs, nor give us the least instance of one thing being done by him, in pursuance of his trust as such a Governor.

These seventeen persons speak not one syllable of the manner of his being chosen Governor ; but perhaps that defect may be thought abundantly supplied in the certificate of Ger. Squire, Esq., which I shall set down at length, that what I shall offer to invalidate it may appear the more plain and unexceptionable.

"I do hereby certify that Dr. Geo. Walker during all the time of the siege of the city of Londonderry, and until Major-General Kirke came into the said city, executed the office and place of Governor of the same joint with Colonel Henry Baker, until the said Baker's sickening (of which he died), and after with Colonel John Mitchelburn, who was in a general meeting of the field and other officers of the said garrison, elected to act as Gover-

* Mackenzie here refers to an anonymous letter appended to his *Narrative a false Libel.* The writer of it makes the following candid observation :—" It is strange the world should be so imposed upon to believe Dr. Walker Governor of Londonderry, if he were not; *or that any should now so soon deny it, if he were.*" P. 17.

nor in the said Baker's place, during his sickness, as well in all things relating to military affairs, as in seeing the provisions gathered and distributed; the management of the provisions to the best advantage, was a great means by which the said city held out so long; and I do also certify that it being agreed upon by the said Governors and Council that I should administer an oath of fidelity, then agreed upon to be taken by the said Governors and Council, I administered the said oath to the said Dr. Walker, and Colonel Baker, as Governors of the said city, the said Dr. Walker having the precedence, as well as to the members of the said Council; all which I am ready to depose upon oath, if required; and I do further certify that I never saw a pamphlet, entitled "A Narrative of the Siege of Londonderry," or any part of it, published by Mr. John Mackenzie, until after it was printed; and having perused it since, I do not approve of it. Witness my hand, the 9th day of April, 1690.

"GER. SQUIRE, *Mayor*."*

I shall not now insist on it, that as Mr. Squire was not then mayor of that city, so his reputation is not of so great weight as this pamphleteer would, in kindness to Dr. Walker, make it; but I shall, by clearing

* When the reader carefully marks the language of this certificate he may see that it is a very lame and unsatisfactory document. In addition to the objections urged against it in the text, we may state that it is otherwise evasive. When it sets forth that the rev. gentleman "*executed* the office and place of Governor *joint* with Colonel Henry Baker" it settles nothing; for Walker was charged with sometime *executing* functions which he had no right to assume; and though he was only assistant to the Governor, he might be said to be *joined* with him in the administration. Squire does not venture to affirm that Baker and Walker possessed *equal* authority, which was, after all, the only point in dispute. The fact that the oath was first tendered to Walker is obviously of no consequence. Knowing that he was the suspected man, he may have deemed it prudent to step forward first, or the other members of the council may have requested him to do so. There is in fact nothing in this certificate which may not be reconciled with the statement made by Squire to Byfield as attested in a subsequent document. Squire was called on to administer the oath because he was Mayor, a fact of which Mackenzie was evidently ignorant. Mr. Campsie died on the 11th of April, and Squire was chosen to succeed him two days afterwards; but during the siege his authority was superseded, so that the fact of his appointment was known to comparatively few.

those matters of fact which this certificate gives a very confused account of, show its weakness and falsehood.

To this purpose, the reader must know that neither Colonel Baker, nor Dr. Walker, were sworn at all at the time of their election, viz., the 19th day of April, nor indeed any of those that were then made Colonels. The occasion of their being sworn was this: the greatest part of the officers of the garrison were in May extremely jealous of the treacherous designs of Dr. Walker; and to a high degree disgusted with Governor Baker himself for giving so much ear to the advice of one of whose integrity they had so deep a suspicion. Governor Baker, to remove all occasion of their fears, and give them full satisfaction in that matter, agreed to the motion of putting the government into the hands of a Council of Fourteen, of which they were contented Governor Baker should be the president, (every regiment deputing one to sit in it, and both city and country having some to represent them.) And if Mr. Squire had pleased to acquaint us what the oath was which he administered, it would have cleared the whole affair; for it was no more than this: "that they should be true to the garrison, and have no treaty with the enemy without the knowledge and order of that Council." Nor was there any difference in the oath, as taken by Governor Baker, by Dr. Walker, or any other member of that Council. Now when this Council of Fourteen had the government put into their hands, when Colonel Baker was the only president of it, when Dr. Walker had no more power than any other member in it (his concern in the stores excepted), when the oath administered to all of them was the same, with what face can this gentleman pretend to have administered this oath to Governor Baker and Dr. Walker as Governors of the said city—nay, to have allowed Dr. Walker the precedency, who was not president of the council? For if he were sworn first in these circumstances, it could be no other than a mere compliment paid to his gown, for the precedency was evidently due to Colonel Baker, and Mr. Squire could not (whatever he might intend), by administering that oath to Mr. Walker, make him any more a Governor of the garrison than each member of that council might as justly pretend to be. Note here, that Mr. Squire, in this certificate, mentions not one word of Dr. Walker being *chosen* Governor.

Having said so much to Mr. Squire's, I need say the less to Captain Bennet's, certificate. For not to mention the obscurity of his expressions concerning Dr. Walker's Governorship, it is strange that he should not only insinuate that Colonel Baker and Dr. Walker were sworn at the time of their election, but that this was during his stay there, both which are notoriously false. The election was on the 19th of April; the oath was administered about the latter end of May; and both by Dr. Walker's Account, and the Relation* that is said to be published by himself, Captain Bennet left Derry about 23rd or 24th of April: and so insignificant is his certificate, as well as false, that were all true that he saith concerning Dr. Walker's signing any writings with Colonel Baker to Lieut.-General Hamilton, or giving him a little money to bear his charges, or being called a Governor in the Irish army, it is all consistent enough with his being Governor of the stores only, if we consider his forwardness, and Colonel Baker's complaisance : and Captain Bennet might, by these weak arguments, be as easily led to fancy that Dr. Walker was chosen Governor of the garrison, as he was that Colonel Murray was chosen the General of their forces, because he usually led them out in their sallies, as is asserted in the printed Relation which is known to be Mr. Bennet's. But that the reader may the better conjecture what it was indeed that moved Captain Bennet to sign such a paper for Dr. Walker, do but observe the following certificate from two of Derry officers :—

"We, whose names are subscribed, do certify that, about the 20th of April last, being in

* The pamphlet here mentioned was published in London about the close of the siege. It is entitled, "A True and Impartial Account of the most material passages in Ireland since December, 1688; with a particular Relation of the forces of Londonderry." The publication is anonymous, but the reference in the text shows that it was written by Bennet. In the *True Account*, under the date of April 20, Walker says—"We sent Mr. Bennet out of the garrison with orders to go to England, and to give an account of our Resolutions to defend the town against the enemy. Our men were ordered to fire after him, that the enemy might think he had deserted us." Bennet was afterwards rewarded for this service. He seems to have been entirely under the influence of Walker; and, probably owing to his patronage, he had now attained the rank of captain. We have here another proof that the rev. author of the *True Account* could not have kept a diary; for Bennet, in his *Relation*, gives a minute description of the battle of Pennyburn Mill, which took place on the 21st of April, and of some subsequent occurrences; whereas Walker alleges that he left Derry on the 20th—a mistake which the assistant Governor could not have committed had he daily noted down passing occurrences.

company with Captain Joseph Bennet, in the city of London, and discoursing about his and our going for Ireland, he demanded whether we had owned or approved of Mr. John Mackenzie's "Narrative of the Siege of Londonderry," declaring to us, that if we did, we needed not go for Ireland with any expectation of employment in the army there, nor any who would not express their dislike or disapproving of the same, by reason of Major-General Kirke's and Dr. Walker's influence there, or words to that purpose. As witness our hands this 12th day of June, 1690.

"SAMUEL MURRAY.
"ALEXANDER HERON."

And as none of the certificates allege anything done by Dr. Walker as Governor in respect of the military affairs, so I would desire his advocate to give us some instances of that kind, which, methinks, it were an easy matter to have done if his pretensions were true; for I hope they will not allow him to have been a mere cipher in that station; and a few such instances would have signified more than all these certificates. And one would think, that as my Narrative mentions so many things done by Colonel Baker plainly show he had the conduct of their military affairs, so Dr. Walker's account should furnish us with the like evidence of his sharing with him in that part of the government. I have, to this purpose, reviewed his narrative; and shall (to supererogate for once) take the pains to examine all the passages that give the least ground to imagine that the military affairs of the garrison were under his conduct.

In page 21 of Dr. Walker's Account it is said the Governors divided the outline into eight parts, and each regiment had its own ground, and each company knew their own bastion; the drummers were enjoined to quarter in one house.

Now the division of the outline was made by the officers themselves; and the quartering the drummers in one house was the contrivance of Governor Mitchelburn, and that not till the last month of the siege. And the enjoining of all parties to forget their distinctions &c., and to betake themselves to their several devotions, mentioned in the same page, was an order I never heard of in Derry. But those who have so liberally given Dr. Walker the conduct of our military affairs might very well (to carry on the humour) give him the conduct of our ecclesiastical too, and make him Bishop, as well as Governor of the city.

In p. 24, Mr. Walker is said to have found

it necessary to mount one of the horses, to make our flying horse rally, and to relieve Colonel Murray.

Now though this grand feat itself be no very convincing argument of his Governorship; because it might be done by him as Colonel of a regiment (it being more proper for a colonel than a governor to expose himself to so eminent hazards), yet the credit of it is much more spoiled by the unhappy disputes that have arisen about the matter of fact. For some have started such cross questions about the armour of the rider, as well as the colour of the horse, as I fear will go near to dismount the Doctor in the next edition of that Account, and leave Col. Murray to get off as well as he can without him.

In p. 25, Mr. Walker is said to draw a detachment of ten men out of each company, and (after putting them into the best order their impatience could allow) to sally out at the head of them, with all imaginable silence at Ferry Quay Gate.

Now I have heard, indeed, that Governor Baker and other officers were about to detach such a number of every company; but the soldiers were too eager, to wait any of those formalities, and ran out in what order best pleased themselves. But I never was informed before, that Mr. Walker was so foolishly prodigal of his life, as to sally out at the head of them; for if he did so, it was not only with all imaginable silence, but with so wonderful secrecy, too, as to be neither seen nor heard by any of those that are said to follow him. No, he understood his post in the stores too well to expose his person in any of the sallies. And therefore the gentleman that wrote the "Vindication" of his "Account" might have spared that long and learned apology he has for the Doctor, as if in the siege he had been forced to do so many things inconsistent with the character of a clergyman. For as to the enemy, he was a man of peace all the time, and was guilty of shedding no other blood to stain his coat with, but that of the grape.

In p. 26, it is said the enemy hung out a white flag to invite us to a treaty, and Mr. Walker ventured out to come within hearing of the Lord of Louth, and Colonel O'Neill, and in his passage had a hundred shot fired at him; but he got the shelter of a house, and upbraided them with this perfidious dealing, and bid them order their men to be quiet, or he would command all the guns on the walls to be fired at them.

Now besides that Dr. Walker might be sent on a treaty without being Governor of the garrison (as several others were), I have heard some incredulous people say that the smoke of the one hundred shot was as invisible as the flying of the bullets: and they could not imagine whereabouts the house stood (all without the gates next the Irish camp being pulled down) that so happily yielded the Doctor a safe shelter, till he could call to the men on the walls to fire the guns at these treacherous villains.

In p. 32, it is but barely asserted, and without the least ground, that Colonel Mitchelburn was appointed during Governor Baker's sickness to assist Governor Walker, that while the one commanded in the sallies, the other might take care of the town.

On the contrary, Colonel Mitchelburn was deputed by Governor Baker to his own post,* and consequently Mr. Walker was only his assistant; and as I presume that Dr. Walker will no more pretend to have commanded in the sallies, so the garrison by this time understood him too well to lay any great stress on his care of the town.

In p. 33, it is said by the contrivance of our Governor and Colonel Mitchelburn, &c., we countermine the enemy before Butcher's Gate.

It is a sign how he minded those affairs that talks of our countermining the enemy; for neither they nor we ever drew a mine. We did indeed counterline them; but this was purely Governor Mitchelburn's contrivance; and it was a double injury in Dr. Walker at once to rob him of the sole honour of that action, and the title of Governor too.

In pp. 37, 38, there is a pleasant story about the suspicions of the garrison concerning Dr. Walker, occasioned by some discourse of one Mr. Cole, whom Dr. Walker is said to have confined on the account of it, &c.

Now the story is strangely misplaced at the end of the siege, whereas Captain Cole came into town about the 9th or 12th of May; but he was confined by Governor Baker, not Dr. Walker, and that not for any discourse against Mr. Walker, but on suspicion of his being an agent for the enemy, among whom he had been detained for some time. And so far were the garrison from being brought to a better opinion of Mr. Walker by anything Mr. Cole discovered (as here idly suggested), that soon after, in the same month, the articles against him were drawn up.

And yet these are the only passages in that Account that carry any colour of an argu-

* This statement is substantiated by the testimony of Captain Ash, who was an Episcopalian. —See an extract from his Diary in the Introduction.

ment for Dr. Walker's being Governor as to the military affairs. And sure if he was such a Governor, he was not so extremely modest but he might have given us some true instances of his military conduct, especially when he had the confidence to impose upon the world so many mistaken ones. Likewise the Doctor will have Captain Darcy to be prisoner in Derry, and one of the signers of the letter with the Lord Netterville, &c., to Lieutenant-General Hamilton, the beginning of July, when it is certain the said Darcy left Derry before May three or four days, Mr. Walker being privy to it.

And as these three considerations are sufficient to blast the credit of these three certificates, so far as they contradict either the narrative or the preface, so for the three letters annexed, viz., of Captain Alexander Sanderson's, Lieutenant-Colonel Blair's, and from the officers of Colonel Lance's regiment, I shall only say, that as they were written to Dr. Walker, to beg his recommendation of them,* so they only give him the name of Governor (which the Narrative owns was often given him, as Colonel Baker's assistant in reference to the stores); and these letters are not the only evidence how fulsome compliments, necessity and hope of preferment (especially hearing that nothing was done at Court for them, but by Dr. Walker's interest), has drawn from too many of them, to one, of whom they expressed other thoughts

* The letter of Lieutenant-Colonel Blair published in Mackenzie's Narrative a false Libel, and adduced to prove that Walker was Governor of Derry, may here be annexed:—

"Londonderry, the 20th of Oct., 1689.
"SIR,—I understand by the King's letter that of the four regiments Major-General Kirke left unreduced at Londonderry, there are now but three of them to stand. I humbly entreat that you would, among the rest of your many favours, add this one, of being an instrument of preserving us by dealing effectually with the King that we may be continued, which we doubt not, by your care therein, and by giving an account of our more than ordinary necessity, you will prevail to the relief of the whole regiment, and also put a singular obligation on, Sir,
Your obedient and humble servant,
THOS. BLAIR.
To the Rev. George Walker,
Governor of Londonderry,
at Old Jury, London.

This is evidently the letter of a distressed gentleman to a powerful patron. Blair knew that Walker was well pleased to be styled Governor, and he here accordingly gives him the title, though he had some months before ceased to have any authority in Derry.

before. As for Captain Alex. Sanderson, how particularly he approved what the Narrative relates concerning the change of the Government, was before observed from the testimony of such as were present. As for Lieut. Colonel Blair, that the title of Governor wherewith he complimented Dr. Walker, was never intended by him any otherwise than I have explained, appears not only by the foresaid testimonial, but by the following certificate also :—

"I do hereby certify that, about the 15th day of April last, Lieutenant-Colonel Thomas Blair declared to me, in the presence of Mr. John Mackenzie, that he was earnestly solicited to sign a certificate contradictory to the said Mr. Mackenzie's Narrative, and was threatened, if he refused, with the danger he might be exposed to by Major-General Kirke's and Dr. Walker's interest when he returned to Ireland. But he refused to sign any such thing. He added also, that though he had in Ireland subscribed two letters, one of his own, the other with some other officers of his regiment, wherein they had complimented Dr. Walker with the title of Governor, in hopes of being, by his interest, put on the new establishment ; yet he knew, and was ready to give it under his hand, that he acted only as Governor of the stores. Given under my hand this 8th of May, 1690.

"JOHN ABERNETHY."

And as this discourse of the Lieutenant-Colonel's unriddles the whole mystery of these seeming contradictions, in what these gentlemen write and speak concerning Dr. Walker, so it gives a shrewd specimen of the articles (of threats as well as flattery) used to suppress the plain truth in these matters : for that such methods have not been tried with him alone, appears by so many of them having changed their note soon after they came to this town.

For the arguments to prove Dr. Walker's Governorship from its being owned by the King, the Parliament, the Privy Council, London, Edinburgh, Glasgow, Cambridge, and Oxford, I shall only add, that as I know not that they have owned him Governor in any such sense as I have here opposed (viz., with reference to the military affairs of the garrison), so if they have done it, it is a much stronger proof of that gentleman's extraordinary confidence in imposing such a mistake on them, than of their weakness in believing it at first, till better informed ; but I suppose it he will inquire better he will find several of them are undeceived, and of another opinion. And if on the force of this small trick, and the admirable success of it, he will needs compare Dr. Walker with the English Rogue, Spanish Gusman, and Crafty Clausy, he may (as being related to him) use the greater freedom with him; but most people will beg his pardon for thinking it so great a piece of wit to lead those who had only his own account of that matter, and the account of such as designedly abetted him into that mistake concerning him.

And so much for Dr. Walker's Governorship.

The only material passage that relates to the Narrative of the Siege against which the pamphleteer has anything to except, is the article against Dr. Walker for embezzling the stores, and the order occasioned thereby, that his note should not be accepted by the storekeepers unless signed by Governor Baker or Major Adams. Against this he produces a long certificate of Mr. Curling's, wherein he affirms that Dr. Walker neither could nor did embezzle the stores, and he never knew the Doctor's orders disputed. Now Mr. Curling does not understand the meaning of that article, for the Doctor was suspected to have embezzled the stores, by disposing of them, when taken out of private houses, to his own advantage, without ever suffering them to come into the store-keeper's hands. And as my Narrative only affirms this to have been one of the articles, so the officers concerned in drawing them up thought themselves capable of proving it, and the order mentioned was really made on that occasion: and if Mr. Curling himself never saw the Doctor's orders disputed, others, as well as myself, have several times seen his note rejected by Mr. Harvey,* on this very account that neither Governor Baker's nor Major Adams's hand were annexed to it, and, after their decease, Governor Mitchelburn's.

But there is one dangerous paragraph in that certificate of Mr. Curling's which I must take notice of. It is the last, in these words: "And lastly, I do declare that some persons concerned in putting out this pamphlet [viz., the Narrative], as I presume, since I came to London, did come to me, and would have drawn me, by great promises, to have bespattered and abused the reputation of the said Dr. Walker."

Upon which clause the pamphleteer thus insults: "And do not your ears tingle? are not your faces covered with a blush, who have plotted, caballed, and contrived such a scandalous libel, and more calumniating Preface; and now to hear-that some of you have been tampering to pervert truth, and to add subornation to bearing false witness."

Here is a desperate charge; but if he that brings it do not blush when I have cleared this matter, it will be only because he has steeled his forehead.

I hope none can be presumed a better interpreter of Mr. Curling's words than Mr. Curling himself, and what he meant by the passage last quoted will best appear by this certificate of his own.

"I, Edward Curling, do hereby declare that, whereas it is mentioned in a certificate under my hand, dated the 25th of April, which is inserted in the pamphlet entitled, "Mr. John Mackenzie's Narrative of the Siege of Londonderry a False Libel," &c., that some persons since I came to London did come to me, and would have drawn me, by great promises, to have bespattered and abused the reputation of Dr. George Walker, that all I meant or intended therein was only a discourse that one Mr. Hugh Galbraith had with me soon after I came to this city, touching a certain letter of Dr. Walker's which he was told I had, and often was very earnest to have seen or procured it, saying it should be £50 in my way, or words to that effect, in case I would procure it for him; neither were any other proposals or promises made to me by him or any other in that behalf, or towards any other bespattering or abusing of Mr. Walker's reputation, or to have sworn anything against him, which was never in the least proposed to me by any person whatsoever, which I certify, as witness my hand this 19th day of May, 1690.

"EDWARD CURLING.

"Witness,
"THOMAS BOULTON."

Here the reader may see by his own explication, the "some persons" mentioned in the former certificate amount only to "one Mr. Hugh Galbraith." And by the way, Mr. Galbraith was no more concerned in the publishing that Narrative, than the Archbishop of Tuam,* George Philips, Esq., or Mr. Wilkinson himself. Their drawing him by promises to bespatter and abuse the reputation of Dr. Walker amounts to no more than Mr. Galbraith's encouraging him to expect so much money for delivering up that letter (which, by the way, is a very improbable story, and expressly denied by Mr. Galbraith himself).

---

* Here is a plain fact which clearly shows that Walker occupied only a secondary position.

* It is highly probable that this Most Reverend prelate is the author of the pamphlet entitled, "Mackenzie's Narrative a false libel."

And now let the pamphleteer and the other gentlemen concerned in procuring that certificate clear themselves as well as they can of the guilt of suborning Mr. Curling to express so innocent a practice of Mr. Galbraith's, as desiring to obtain a real letter of so considerable importance, by so suspicious words as these: that some persons concerned, as he presumes, in publishing that Narrative, would have drawn him by great promises to have bespattered and abused the reputation of the said Dr. Walker. I am sure this looks in good earnest like shrewd tampering to prevent truth.

But perhaps the reader may be curious to know what this letter of Dr. Walker's was which Mr. Galbraith was so solicitous to procure, and what is become of it. To gratify him therein, I shall give the best account I can of it, from the relation of Mr. Curling, mentioned in the following certificate, and the rather because it confirms what is said concerning Dr. Walker in the Narrative, and shows how little regard is due to all the good words Mr. Curling has bestowed on him in his first certificate.

"We, the subscribers, do certify that on the 3rd of February last, or thereabouts, we heard Mr. Edward Curling, who had been in Londonderry during the siege, say publicly, on the Exchange, that Mr. George Walker was never Governor of that garrison, but only of the stores; and he further said that Mr. Walker was a great rogue and villain, and had endeavoured to betray the said city into the enemy's hands; and for that end had corresponded with Lieut.-General Richard Hamilton, which the said Curling affirmed he could prove by a letter now in his custody, written by Mr. Walker to the said Lieut.-General Hamilton, the which letter he offered to show to Mr. John Mackenzie and us, the subscribers, at six o'clock that evening; in expectation whereof Mr. John Mackenzie and we waited on him at the time and place appointed, and he accordingly met us, and having searched many papers he had in his portmanteau, found not the letter; for which he appeared to be much troubled, declaring that he believed that Captain Godfrey* (to whom he had given the key of his portmanteau that morning, to get out some clothes he had in it) had stolen the letter; notwithstanding the said Edward Curling very solemnly declared that he fully remembered the contents of the said letter, and could prove the same by divers that had seen it; the contents of which letter he solemnly affirmed were as followeth, viz.:—Mr. Walker first excused himself for not performing his engagement to the said Lieutenant-General, showing that the mobile were in a great tumult and rage against him, but he hoped they would be soon quieted, faithfully promising that he would perform his engagement, only requested the Lieutenant-General's patience for a little time, and that he confidently expected the Lieutenant-General would not fail the payment of £500, and the securing his life and fortune, and procure King James's favour to him. The contents of this letter, as related here, he promised to swear before any magistrate in the city of London, if desired; all which was Mr. Curling's own voluntary proposal (neither expected nor desired by us), upon our first meeting with him in London. Subscribed this 7th of May, 1690.

"JOHN ABERNETHY.
"HUGH GALBRAITH."*

And now, unless the letter itself could be produced, we cannot expect any clearer evidence what the contents of it were than these two last certificates compared together. And as I hope Dr. Walker's advocate will no more upbraid me with Mr. Curling's certificate, so he must thank his own folly (to say no worse) that his senseless triumphs upon it have made it necessary to lay open this whole matter, which indeed does sufficiently bespatter, but (if Mr. Curling, his own witness, may be believed) does no way abuse, i.e., injure or wrong the reputation of Dr. Walker.

As for the Appendix relating to Captain James Hamilton,† and the passage concerning him in Sir Arthur Rawdon's memoirs, I need only quote Sir Arthur Rawdon's own ingenuous reply in a letter to a person of quality, a friend of his in town:—

"There is one passage in that pamphlet, because it belongs something to me, I beg leave to take notice of, which is about Lundy's being sworn aboard the ship. In the first place I must needs say I meant no particular reflection on Colonel James Hamilton, whose forwardness everywhere, especially at Cladyford, are too great demonstrations of his zeal and integrity to the cause to be at all blemished, but as it was matter of fact I could not omit it, for being accidentally

---

* This gentleman belonged to Colonel Lance's regiment.

* It must be admitted that the testimony of this document is most damaging, especially when it is considered that the witnesses are so trustworthy. Mr. Abernethy was a minister of the highest character for integrity, and Galbraith was a respectable gentleman.

† See p. 64.

in the ship with William Ponsonby and others that I have forgot, and Lundy coming aboard, after some small discourse we were told they had private business, so that we withdrew out of the cabin and stayed above deck with Captain Beverly till we were wet with rain. What was done in the cabin in the meantime I know not, nor did I hear till next day that most people were dissatisfied with Lundy for refusing to take the oath publicly again, though much pressed to it, particularly by Colonel George Phillips; and though now the excuse is that the Mayor was a Papist, yet they found a Protestant Mayor there who proclaimed the King, &c., namely, Mr. Campsie.* There is a mistake of mine taken notice of too in the book, viz., saying that the officers, civil and military, &c., which was from my not remembering the instructions, which I never heard but once. I find in the printed book, inserted in my memoirs, that the bishop was by at the proclaiming the King, &c., though I suppose I meant the Mayor,† but the mistake is not great, and of no consequence. I beg your pardon for this trouble, &c.

"ARTHUR RAWDON."

I shall only add here that, as all that Sir Arthur Rawdon's memoir saith about the swearing of Lundy is, that if he were sworn it was very privately, so this may very well consist with the truth of what Captain Mervyn and Captain Corry certify;‡ and yet his refusing to swear publicly in those circumstances was a very suspicious sign of his ill intentions, and therefore justly taken notice of.

For the grave letter at the end§ I see nothing in it of argument against anything in

* The first meeting of the old Protestant Corporation after the shutting of the gates appears to have taken place on the 2nd of January, 1689. Mr. Campsie, the Presbyterian Mayor, then resumed his former position.
† See p. 26.
‡ Their certificate is as follows:—
"We, whose names are underwritten, do hereby certify that we were present when Captain James Hamilton administered to Colonel Lundy both the oaths of fidelity mentioned in his Instructions; and do likewise testify that he administered them to him before he delivered up to the said Colonel Lundy any part of his trust. In witness to the truth whereof, we have hereunto set our hands, this one and twentieth day of April, 1690.
"HEN. MERVYN.
"JAMES CORRY."
—*Mackenzie's Narrative a false Libel*, p. 16.
§ This letter has been already noticed.—Note, p. 86.

the Narrative. But sure it is but a sorry proof of Dr. Walker's being Governor of the garrison that some who were at first so charitable as to believe what he pretends to, altered their sentiments when better informed. But that this was owing to any mistake about his persuasion is only an idle fancy of the writer's. But sure those have little reason to complain of Dr. Walker's Account being atributed to the Archbishop of Tuam, who, with far greater confidence father the Preface of my Narrative on Mr. Boyse, and thence take occasion to say whatever their wit and malice could suggest against him. But how little either of them could furnish them with to his prejudice appears by what this pamphleteer has said; for he is forced here to renew the same accusation he had brought in the "Remarks on Mr. Osborne's Vindication," viz., "that when Dr. King and Dean Manby were pickeering, he took up a flail, and threshed them both;* and while the Doctor was engaged in a duel with a pernicious apostate from the Protestant religion, he came behind his back and stabbed him, only because he incidentally reflected on that persuasion whereof Mr. Boyse is ambitious to be the celebrated champion." And in his "Remarks on Mr. Osborne's Vindication," he saith he could tell Mr. Boyse what harm his book did the Protestants, and what use the Papists made of it against the Church at that time.

Now if the pamphleteer's passion had not blinded his wit, he would in prudence have concealed what casts so unhappy a reflection on some of his own coat, but can never lessen the reputation of Mr. Boyse in the judgment of any but such ignorant bigots as himself. For since he will bring that matter on the stage, the plain truth was this.

Dean Manby printed his Considerations that moved him to change his religion, which were nothing else but the old banter about the mission of Protestant bishops and priests revived. Dr. King in his answer chose to insist on such principles as were only calculated to defend the mission of the English bishops and their clergy, but left the ministers of other Protestant Churches that had not bishops for their reformers in the lurch; nay, he laid down such notions as made church rebels of them, as well as the Dissent-

* Manby, the Dean of Derry, turned Papist, and published a work in defence of his apostacy, which called forth a reply from Dr. King, afterwards Bishop of Derry, and then Archbishop of Dublin. King was a high churchman; and his reply was based on such narrow and exclusive principles, that Mr. Boyse felt it to be his duty to expose its errors.

ing ministers, whom, with their flocks, he expressly excluded from the Catholic Church. Mr. Boyse wrote reflections on both these papers, wherein he laid down the true and common notions of Protestant writers about mission, and on those endeavoured to justify the Reformed ministry abroad, and particularly those at home. And now can this scribbler have the impudence to pretend that that book should injure the Protestants, and give the Papists advantage, which vindicates the mission of all the ministers of Protestant Churches (those of the Church of England included as much as any) from the schismatical principles of the Papists on the one hand, that deny the validity of all Protestant orders, and those of Mr. Dodwell* and his followers on the other, that deny the validity of any orders but what are derived from diocesan bishops. If Mr. Boyse's flail did on this occasion thresh them both, it was because both deserved it; nor did he stab Dr. King, but rather warded off the stab which his unhappy notions would have given, not only to his brethren in Ireland, but to those in France, Piedmont, &c., too; and all out of a narrow zeal for the Church of England. I shall only add that Mr. Boyse was so far from opposing any just endeavours then used to stem the tide of Popery, that he preached as many sermons against it in the late King James's reign as perhaps any one clergyman in that kingdom.

And on this occasion I can heartily join with the writer of this Epistle in his prayers that God would rebuke that spirit of bitterness and evil-speaking that exposes us to the scorn of our common adversary, and contempt of all : and I could wish he had given some good advice of this kind both to this pamphleteer, and to the Archbishop of Tuam, who in a sermon preached at Windsor, 1684, and since printed, vents his passion in such expressions as these, p. 32, "But while I am speaking of these things, methinks I hear a voice saying to me, as to the Prophet 'Son of man, seest thou what they do, they of the Church of Rome? Turn thee, yet again, and thou shalt see greater abominations, a people,'" &c.—and so he goes on to describe the Dissenters. And so, pp. 35, 36—" In return of all which, I hear her [speaking of the Church of England] crying out in the words, and with the tears and compassion of our blessed Saviour, 'O Jerusalem, Jerusalem! thou that killest the prophets,' &c.—'O ye of the foreign Reformation, how often would I have gathered you under my communion, and covered or excused your defects, but ye would not ; but now these things are hid from your eyes, and your house is left to you desolate. And O ye, of the domestic separation, how often would I have gathered you, but so often have I stretched forth my hand to a gainsaying and disobedient people.'" And the same person in a sermon preached at Bow Church, October 23, 1689, speaks to the same purpose. Page 15—" That Church (viz., the Church of England) would gather all the parts of the Protestant religion under her wings as a hen doth her chickens, but they would not. But as soon as the sun shines, and the bird of prey is removed, too many begin again to scatter, and divide, and quarrel, as if they would pick out their mother's eyes, and then one another's," &c. The reader may observe what a spirit of meekness, healing, and moderation is in the mouth of this great prophet, as well as what a spirit of truth, ingenuity, and candour is in the mouth of this ignorant and scurrilous pamphleteer.

For my part I am not in the least conscious to myself of having said anything against any party of Protestants; and if some have the cunning to interest a party in their reputation, as if whatever is said to expose their treacheries were levelled against all others that are of their persuasion, I cannot help their weaknesses who so grossly misunderstand the design of my Narrative. But what I have said concerning two or three particular persons, is no more than what was not only true, but necessary to have been said, in giving that plain account of these transactions, which the misrepresentation of others gave too just occasion for. And if the pamphleteer will needs draw that perverse inference from my Narrative, "that all the brave and glorious actions in the siege were performed by the Dissenters, and Colonel Murray at the head of them ;* all inglorious actions and treacherous attempts are to be imputed to the other part of the garrison, and principally to Dr. Walker"—let him look to his conclusion, for the premises are true; but I confess I should deny the

---

* Dodwell was what would now be called a Puseyite. He was a very learned man, and a Nonjuror.

* Colonel Murray was a high-principled Presbyterian, and the reputation he acquired during the siege of Derry placed him at the head of his co-religionists. It is said that the laird of Philiphaugh, to whom he was related, conformed to prelacy in the reign of Charles II.; but, at least on one occasion, he offended the Government by refusing to become a persecutor.—See *Wodrow* II. 366, 368. Some of the Murrays of Scotland are among the Presbyterian worthies. — See *Wodrow, II.* 37 ; *IV.* 39.

inference, because several of the officers that are much commended were of the Church of England, though but very few of the common soldiers.

To show further how little credit is due to Mr. Squire's certificate, which the pamphleteer boasts so much of, I shall produce Mr. Squire to confute himself in the following certificate, though not in its due place, because it came but late to my hands:—

"I do hereby certify that Gervais Squire, Esq., of the city of Derry, did, soon after his coming over for England, upon my enquiry concerning Mr. Walker, inform me that he was not Governor of the said city, but Colonel Baker, and that he had only the stores committed to his trust. Given under my hand this 14th day of June, 1690.

"GERVAIS BYFIELD."*

† Gervais Byfield was probably related to Gervais Squire. He was Comptroller of the Customs at Leith.—See *Chamberlayne's Magnae Britanniae Notitia, Part II., Book III.*, p. 41.

I should not have taken notice of another small mistake relating to Derry, suggested in Mr. Walker's Narrative, if it had not been also inserted in a letter, subscribed H. R., (probably Hugh Rowley,) set down in Mr. Cox's History of Ireland, part 2nd, that Mr. Phillips should have sent to the citizens of Derry, on approach of the Irish forces, to shut their gates, and that they accordingly did so; ascribing that to him which was inconsistent with the city's declaration, letters subscribed by himself,* in my Narrative mentioned, and the account given by those who were principally concerned in that affair.

Having said so much to clear my Narrative from the aspersions cast upon it by this idle pamphlet, I think fit to desire the author, if he scribble again, to be so honest as to set his name to it, for I shall not think myself concerned to encounter any longer with spectres and hobgoblins.

* See Note, p. 60 of this volume.

By the same Author, Second Edition, 8vo, 12s. Cloth,

THE ANCIENT CHURCH;

ITS HISTORY, WORSHIP, DOCTRINE, AND CONSTITUTION TRACED FOR THE FIRST THREE HUNDRED YEARS.

"It is your distinction to have among you the author of the best history of the Ancient Church that has yet been written from the Presbyterian stand point. I trust the volume which has appeared is but the first of a complete series that are yet to be text-books in all our Presbyterian Theological Seminaries."—*Rev. Dr. Kerr, Professor of Church History for the United Presbyterian Church of North America. Speech in General Assembly of Presbyterian Church in Ireland, July 4, 1860.*

"We hail Dr. Killen's 'Ancient Church' with great delight. We hail the appearance of it because of the decided views which he expresses, and because of the full and complete and able discussion of them, with which God has enabled him to favour the Church. . . . . As to the new recension of the Ignatian Letters, we are confident that every honest mind will acknowledge the ability and thoroughness of Dr. Killen's investigations. Our author thoroughly investigates anew this old controversy, and sheds a flood of new light on it."—*Rev. J. B. Adgar, D.D., Professor of Ecclesiastical History in Columbia College, U.S.*

"This is a work of great value and importance, and will, we have no doubt, take a high and permanent place in the department of the theological literature to which it belongs. . . . . Dr. Killen is evidently possessed of very high and thoroughly cultivated powers, and of a very complete mastery of the subjects of which he treats. He has brought very fine talents and extensive erudition to bear upon an investigation of all the most interesting and important questions suggested by a survey of the Church of the first three centuries, especially those connected with its constitution and government."—*British and Foreign Evangelical Review.*

"We have received this noble volume, which we welcome both as an additional and interesting proof of intellectual activity in our mother Church, and as a further bond of union with ourselves. In keeping with the external dress is the simple and transparent style, sometimes rising with chastened but impressive eloquence. The author appears equally familiar with the ancient and modern literature of the subject. It contains original and novel views, especially in reference to the genesis of Prelacy, and the genuineness of the writings of Ignatius."—*Princeton Review.*

"We have not previously met with Dr. Killen as an author, but he writes with an honest purpose and is well read in his subjects. . . . . Amongst Church historians he is fairly entitled to a' respectable rank. . . . . Dr. Killen has given us a few chapters in which the inner life of a spiritual people is comprised; and they are worth all the rest. He understands the subject."—*Christian Observer.*

"We have read it with great care, and we must add, with almost unmixed satisfaction. It is a monument of vast erudition, reared by the hand of a master. The materials are enormous, but complex, confused and multifarious; in the hands of Dr. Killen, however, they soon become disentangled, disencumbered, arranged, and adjusted, and ready for putting together. This done, the enterprise begins, and the goodly fabric forthwith displays its noble proportions. Here the question of Church Government is exhibited in all its aspects with much learning, candour, and force. There is both correction and instruction for the disciples of the several systems, and they will do well to listen to so profound and judicious a monitor. It is by far the richest contribution that has been made to British Ecclesiastical Literature during the nineteenth century."—*Christian Witness.*

"Dr. Killen reviews the first three centuries from a Presbyterian point of view. His work is elegant, learned, comprehensive, and in the main thoroughly convincing. We would at once draw special attention to the sections on the Literature and Theology of the Church, including the author's examination of the Epistles ascribed to Ignatius."—*Wesleyan Methodist Magazine.*

"There is certainly no book in the English language to be compared with this work of Dr. Killen's, as exhibiting very high literary excellencies, in combination with a full exposition and defence of the views upon the different departments of the subject, which have commended themselves to the ablest and most learned defenders of Presbyterian principles. The work is entitled to our cordial recommendation, and is in all respects one of great excellence and value."—*Edinburgh Witness.*

London: JAMES NISBET & Co.

www.ingramcontent.com/pod-product-compliance
Lightning Source LLC
Chambersburg PA
CBHW020133170426
43199CB00010B/735